COMPLETE IN HIM

A GUIDE TO UNDERSTANDING AND ENJOYING THE GOSPEL

BY
MICHAEL P. V. BARRETT

AMBASSADOR-EMERALD INTERNATIONAL
GREENVILLE, SOUTH CAROLINA • BELFAST, NORTHERN IRELAND

Complete in Him
A Guide to Understanding and Enjoying the Gospel

ISBN: 1-889893-58-7

Published by:
Ambassador-Emerald International
427 Wade Hampton Blvd.
Greenville, SC 29609 USA

and

Ambassador Productions
Ardenlee Street
Belfast, BT6 8QJ
Northern Ireland

www.emeraldhouse.com

Cover and internal design by Brad Sherman

Printed in Canada

To my former colleagues in the Seminary of Bob Jones University
And especially
To Thurman Wisdom–my long-time Dean
For his loyalty and humble leadership

TABLE OF CONTENTS

Preface

"Wisdom is the principal thing; therefore get wisdom: and with all thy getting get understanding" (Proverbs 4:7). Obtaining wisdom and understanding is possible because "the Lord giveth wisdom: out of his mouth cometh knowledge and understanding" (Proverbs 2:6). Ultimately, getting wisdom is getting Christ. Getting understanding is increasing in the knowledge that as Christians we are "in Christ Jesus, who of God is made unto us wisdom, and righteousness, and sanctification, and redemption" (1 Corinthians 1:30). Christ is the gospel, and there is nothing more vital for life than understanding the gospel and nothing better in life than enjoying it. It is my prayer and desire that *Complete in Him* may help guide you to a deeper understanding and a greater enjoyment of what it means to be a Christian.

The Lord has given me the privilege for many years of teaching the Bible and ancillary subjects. Whether teaching theology or advanced Hebrew grammar or biblical archaeology, it has been my supreme objective and desire to set before my students the importance of knowing the Lord Jesus Christ and His glorious gospel. It is my prayer that to some degree my testimony may begin to approach that of Paul's: "For I determined not to know any thing among you, save Jesus Christ, and him crucified" (1 Corinthians 2:2). That is my objective for this book as well. May the Lord grant it to be true.

This book is not designed to be a scholarly analysis of the doctrine of soteriology, filled with critical analysis or interaction with scholars of differing schools of thought or theology. I have intentionally avoided footnotes, whose very presence tends to intimidate some readers. Yet I have not designed this for casual reading either. There will be times when I want you to slow down and think carefully about the issues. I hope that you will find devotional blessing as well as increased spiritual insight. After all, this is to be guide to both understanding and enjoyment.

Although I am not interacting with other literature, I will from time to time quote or refer to the historic, orthodox confessions and catechisms. The confessions give summary statements of the doctrines of Scripture in declarative paragraphs. The catechisms teach the truths in a question–answer format. I think you will find these references to be most instructive if you take the time to read and think through them. I quote them not only because they are classic statements, but because I want to emphasize that what I am saying is not novel: It is the old-fashioned gospel. I have used both the Westminster and London standards in order to show that I am not just proffering a particular denominational slant or peculiarity. The Westminster standards (1646-1648) are those generally adopted among conservative, orthodox Presbyterians, and the London Baptist Confession (1689), the precursor to the Philadelphia Confession, is the historic Baptist statement of faith. Bible-believers differ on some points of interpretation, and that's okay. But regardless of denominational distinctives, all fundamental, conservative, orthodox believers should rejoice in the gospel of Jesus Christ. We are part of His body, and one day we will all be with Him. What a day that will be!

Admittedly, I am responsible before God for what I have written, but I am indebted to many. I want to acknowledge those who introduced me to and taught me the gospel. I have enjoyed godly influences all of my life. I must first express my gratitude to God for Christian parents who from my youth provided an environment in which the claims of Christ were put before me. I especially thank the Lord for the memory of my grandmother– to this day the godliest woman I have ever known. I had the privilege of growing up next door to her and witnessing a life that, through immense suffering, testified daily to the reality of the gospel. She now enjoys the presence of her Savior. For the first 18 years of life I had the advantage of growing up in a church that faithfully preached the gospel. My preacher, Rev. Kinnamin Crawford, had an evangelistic passion that remains an example. It was in the basement of that church that Mrs. Weir, my Sunday school teacher, used Romans 3:23 to convince me as a young child of my need of Christ. I owe much to my professors at Bob Jones University who taught me as a young man how to rightly divide the Word of Truth. It is impossible to express how deeply appreciative I am to Alan Cairns, my minister for over 20 years. I esteem him very highly in love for his work's sake. He knows what it is to preach the gospel.

I must express thanks as well to those who have helped in the preparation of this manuscript. Dr. Cairns made invaluable suggestions to help me refine some of my theological statements. His knowledge of Systematic Theology far exceeds mine, and it was nice to have him around. I would highly recommend his *Dictionary of Theological Terms* (Ambassador-Emerald International, 1998). You can find in his dictionary succinct definitions of many of the themes and terms I will discuss in this book. Were it not for the fact that he was laboring on a manuscript of his own while I was working on this project I would have taken more advantage of his expertise. Perhaps my timing will be better next time. Dr. Marshall Neal, my teacher, Dean, colleague, and friend read the manuscript to evaluate the theological content. I appreciate his taking time from retirement to help a former student. He and I shared many cups of coffee and conversation about the things of God over the years that we occupied adjacent offices. I may have learned more from him during those informal times of fellowship than in the classroom. Dr. Hugh Clarke, a friend and neuro-surgeon with an insatiable appetite for God's Word, read the manuscript and made helpful suggestions from a layman's perspective. Dr. Caren Silvester of the English Department of Bob Jones University deserves much credit for her tedious labors in editing my style and grammar. Her suggestions were always helpful and to the point. She is most gracious, and we work well together–something that is not always true of writers and editors. I also must thank my wife Sandra for her patience and encouragement throughout the project, as well as for her labor in collecting the data for the Scripture index.

Of course, I thank Ambassador-Emerald International for its support and offer to publish this work. I should thank as well

Wade Kuhlewind for proposing the idea for this book. Some years ago, I preached a series on the inseparable links of the gospel at the annual Faith Bible Conference near Pittsburgh. Wade, pastor of one of the participating churches, suggested developing the series in book form. That thought never left me.

Ultimate thanks and praise belong to the Lord for His faithfulness throughout the undertaking. I trust that this exposition of the gospel will be to the praise of the glory of His grace.

Michael P. V. Barrett
Vice President for Academic Affairs
Whitefield College of the Bible
Theological Seminary of the Free Presbyterian Church of North America
Greenville, S.C.

Introduction

What is the gospel? What does it mean to be saved? The answers to these questions are simple yet profound. The gospel is Christ, and being saved is having Christ: "He that hath the Son hath life" (1 John 5:12). That is elemental enough for a child to understand, yet complex enough to challenge every believer to a greater understanding and enjoyment of saving grace. Being saved does not require an academic degree in theology, but the more any believer understands the fullness and vastness of salvation, the more he can enjoy all the blessings that God has graciously provided in His Son and our Savior, the Lord Jesus Christ. The Scripture declares that Christ is "full of grace and truth" (John 1:14) and that believers are "complete in him" (Colossians 2:10). For the Christian, everything–both his eternal destiny and his earthly journey–depends on what he thinks of Christ. That *Christ is everything* and that *Christians are complete in Him* ought to generate joyous satisfaction in every believing heart.

The Problem

Tragically, however, many genuine believers plod along the earthly journey on their way to eternal glory without much conscious thought of Christ. Testifying that they have been saved, these plodders tend to relegate salvation to a past decision and then struggle through life with little more than a "cross-your-fingers" assurance that all will be well in the end. They define Christian life in terms of rigid, conservative lifestyles fueled more by guilt than by faith. On the whole, they exhibit a woeful ignorance of how to apply gospel truths. In my teaching ministry over the years, I have encountered many young people who have grown up in professedly Christian environments. They have been immersed in rules and regulations that may be good and proper, but either they have never been taught or they have never personally put forth the faith to link the code of conduct to the core truths of the gospel. Consequently, I have seen professing believers either rebelling against the Christian lifestyle because they don't know the why of it or burdened by guilt because their performance of duty does not measure up to some perceived standard. The extremes of excessive license or oppressive bondage result. Neither of these extremes includes the joy or utilizes the power of the gospel.

One of the foremost objectives in my ministry has been to bring students to see and understand something of the Savior: who He is, what He has done, and what their place in Him is. I have often grieved, having expounded some essential gospel truth such as justification by faith or union with Christ, that so many students confessed they had never heard such truths before. The general consensus seems to be that whereas the gospel message is essential for evangelism, edification requires something beyond those simple facts. Such a reaction to the gospel betrays a sad unfamiliarity with its power and scope. Although I have rejoiced to see many come into the true liberty of the gospel, I have lamented that what I teach from the Scripture seems so novel to so many.

Why is it that what is so common in the Bible has become so foreign to those who profess belief in the Bible? Too often there has been a rush to achieve visible results without giving the necessary attention to the means to and reasons for those desired results. Inviting people to walk an aisle has been equated with "getting people saved." Motivating people to live by conservative standards has been equated with living for Christ. Reminding people that "once saved always saved–after all you can't make God a liar" has become the only thread of assurance for doubting hearts to cling to. Consequently, the best of churches are filled with genuine Christians whose only argument for salvation is a date written on the flyleaf of a seldom-used Bible and whose only concept of living for Christ is being in church whenever the doors are open. Sadly, the best of churches are filled with professing Christians who have "done it all" and convinced themselves that all is well with their souls when in reality they have no saving interest in Christ.

The Solution

Attempting to assign blame for this tragic state of spiritual affairs is not really the solution. Pulpit and pew alike share the culpability, and both must strive to sharpen the focus on Christ and the gospel if there is to be a resolution to the problem. I have told my students, perhaps thousands of times over the years, that *right thinking about the gospel produces right living in the gospel*. It is truth, not activity, which makes Christianity distinct. We cannot ignore the link between gospel doctrine and gospel duty if we hope to approach genuine Christian life and successful Christian living. Contrary to some notions in modern fundamental and evangelical Christianity, doctrine does not destroy life: it defines it. Therefore, it is the responsibility of preachers to proclaim the essential truths of the gospel and point their people to the proper implications and applications of those truths to daily life. It is likewise the responsibility of each individual believer to appropriate by faith the unchangeable truths of the gospel and to live consciously in the reality of those truths.

The Purpose and Plan

What I have tried to do in my classroom and pulpit ministry is what I want to do in this venue. I want very simply to expound and apply the gospel of saving grace: what the gospel is and what it means to be saved. The Bible defines the gospel and salvation in both general and specific terms. Comparing salvation to a strong, unbreakable chain composed of many individual yet inseparable links illustrates this general and specific revelation. Sometimes the Scripture presents the entire chain in overview (macroscopically); sometimes it examines the individual links in particular (microscopically). Although a particular passage may be focusing on just a single link, that link does not and cannot exist alone. If one link exists, the whole chain exists. It is impossible to have one element of salvation without having the whole of salvation. If there is election, there is justification. If there is justification, there is sanctification. If there is sanctification, there is glorification. And on it goes. These components are so closely linked that even when the Bible is concentrating on one microscopically, it is impossible for us to keep the related components out of our field of vision.

As expected in any chain construction, there will be overlaps–something that keeps the whole together. What secures all the components of salvation is the gospel of Jesus Christ. So regardless of the specific aspect of salvation in focus, the Scripture consistently couples it to some truth about the person or work of the Savior. The Bible always defines salvation in terms of the Savior, and we must, too, if we are going to understand the gospel as we ought. Every link has its objective cause in Christ and must be subjectively understood and enjoyed in terms of Christ. That is why, on the one hand, salvation is as simple as having Christ. Yet on the other hand, the more those who have Christ can learn about the chain of salvation, the more confidence they will enjoy and the more guilt-free motivation they will experience as they seek to live the Christian life.

Salvation does not and cannot exist in a mental vacuum. Truth must be known before it can have any effect. Orthodoxy (doctrinal truth) isolated in the head is dangerous, but the head is nonetheless where it starts. Remember my statement: "Right thinking about the gospel produces right living in the gospel." The Bible sets the pattern of first knowing (Romans 6:3, 6, 9), then believing (Romans 6:11), and then doing (Romans 6:12, 13). To reverse that order or to omit a step is deleterious to a successful Christian life. I want us first to know and then to do. So that is the objective of this book: to teach the truth and to offer guidance in using truth practically.

Each of the following chapters will focus on a fundamental of the gospel. Before beginning the analysis of the benefits of the gospel, I will lay the foundation with two chapters: condemnation as the need of the gospel and Christ as the essence of the gospel. Truths from these chapters will necessarily reappear throughout the entire book. Next I will consider such themes as conversion, regeneration, justification, adoption, reconciliation, union with Christ, and sanctification. As we contemplate together these great gospel truths, I want not only to define biblically and precisely the particular doctrine (component or link of the gospel), but also to suggest the relevant implications and application. Sometimes I will collate key texts from throughout the Bible and discuss the doctrine thematically. I will do my best not to interpret or use any passage out of its context–always a potential problem of "proof-texts." In other instances I will discuss the doctrine by expounding a key passage that comprehensively elucidates the specific truth. In every chapter I intend to demonstrate conclusively that the particular benefit of salvation under discussion links to Christ. Please do not tire of what may appear to be mere repetition. Linking everything to Christ is what I want us all to learn and to practice. It is my prayer that we Christians live in the reality of what we are in Christ, that we become increasingly overwhelmed with our salvation–in short, that we reach a state in which we can't get over being saved.

The title of this book, *Complete in Him*, suggests the overriding and underlying premise that is foundational to any true understanding and enjoyment of salvation. Paul's emphasis on the preeminence of Christ in the book of Colossians sparked the title. In chapter 1 Paul highlights the imperial Christ who is our confidence, the incarnate Christ who is our peace, and the indwelling Christ who is our hope. In chapter 2 he expresses his desire that those to whom he has ministered might experience "all [the] riches of the full assurance of understanding, to the acknowledgement of the mystery of God, and of the Father, and of Christ; in whom are hid all the treasures of wisdom and knowledge" (2:2-3). Then having declared that in Christ "dwelleth all the fulness of the Godhead bodily," he proclaims, "Ye are complete in him" (2:9-10). That's the secret. The thrill of all the benefits and blessings of saving grace will be in proportion to how much we reflect on the completeness of Christ and our completeness in Him. So as we consider what it means to be saved, let us echo the words of the hymn:

Complete in thee–each want supplied
And no good thing to me denied;
Since Thou my portion, Lord, wilt be,
I ask no more–complete in Thee.

CHAPTER 1

Condemnation: The Need of the Gospel

"No news is good news." That adage may have happy relevance to the ordinary routines of life, but it does not apply to man's spiritual condition. Spiritually speaking, no news is bad news. Without the good news of the gospel of Jesus Christ, the headline over humanity reads nothing but Bad News. Without Christ, man is without God and, consequently, without any hope in the world (Ephesians 2:12). But the good news is that "There is therefore now no condemnation to them which are in Christ Jesus" (Romans 8:1). Let me go ahead and state the obvious: That there is no condemnation to those in Christ means that those not in Christ are under condemnation. The news could not be worse.

It may, perhaps, appear odd for me to begin a book about understanding and enjoying the good news of the gospel with a chapter on the bad news about man's guilt and condemnation before God. I submit, however, that we will never understand the greatness of the gospel until we understand the need for the gospel. We cannot appreciate the good news if we are unaware of the bad news. Unless and until a sinner knows he is lost and without hope, he will never see his need for Christ. The common advice given to aspiring evangelists is that you have to get a sinner to see his lost and desperate condition before you can lead him to Christ for his only hope of salvation.

The point is that you have to know you're lost before the panic sets in. Let me offer this illustration. I love to hunt and to be in the woods, but admittedly, I am not the best woodsman around. My sense of direction is often skewed. My tendency, when walking through the woods scouting for deer sign, is to take the paths of least resistance. It is much easier walking around a brier patch than through one. More than once, my sense of relaxation at being in the woods has turned to panic when it dawns on me that I have no idea where I am. When I look at my compass to get my bearings, I realize that knowing where north is helps little in knowing where my truck is. You have to check the compass before going into the woods if it is going to help coming out. It is always a great feeling when I either recognize a landmark or aimlessly find my way out. Being lost in the woods can be scary; but being lost in sin means eternal damnation. And in contrast to my fortuitous exits from the woods, there is no way a sinner is going to find his way out on his own. That ought to be a fearful thought for every sinner.

This is unmistakably the logic used by the most prolific of gospel writers in the New Testament, and particularly so in the most extensive of his inspired gospel treatises, the book of Romans. Before Paul says anything about justification, reconciliation, redemption, adoption, sanctification, glorification or any other aspect of the gospel, he first announces the bad news that "the wrath of God is revealed from heaven against all ungodliness and unrighteousness" (Romans 1:18). He then presents irrefutable evidence of man's sin, taking away every excuse and rendering the whole world guilty before God (Romans 3:19). In the light of God's just sentence upon guilty sinners, how magnificently wonderful is the good news that God has given His Son to be the only way whereby guilty sinners can escape their lost estate.

To understand the full weight of this just condemnation requires some comprehension of the serious nature of sin and why, as an affront against the holy and righteous God, it deserves such a terrible penalty. Without developing the biblical theology of sin and defining all the terms for it, let me remind you of the apostle John's simple definition of sin: "For sin is the transgression of the law" (1 John 3:4). Translated more literally, it reads: "sin is lawlessness." The word "sin" is the most general New Testament term for sin that reflects the image of its Old Testament counterpart, which pictures sin as the missing of a target. It defines sin as the failure to meet the demands and requirements of a fixed standard–God's inflexible law. Hence, sin is breaking the law of God, either by deliberate violations or unwary infractions.

Law without penalty for breach of law is impotent. Since "the righteous Lord loveth righteousness" (Psalm 11:7), any and all breaches of His righteous law deserve the severest penalty: "Upon the wicked he shall rain snares, fire and brimstone" (Psalm 11:6). The apostle Paul summed up the horrible consequence of sin when he concluded, "The wages of sin is death" (Romans 6:23). Succinctly and scripturally, the *Westminster Shorter Catechism* captures both the essence of sin and the extent of its consequence:

> Sin is any want of conformity unto, or transgression of, the law of God. (question 14)
>
> All mankind by their fall lost communion with God, are under his wrath and curse, and so made liable to all miseries in this life, to death itself, and to the pains of hell forever. (question 19)

Remembering the misery of our lost estate will aid both in increasing our appreciation for God's wondrous grace that is greater than our sin and in motivating our love and praise for Christ as our Savior. This is the very point Christ intended in His parable to Simon concerning the two debtors who were incapable of repaying their debt (Luke 7:40-50). One owed five hundred pence and the other fifty, and both were graciously forgiven. Christ asked Simon, who was appalled at the sinful woman's anointing Christ's feet with expensive ointment and tears, "Tell me therefore, which of them will love him [the creditor] most?" According to the Lord Jesus, Simon answered correctly when he replied, "I suppose that he, to whom he forgave most." Just as the debtor in the parable and the sinful woman responded with gratitude because they were forgiven much (Luke 7:47), the more conscious we are of the depths of our sin and its horrific consequences, the more conscious we will be of the greatness of our salvation.

Do not misunderstand what I want us to think about. It is not good for Christians to dwell on the specifics of past sins. But it is good for each of us to remember that God through Christ has "brought [us] up also out of an horrible pit, out of the miry clay, and set [our] feet upon a rock, and established [our] goings" (Psalm 40:2). For this reason, I want us to consider what the Bible teaches about man's sinful condition that justly condemns him before God and to rejoice in the amazing truth that man's total depravity is cured by God's infinite grace. God's indictment against sinners is all-inclusive: "There is none righteous, no, not one" (Romans 3:10; see also Psalm 14:1-3). The evidence that proves the indictment is undeniable: "For all have sinned [missed the target], and come short [constantly lacking] of the glory of God" (Romans 3:23). I want very simply to consider what sinners are by nature (Ephesians 2:3) in order to heighten the beauty of what saints are by grace (Ephesians 2:5). Because of what sinners are, *sinners need a gospel.*

SINNERS ARE SPIRITUALLY DEAD

In Ephesians 2:1, Paul identifies the state of believers prior to salvation as being "dead in trespasses and sins." In this context, being dead refers to the absence not of physical life but of spiritual life. Being spiritually dead renders one insensitive and unresponsive to the things of God (1 Corinthians 2:14). The most important part of man's person–his eternal soul–is dead to the most vital part of life–God. The grammar of this statement (particularly, the function of the dative case) means either that sinners are dead within the sphere of trespasses and sin (surrounded by sin) or that they are dead because of trespasses and sins. Both ideas are tragic and theologically true. Because of trespasses and sins, man is spiritually dead. It is the fact of original sin that renders every man spiritually dead; it is the fact of spiritual death that impels every man to actual sin. Spiritual death buries a man in the dirt of sin. Spiritual death renders man thoroughly corrupt (a stinking corpse) and completely incapable of generating spiritual life. Theologically, we refer to this condition as man's total depravity and total inability. The Scripture presents two important perspectives of this universal problem of spiritual death.

Dead in Adam

The Bible teaches and experience verifies that sin is universal. According to Scripture, the explanation for this universal presence of sin in the human heart lies in Adam's first sin, the fall of the human race. 1 Corinthians 15:22 declares explicitly, "In Adam all die." Romans 5 is a weighty text for many reasons, particularly for its explanation linking our guilt to Adam's sin. "Wherefore, as by one man sin entered into the world, and death by sin; and so death passed upon all men, for that all have sinned" (5:12). Consider also these statements: "For if through the offense of one many be dead . . ." (5:15); "For the judgment was by one to condemnation . . ." (5:16); "For if by one man's offence death reigned by one . . ." (5:17); "By the offence of one judgment came upon all men to condemnation . . ." (5:18); and "For as by one man's disobedience many were made sinners . . ." (5:19).

All this raises an important and legitimate question: If Adam did it, how come I'm guilty? Theologians have long debated the answer to this question, often allowing the limitations of finite reason and a perverted, selfish sense of fairness to cloud the evidence of the Scripture. There are many wrong answers to this question, and what I believe to be one right answer. Properly understanding the relationship between Adam's sin and our guilt is essential to understanding the relationship between Christ's righteousness and our freedom from guilt. Even the doctrine of condemnation relates to the doctrine of Christ.

Some Wrong Answers

To examine critically all these wrong answers in detail would require more space and more knowledge than I have. Trying to adhere strictly to my prospectus accounts for the space issue. Admitting that I am neither a church historian nor a systematic theologian explains the ignorance factor. Notwithstanding these limitations, it will not hurt to present a cursory synopsis of these wrong theories. Keep in mind that each of them has tenets related to but beyond the specific issue of our relationship to Adam.

For instance, a theory called Pelagianism denies that there is any constitutional connection between Adam's sin and the guilt of humanity. This view holds that all humanity, just like Adam, comes into the world balanced on the fence of morality, with an equal chance of sinning or not sinning. Accordingly, Adam, being morally indifferent, alone bore the responsibility for his sin, and neither his sin nor its consequences affect the human race. At worst, Adam set a bad example, and his descendants simply follow his bad example by sinning themselves. On the surface, the notion of individual responsibility sounds fair, but it ignores the explicit biblical data and wipes away the other side of Paul's argument in Romans 5 that links Christ's obedience to justification. If Adam's sin was just a bad example, then it follows that Christ's obedience was just a good example that ultimately contributes nothing to the salvation of sinners. Every man would be left to his own attempts to be perfect, attempts that are doomed to failure. That is hardly good news. This is an obvious and deleterious error.

An adaptation of Pelagianism called Semi-Pelagianism teaches that man inherited from Adam a moral corruption that renders him spiritually sick but not dead. Semi-Pelagians define sin as conscious voluntary acts; sin is not a condition, just a type of behavior. Since man was not a voluntary participant in Adam's transgression, he cannot be liable for Adam's guilt. Inherited corruption, though not sin, gives occasion to actual sins. Although man may theoretically be capable of not sinning, this sickness and corruption render man hard-pressed not to sin without God's help. Notwithstanding sinful urges, man in spite of his innate moral sickness can, without divine intervention, initiate right behavior toward God, who then responds to man's feeble efforts with aiding grace. Semi-Pelagianism led eventually to what we know more commonly as Arminianism. Arminianism, rather than saying God responds with aiding grace to man's initiating efforts, asserts that God gives grace equally to all men enabling them to believe if they so choose. This is generally designated as prevenient grace, a term derived from Latin meaning "to come before." Arminianism argues that it is God's prevenient grace in the soul of every man that renders a spiritually sick man capable of responding to the gospel and thus by his response making the gospel personally effective. Again, the emphasis on individualism and personal responsibility makes this sound fair, but it hardly agrees with the biblical data that declares man spiritually dead, not just morally sick. Salvation is reduced to possibility rather than actuality.

There is one more wrong answer that I will mention. This system of doctrine is called New School or New Haven theology because it evolved out of Yale in the early nineteenth century. Concerning the matter of Adam's sin, this theory teaches that man inherits from Adam an inherent tendency to sin. Although this tendency invariably leads to sin, the tendency itself is not sin because, according to this view also, sin consists exclusively in conscious, intentional violations of the law. Interestingly, this "guiltless tendency to sin" is remarkably similar to the Roman Catholic doctrine of concupiscence, the inherent lust, which although not sinful does occasion sin. In simple terms, men are not corrupt because they are guilty in Adam; they are guilty because they are corrupt. Men are guilty sinners only because they sin. This view essentially claims that behavior determines nature, whereas the Bible teaches that nature determines behavior. Bob Jones, Sr., an evangelist of the early twentieth century and founder of Bob Jones University, had a saying that nicely counters the error of New Haven theology: "Men are not sinners because they sin; men sin because they are sinners." A most insightful and a most Scriptural aphorism.

The Right Answer

The answer of Federal Theology best explains the connection between Adam's sin and man's consequent guilt. Federal Theology essentially affirms that God ordained Adam as the representative head of the human race. This is going to get a bit thick, but stay with me. I believe this best explains the language of Scripture, particularly in Romans 5 and 1 Corinthians 15.

As the first man, Adam stands naturally as the father of mankind. Every human being who has ever lived can trace his ancestry back to Adam by natural generation. In fact, as evidence of the real humanity of Jesus Christ, Luke traced the Savior's lineage right back to Adam (Luke 3:38). If we believe what the Bible teaches about creation, recognizing the natural headship of Adam is easy enough. Federal Theology also maintains that Adam was the covenant head of the human race. God established Adam as the representative head not only in a parental sense but also in a federal sense–the human race was in union with him. In the first covenant, which dictated the terms of life and death (Genesis 2:16-17), God would deal with the race as He dealt with Adam. After all, when God dealt with Adam in this covenant, Adam was the human race.

As the covenant head, Adam's behavior toward the terms of the covenant affected the whole race both because he represented the race and because very literally the entire race was in him. Had Adam obeyed the conditions of the probation placed on him in Eden, he would have earned for himself and his descendants eternal life. Unlike the Pelagian notion, Federal Theology maintains that Adam was not created tottering precariously on the edge of right and wrong, but was created with a positive bias toward God with spiritual knowledge, righteousness, and true holiness (see Colossians 3:10; Ephesians 4:24). Since God gave Adam every spiritual advantage, it was hard for him to sin. This increases the heinousness and seriousness of his sin. Adam did not uncontrollably slip and slide into sin. Solomon said that God made man upright but that contrary to that original righteousness he sought out many schemes (Ecclesiastes 7:29). Remember how plainly Paul explained it: "Adam was not deceived . . . in the transgression" (1 Timothy 2:14). Let's be sure to base our theology of Adam's fall on the Scripture and not on nursery rhymes. I certainly agree that Humpty Dumpty had a great fall and that despite the efforts of all the king's horses and all the king's men, Humpty could not be put back together again. But Humpty–i.e., Adam–was not an egg balanced on a wall. He was put in the middle of Paradise, and he had to take a long, running jump to get over the wall God had erected. Not easy for an egg.

When Adam deliberately and willfully disobeyed God, he corrupted himself, incurred guilt, and became subject to death. But Adam's disobedience was not confined to himself. Because he was our federal representative, we shared equally in his disobedience and consequent guilt. God justly imputed Adam's sin in breaking the terms of the covenant to the human race, which was in Adam and which consequently was involved in his sin. Through the disobedience of Adam, the entire race is justly considered guilty and is condemned before God (Romans 5:17-19). Therefore, all men are conceived in iniquity, born in sin, and naturally guilty. The immediate results of Adam's first sin have persisted throughout his race: shame (Genesis 3:7), alienation from God (Genesis 3:8), guilt (Genesis 3:10), and the sentence of death (Genesis 3:19, 22). Note that we are not responsible for any of Adam's subsequent sins, only the first sin that plunged humanity into guilt and spiritual death. Listen again to Paul: "By one man sin entered into the world, and death by sin; and so death passed upon all men, for all that all have sinned" (Romans 5:12). That's pretty clear. From the very beginning of our existence, therefore, we need a gospel.

Although our guilt in Adam may seem logically complicated and the implications of it unflattering, the biblical declarations of it are forthright. Consider the statements of the *Westminster Larger Catechism* and the *Baptist Confession of Faith*, which remarkably abstract the key points of Scripture.

> The covenant being made with Adam as a publick person, not for himself only, but for his posterity, all mankind descending from him by ordinary generation, sinned in him, and fell with him in that first transgression. (question 22)

> This sinfulness of that estate whereinto man fell, consisteth in the guilt of Adam's first sin, the want of that righteousness wherein he was created, and the corruption of his nature, whereby he is utterly indisposed, disabled, and made opposite unto all that is spiritually good, and wholly inclined to all evil, and that continually; which is commonly called Original Sin, and from which do proceed all actual transgressions. (question 25)

> Our first parents, by this sin, fell from their original righteousness and communion with God, and we in them whereby death came

> upon all: all becoming dead in sin, and wholly defiled in all the faculties and parts of body and soul. They being the root, and by God's appointment, standing in the room and stead of all mankind, the guilt of sin was imputed, and corrupted nature conveyed, to their posterity descending from them by ordinary generation, being now conceived in sin, and by nature the children of wrath, the servants of sin, the subjects of death, and all other miseries, spiritual, temporal and eternal, unless the Lord Jesus set them free. (*Baptist Confession*, Chapter 6, sections 2, 3)

This, in a nutshell, is what I have been trying to say.

Let me address one final question related to Adam's sin and our guilt that bears directly on the gospel: How was Christ affected by Adam's sin? I think you can see the surface problem. If all men are guilty in Adam and Christ is truly human, then how can it be that unlike every other descendant of Adam, Christ is absolutely sinless? I believe the Scripture unequivocally teaches the impeccability of Jesus Christ. He was not sinless just because He did not sin; rather, He did not sin because He is sinless. Remember this principle: Behavior does not determine nature; rather, nature determines behavior. That applies to Christ just as it does to us. Remember, as well, that sin is not an essential element of human nature as it was originally created. Follow again Paul's logic in Romans 5 and 1 Corinthians 15 and you will find that God established both Adam and Christ as the representative heads of a people. Note how Paul says that Adam was a figure of another to come (Romans 5:14) and how he speaks of the first Adam and the last Adam, the first man and the second man (1 Corinthians 15:45, 47). Although Jesus was a natural descendant of Adam and a real part of the human race, He was not subject to the sin that incurred guilt on the rest of humanity. Mysteriously and miraculously, the Holy Spirit took true human substance from the seed of the woman and produced the sinless humanity of Christ (see Genesis 3:15 and Galatians 4:4). I cannot explain this great mystery, but can only take the angel's word of explanation to Mary as the indisputable fact. "The Holy Ghost shall come upon thee, and the power of the Highest shall overshadow thee: therefore also that holy thing which shall be born of thee shall be called the Son of God" (Luke 1:35). Therefore, Adam's sin had no effect on Him, and with His sinless nature He fulfilled all the terms of the covenant of works that Adam violated. As the second Adam, He is the representative Head whose complete obedience is the basis for redeeming a believing humanity from Adam's curse. I believe that although he failed as the representative head, Adam–perhaps ironically but certainly by divine grace–personally believed God's promise of the Seed of the woman who would reverse what he had just done (Genesis 3:15). Adam received grace and was in Christ. As a public man, he condemned his race. As a private man, Adam knew Christ as his representative Head and was a member of Christ's redeemed race. The truth is that grace is greater than sin, even original sin. But we must understand that God ultimately deals with all humanity in terms of these two men. In union with Representative Adam, all die; in union with Representative Christ, all live. This is why I say we have to understand condemnation if we are going to understand grace.

Dead in Person

Although we are guilty in Adam, we cannot be blaming Adam for our own spiritual lifelessness. Other than Jesus Christ, no man is personally exempt from guilt and corruption. There is not a just man on the earth (Ecclesiastes 7:20). We have to face it: Every man from the beginning of his physical life bears the defilement and guilt of sin. David confessed, "Behold, I was shapen in iniquity; and in sin did my mother conceive me" (Psalm 51:5). When excoriating the people of Israel because of sin, the Lord declared, "Thou . . . wast called a transgressor from the womb" (Isaiah 48:8). We are by nature children of wrath and children of disobedience (Ephesians 2:2-3).

What the Scripture expressly asserts, it also vividly illustrates. Two significant object lessons in the Old Testament dispensation depicted the natural corruption that coexisted with the beginning of life. Though the object lessons are no longer operative, the truth portrayed is still the truth. The first was the ceremony of circumcision. Circumcision required the excision of the foreskin of the flesh, itself a symbol of sin and corruption. Significantly, the New Testament equates being dead in sins to the uncircumcision of the flesh (Colossians 2:13). Although the significance of circumcision as a sign of the covenant has many important implications (see Genesis 17:10-14), at the very least the fact that it was performed on the infant suggests that the problem of sin is a problem from birth.

The second object lesson was one of the laws defining ceremonial cleanness and uncleanness. The overall purpose of these laws–dealing with everything from diet to household scum–was to teach the people that fellowship with God demanded purity and that sin precluded such fellowship. Interestingly, one of the natural circumstances of life that rendered a woman ceremonially unclean was childbirth (see Leviticus 12). Children are without question a wonderful gift from the Lord, and having children is an occasion for happiness (Psalm 127). But regardless of how cute and cuddly the newborn child, God wanted all to know that that child was born a sinner. Job's question and his own answer sum up the perpetual problem of "man that is born of a woman" (Job 14:1): "Who can bring a clean thing out of an unclean? Not one" (Job 14:4).

Not only does the Bible make clear that man is a sinner from the start of life, but it also teaches that guilt and corruption infest man's innermost being. Not only are all men sinners, but all of man is sinful. Man is totally depraved. He is void of any good that can please God; he is without any spark that could possibly flame into spiritual life. Sin is a matter of the heart: "The heart is deceitful above all things, and desperately wicked" (Jeremiah 17:9). Jeremiah describes the heart as being a "Jacob" (same basic word as deceitful) and completely malignant and pernicious. Throughout the Scripture, the heart designates the inner man–the mind, the emotions, and the will. The natural mind is incapable of understanding anything spiritual (1 Corinthians 2:14) because the understanding is darkened (Ephesians 4:18). The whole "mind and conscience is defiled" (Titus 1:15). The natural affections are void of any love of God (John 5:42), being spiritually callous–past feeling (Ephesians 4:19). The natural will deliberately chooses the way of death, rejecting the way of life (Proverbs 8:36–note that the words "hate" and "love" are primarily volitional rather than emotional terms).

Romans 3:11-18 is perhaps the most extensive catalogue of man's sin nature in the New Testament. Note the following statements that particularly focus on the condition of the naturally depraved heart. First, that "there is no fear of God before their eyes" (3:18) suggests the depraved disposition of natural man. The sinner lives without the awareness of God that checks and restricts the evil passions. If Job's fear of God caused him to turn from evil (Job 1:1), it follows that without the fear of God, men turn to evil following a mindset that is hostile to God (Romans 8:7). The sinner lives without any holy motive or impulse. Second, that "there is none that understandeth" (3:11) suggests the imbecility of the depraved mind. In this total spiritual ignorance, even the beauty of Christ and the claims and offer of His gospel make no sense. Third, that "there is none that seeketh after God" plots the course of the depraved will. Nowhere is the depravity of man more painfully vivid than in the exercise of the fallen will. The first act of Adam's fallen will was not to seek God but to hide from Him. That is always the direction taken by the sinner when following his natural inclinations. Those who are in the flesh can mind only the things of the flesh (Romans 8:5). Similarly, Jeremiah described the cursed man as one "whose heart departeth from the Lord" (17:5). To have such a heart is death (Romans 8:7).

Left alone, man is in serious trouble because he cannot resurrect himself from this spiritual death or cure himself from this spiritual depravity. As the Ethiopian (or anyone else for that matter) is incapable of changing his skin, and a leopard (or any other animal) is incapable of changing its appearance, so sinners, who are "accustomed to do evil," are unable to do anything that is good (Jeremiah 13:23). "They that are in the flesh cannot please God" (Romans 8:8). Total inability to change nature is the inevitable corollary to total depravity. Admitting and remembering our helpless estate puts the grace of the gospel in the right perspective.

SINNERS ARE MORALLY CORRUPT

Man may be dead in trespasses and sins, but paradoxically he is quite active living in sin. Like spiritual zombies, sinners live unconscious of their death. The apostle Paul describes this zombie-like condition in Ephesians 2:1-3 when he details how the spiritually dead walk:

> You . . . who were dead in trespasses and sins; Wherein in time past ye walked according to the course of this world, according to the prince of the power of the air, the spirit that now worketh in the children of disobedience: Among whom also we all had our conversation in times past in the lusts of our flesh, fulfilling the desires of the flesh and of the mind; and were by nature the children of wrath, even as others.

The ideas of "walking" and "conversation" both imply the course, habits, and tendencies of life. The text identifies the three morbid guides that the spiritually dead follow. (1) They follow the world. This refers to that transient system that is inherently opposed to truth, righteousness and God. To follow this world and the spirit of this age is to be at enmity with God. (2) They follow the devil. This accuser, tempter, corrupter, and arch-liar is at the head of the parade leading to eternal death. Elsewhere, the Bible calls him "the god of this world" who blinds the eyes of unbelievers (2 Corinthians 4:4) and holds them captive at his will (2 Timothy 2:26). (3) They follow the lusts of the flesh. Nature again rules. The bent of natural inclinations yields to the passions of sin, and the desires of the mind are inherently predisposed to evil. It would be impossible to list all the conceivable sins that man is capable of committing against God and His law that render him culpable before God and subject to the just penalty of the broken law. Some sins are outward acts; others are inward thoughts. Some sins are against fellow men; other sins are against self. Some sins are more heinous than others, but all sins are against God (Psalm 51:4).

This is the problem with having a rotten heart: Out of the heart come all the issues of life (Proverbs 4:23). Consequently, from the evil heart proceed all kinds of defilement (Matthew 5:19; Luke 6:45). The original sin that corrupts the heart always issues forth into actual sins. We do what we do because we are what we are. We don't necessarily do everything we are capable of doing in the sphere of sin, but the great pity is that we are capable of doing the worst. In that catalogue of sin in Romans 3, Paul's attention to man's depraved nature leads to his focus on man's depraved behavior. Since there is none righteous (3:10), it follows that "there is none that doeth good, no, not one" (3:12). Read verses 13-14 and see how the mouth mirrors the heart. From the abundance of the spiritually dead heart emanate untruthfulness, slander, and profanity. Verses 15-17 describe a lifestyle characterized by violence, ruin, distress, affliction, and wretchedness. Sin defiles everything. If we are left alone, it doesn't look good for us.

SINNERS ARE JUSTLY CONDEMNED

God warned man from the start that the penalty of sin would be death (Genesis 2:17). Along with all the other miseries earned by sin (Genesis 3:16-19), death entered the world–immediate spiritual death, inevitable physical death, and eventual eternal death. To be spiritually dead and morally corrupt is to be under divine wrath and condemnation (Ephesians 2:3). To be under that divine wrath is to be inexcusable at the judgment (Romans 3:19). The Bible makes it unmistakably clear that God's judgment is "according to truth" (Romans 2:2) and that He will infallibly and impartially "render to every man according to his deeds" (Romans 2:6, 11). There is hardly a more fearful and sobering thought than to receive from God on that Day of Judgment what we deserve. What the sinner deserves and what he will certainly receive is "indignation and wrath, Tribulation and anguish" (Romans 2:8-9). Outside of Christ, the sinner's only prospect is the "certain fearful looking for of judgment and fiery indignation" (Hebrews 10:27). After that judgment, condemned sinners, having been sentenced "according to their works", are cast–body and soul–into the everlasting lake of fire, designated as the second death (Revelation 20:12-14). Eternal death is the certain end of spiritual death. The prophet's questions should haunt every sinner: "Who can stand before his indignation? and who can abide in the fierceness of his anger?" (Nahum 1:6).

It is beyond my purpose to discuss what the Bible teaches about eternal punishment; rather, for now I just want us to see the reality and the justice of God's condemnation of sinful men. Reflecting on the horrors of sin's punishment, however, should be an incentive for sinners to seek the Lord while He may be found and for saints to rejoice that Christ has delivered us from the wrath to come (1 Thessalonians 1:10) and that we therefore will never see hell. Let me refer you to the statements in the *Westminster Larger Catechism* that detail the sinner's punishment both in this world and in the future. They are sobering words which deserve serious reflection. David summed it well when he said, "Many sorrows shall be to the wicked" (Psalm 32:10).

> The punishments of sin in this world are either inward, as blindness of mind, a reprobate sense, strong delusions, hardness of heart, horror of conscience, and vile affections; or outward, as the curse of God upon the creatures for our sakes, and all other evils that befall us in our bodies, names, estates, relations, and employments; together with death itself. (question 28)
>
> The punishments of sin in the world to come, are everlasting separation from the comfortable presence of God, and most grievous torments in soul and body, without intermission, in hell-fire for ever. (question 29)

Note particularly how part of the punishment of sin in this world is sin itself. God's abandoning a sinner to his own ways is condemnation in action. Condemnation is bad now, but the worst is yet to come.

I hope the point is clear. By nature, we are dead, corrupt, and condemned, and by ourselves we can do nothing about it. We desperately need a gospel. If God were to leave man alone to receive the wages for sin, He would be perfectly just. But the beauty of the gospel is that God has not left man alone. No news for sinners would be bad news indeed, but there is good news. I have drawn attention in this chapter several times to the first three verses of Ephesians 2–bad news. I love the transition in verses 4-5: "But God, who is rich in mercy, for his great love wherewith he loved us, Even when we were dead in sins, hath quickened us together with Christ"–good news. Spiritual life is the only answer to spiritual death. God by His grace gives undeserving, condemned sinners that life in union with His Son. As we begin to consider all that we have in Christ and what it means to be saved, let us with the inspired apostle "thank God through Jesus Christ our Lord" because He has delivered us from the body of this death (Romans 7:24-25). Amazing grace–I once was lost, but now I'm found.

CHAPTER 2

CHRIST: THE ESSENCE OF THE GOSPEL

Far too often the missing element in Christianity is Christ. Modern Christianity–even that which is evangelical and fundamentalist–tends to focus attention on all the accompanying circumstances of Christian living without much direct conscious reference to the Savior Himself. This misguided emphasis leads naturally toward a conservative, "anti-modern culture" lifestyle, but such a lifestyle in itself is not necessarily Christian. We render lip service to the creed that being saved entails a personal relationship with Jesus Christ, but in reality do little practically to foster the knowledge and experience of that personal relationship. While we focus on the do's and don'ts of life and service, the One we say we serve is often simply a relic that we pull out for song or occasionally interject into duty. Considering the actual Person and work of Christ is something that we limit to designated dates on the calendar–the incarnation at Christmas, the resurrection at Easter. Such anniversary celebrations will not do much in helping us to maintain and enjoy the personal relationship with Christ that is indeed the distinctive feature of genuine Christianity.

Anniversary times are special, but relationships do not thrive on anniversary celebrations alone. Pardon the personal example, but it so happens that as I am writing this chapter, my wedding anniversary is approaching. It will be a special time because I am a romantic kind of guy. Yet my relationship with Sandra consists of more than once-a-year memories of our wedding day. I have lived with her daily for almost thirty years. I know her far better today than I did on our wedding day, and consequently, I can honestly say that I love her more today than I did then. Without question, my marriage has dictated aspects of my behavior. For instance, my marriage vows preclude my dating other women. I have gladly kept that vow not only since marriage, but also for some considerable time beforehand. In fact, dating someone else has not crossed my mind since the late '60s. To follow that restriction rigidly, however, while at the same time ignoring Sandra, may conform to the letter of the marriage law and be the right thing to do, but my solitary social life would not by itself make for a happy marriage. The time that we share together, learning more about each other, and what pleases each other contributes to a happy marriage. Pleasing her, not just keeping the rules of marriage, is my motive. It is my love for Sandra that makes my singular devotion and allegiance to her my desire. When you love, duty and desire merge. Love grows with knowledge of the loved one, and knowledge of the loved one increases with companionship. As far as I am concerned, Sandra defines marriage.

Now here is my point. What is true in the marriage relationship is true in the personal relationship that believers have with Jesus Christ. Knowing Christ more deeply and increasingly enjoying Christ are the secret to happy Christianity. Too often believers tend to think of the personal relationship with Christ in terms of the wedding rather than the marriage. Thoughts of Him are limited to the time of conversion and seldom recur for the routine experiences of life. So many believers try to restrict their behavior to what is right while at the same time ignoring the Savior. Duty is fulfilled without the passion of desire. That's not much of a personal relationship with a living Savior. The apostle Paul said that it is the love of Christ that constrains every believer (2 Corinthians 5:14). That cannot be our conscious experience unless Christ is the focus and center of our thoughts. The more our lives revolve around the Savior, the more we will enjoy the benefits of being saved and the more we will desire to live in a way that reflects that relationship and pleases Him. If it is true that right thinking about the gospel produces right living in the gospel, then right thinking about Christ is paramount. Christ defines Christianity: He is the *essence of the gospel*.

In this chapter, I want to lay the foundation for every component and benefit of the gospel that we will consider in the rest of the study. Every aspect of gospel grace flows from Christ, who is the Gospel. To begin to do justice to this grand theme of the Person and work of Christ would require a separate and extensive treatise. However, the scope and purpose of this book require that I restrict discussion to summary statements about the work of Christ that are fundamental to our salvation. I do not mean to imply that the Person of Christ is not relevant to the issue. Who He is gives infinite worth to His work. His uniqueness as the God/Man–one Person with two distinct natures–is essential to His being the one and only Savior of sinners, the only Mediator between God and men. In my book *Beginning at Moses: A Guide to Finding Christ in the Old Testament* (Ambassador-Emerald International, 1999), I devote three chapters to the identity, person, and work of Christ. You may want to consult those chapters for a more detailed, but still far from exhaustive, study. So taking for granted that we understand that Jesus is absolutely God and absolutely Man, I want to develop some thoughts about His work. Using Peter's twofold classification of "the sufferings of Christ, and the glory that should follow" (1 Peter 1:11), I want to consider key aspects of Christ's humiliation and exaltation. Regularly thinking about these truths will help us to grow in our knowledge and enjoyment of salvation because it will fix our hearts on the Savior.

In his classic definition of the gospel (1 Corinthians 15:3-4), Paul isolates the two principal elements of the humiliation and exaltation: the death and resurrection of Christ. The death of Christ was the climax of His humiliation; the resurrection of Christ was the commencement of His exaltation. This definition of the gospel consists of four statements introduced by the word "that," two of which end with the statement "according to the scriptures." Let me set it up this way to illustrate the structure:

That Christ died for our sins according to the scripture
that he was buried

That he rose again the third day according to the scripture
that he was seen

The two "according to the scripture" statements frame the structure and constitute the main facts of the good news. The two subordinate "that" statements establish the irrefutable proofs of the main facts.

The first irrefutable fact of the gospel is the death of Christ. This simple statement is rich with theological significance. The tense of the verb "died" indicates that it was a real, historic, once-for-all-time death. The prepositional phrase "for our sins" suggests the sacrificial and substitutionary intent of the death. The prepositional phrase "according to the scripture" indicates that Christ's death was the fulfillment of the eternal purpose and will of God. The gospel of the death of Christ is God's one and only plan for saving sinners. The proof statement "that he was buried" underscores the certain reality of the death. Christ was not buried alive.

The second irrefutable fact of the gospel is the resurrection of Christ. The tense and voice of the verb "rose" are most significant. Although the Authorized Version translates the verb as an active (the subject is doing the action), the Greek verb is actually passive (the subject is being acted upon). Both are biblically true statements, but interestingly the New Testament most often speaks of Christ's being raised by the will of the Father through the power of the Holy Spirit. As we will see, this stresses God's approval and acceptance of the sacrifice of Christ. The tense of the verb vividly refers to an action that has historically been accomplished but that has continuing consequences. The point is that Jesus, having died and having been buried, was supernaturally brought back to life and continues to live. He will never die again. That all this was "according to the scripture" means that the glory that followed the suffering was part of God's eternal plan for Christ as well. The proof statement "that he was seen" verifies that His was a real, bodily resurrection. The theology of the resurrection is based on the historic fact of the resurrection.

These are the simple and far-reaching facts. Let's now consider some of the aspects of Christ's humiliation and exaltation in a little more detail to give us something to think about as we learn to apply Christ to our salvation. It is thinking about Christ and His gospel work that will direct our lives toward pleasing Him. Those who think about Christ's death can no longer "live unto themselves" but must instead live "unto him which died for them, and rose again" (2 Corinthians 5:15). Right thinking produces right behavior.

In order to avoid excessive repetition, my purpose at this point is simply to identify and briefly to explain the facts. In the following chapters I will suggest the implications and applications of these truths for our understanding and enjoyment of the specific benefits of the gospel.

Key Aspects of Christ's Humiliation

Although the death of Christ is central to the gospel, Christ could not have died without His having lived. That may appear to be a self-evident statement, but the life of Christ is a crucially necessary element of Christ's redemptive work. The earthly sojourn of Jesus from the womb of the Virgin Mary to the tomb of the rich man Joseph was part of His humiliation, contributing to His qualification as our Savior. If we are going to understand the gospel, we must understand that His life was as vicarious as His death. What He accomplished in His perfect life qualified Him for dying a vicarious death. Since I will highlight the specific implications of this in subsequent chapters, here let me note only the salient and foundational points of our Lord's voluntary humiliation. Note how the *Westminster Larger Catechism* identifies the integral parts of the estate of Christ's humiliation:

> The estate of Christ's humiliation was that low condition, wherein he for our sakes, emptying himself of his glory, took upon him the form of a servant, in his conception and birth, life, death, and after his death, until his resurrection. (question 46)

Christ's Condescending Incarnation

Although man stands as the apex of God's creation, the apex of creation is infinitely beneath the Creator. For the Creator to stoop so low by assuming the frailty and limitations of human nature is the great mystery of godliness (1 Timothy 3:16) that reveals a condescension defying comprehension. Too often the wonder of the incarnation is lost to exalted views of humanity rather than magnified by exalted views of God. If we can begin to understand even a little of how great God is and how small man is, then the fact of the incarnation of the eternal Son of God will not only boggle our minds but overwhelm our hearts in love for the grace it reveals. To realize that Christ is the brightness of the Father's eternal and immutable glory increases our sense of wonder at His becoming man.

Follow, for example, the logic of John 1:1-14 and stand amazed. Several astounding statements jump out that point to the humiliation involved in the incarnation of the Lord Jesus. (1) He is eternal–verse 1. (2) He has an eternal, intimate relationship with God–verse 2. (3) He created everything–verse 3. (4) He is the essence and source of life–verse 4. (5) He is the revealer of true knowledge and holiness–verses 4-5. (6) He entered the world that He created–verses 9-10. (7) He assumed human nature by becoming flesh–verse 14. (8) He revealed God's glory as the only begotten Son of God–verse 14. This incarnation established the Lord Jesus as one with the human race; it was achieved by a supernatural conception and virgin birth, and it was necessary because of man's sin. From the first gracious promise of salvation given to sinful man, God made it clear that the Savior from the curse would have to be a man, the Seed of the woman (Genesis 3:15). In the fullness of time–when every thing was ready according to God's eternal schedule–He sent forth His Son, made of a woman (Galatians 4:4). The old hymn expresses something of the wonder that the incarnation ought to generate within us:

Give me a sight, O Saviour, of Thy wondrous love to me,
Of the love that bro't Thee down to earth, to die on Calvary.
Oh make me understand it, help me to take it in,
What it meant to Thee, the Holy One, to bear away my sin.

Perhaps there is no other text in the Bible that accents the humiliation of the incarnation more than Philippians 2:6-8.

> Who, being in the form of God, thought it not robbery to be equal with God: But made himself of no reputation, and took upon him the form of a servant, and was made in the likeness of men: And being found in fashion as a man, he humbled himself, and became obedient unto death, even the death of the cross.

The inspired apostle emphasizes both the depths to which Christ stooped and the reason He so stooped. The language is rich, explicit, and significant. Four notable points stand out.

(1) Jesus was, is, and continues to be in the form of God. The word "being" denotes a continuous existence, without beginning and without ending. Christ's unceasing existence is "in the form of God." The word "form" refers to the essential nature or essence of something. Jesus is everything God is–He always has been and always will be.

(2) Jesus knew He was God; He was conscious of His absolute deity. Here is a literal translation of verse 6 that shows the precise logic of the statement: "Who, because he was the very essence of God, did not regard equality with God to be something seized." The point is that equality with God was not something Jesus had to acquire; it was already His by virtue of His eternal existence. He did not grow into deity or divine awareness. Striving for deity was not necessary, because He was God. This is the essential truth that makes the next point such an amazing assertion of humiliation and grace.

(3) The Son of God became man. As He was the essence of God, so He became in essence a servant and assumed the appearance of ordinary man. Eternally used to

glory, our Savior entered the realm of natural frailty and infirmity. His making Himself of no reputation means that in self-renunciation He emptied Himself. The irony is that He emptied Himself not by setting something aside but by adding something—human nature. The infinite bowed to live among the finite; the Master of all became a servant.

(4) The Savior submitted to death. This indeed was the purpose of His coming. He came to pay the price for our sin and redeem us by His blood. This submission is defined in terms of humble obedience that led Him to the death of the cross, which encompassed the depths of suffering and shame. From the manger to the cross, the blessed Lord Jesus trod a path of humiliation that culminated in indescribable misery and reproach. But it is because of His voluntary humiliation to manhood and its limitations and consequences that we have salvation.

The *Westminster Larger Catechism* sums up concisely the elements of the humiliation of Christ in His incarnation:

> Christ humbled himself in his conception and birth, in that, being from all eternity the Son of God, in the bosom of the Father, he was pleased in the fulness of time to become the son of man, made of a woman of low estate, and to be born of her; with divers circumstances of more than ordinary abasement. (question 47)

His Suffering Life

Theologians define the life of Christ in terms of active obedience and His death in terms of passive obedience. Active obedience specifically refers to His perfect conformity to every requirement of the law of God, whereby for His people in His humanity He earned life by fulfilling righteousness. The merited righteousness of Christ is an essential factor in our justification. Passive obedience refers to the death of Christ whereby He suffered the penalty of the broken law in behalf of and instead of His people.

The death of Christ satisfied justice and established the grounds for the forgiveness of sin. Keep in mind that the term *passive* in no way implies that Christ was inactive or simply an inert victim. Rather, the term plays on its Latin root meaning "capable of suffering." I am happy enough with these designations and use them regularly in my teaching about the work of Christ. It is important to understand, however, that Christ was most active in His death and was highly capable of suffering throughout His life. Indeed, it is the entire suffering life of Christ that constitutes a necessary aspect of His humiliation. The *Westminster Larger Catechism* again expresses it cogently:

> Christ humbled himself in his life, by subjecting himself to the law, which he perfectly fulfilled; and by conflicting with the indignities of the world, temptations of Satan, and infirmities in his flesh, whether common to the nature of man, or particularly accompanying that his low condition. (question 48)

Because of Christ's lifelong misery, we have a Savior who is "touched with the feeling of our infirmities" (Hebrews 4:15). Through suffering, the Captain of our salvation was perfected (Hebrews 2:10). Similarly, "Though he were a Son, yet learned he obedience by the things which he suffered; And being made perfect, he became the author of eternal salvation unto all them that obey him" (Hebrews 5:8-9). In simple terms, Jesus earned His qualification as the Savior through real life experiences. His humanity was real. Throughout His life, Christ suffered in body and soul from various causes ranging from privations of life's goods to living in the polluted atmosphere of a sinful world. He suffered assaults by Satan from the time of His birth to His temptation in the wilderness to the unfathomable agonies of Gethsemane. In the midst of His sufferings, He evidenced a perfect trust in and reliance upon His Father and the Word of God (see, for instance, the express statement of trust in Psalm 22:8 and Hebrews 2:13 as well as His use of Scripture in resisting temptation–Matthew 4:4, 7, 10). In so doing He fulfilled all righteousness in behalf of His people and also taught by example the godly way through the sufferings and temptations of life. Another substantial benefit accrues to us in that because "he himself hath suffered being tempted, he is able to succour [come to aid] them that are tempted" (Hebrews 2:18). Furthermore, His being rejected by His people hurt His soul deeply, as evidenced by His compassionate lament over Jerusalem (Luke 13:34). With what marvelous precision did Isaiah foretell, as though in echo, the intensity, extent, and substitutionary purpose of the Savior's suffering life: "He is despised and rejected of men; a man of sorrows, and acquainted with grief . . . Surely he hath borne our griefs, and carried our sorrows" (Isaiah 53:3-4). Man of Sorrows–what a name! Hallelujah, what a Savior!

His Experiencing Death

Since death is a human experience (Hebrews 9:27), it was necessary for Christ to become man in order to die. Very simply, Christ was born to die; the ultimate purpose of Christ's incarnation was death. Consider how the Scripture so often links the fact of the incarnation to the end and purpose of His death. For instance, Paul says, "We see Jesus, who was made a little lower than the angels for the suffering of death" (Hebrews 2:9). Again the apostle declares, "Forasmuch then as the children are partakers of flesh and blood, he also himself likewise took part of the same; that through death he might destroy him that had the power of death, that is, the devil" (Hebrews 2:14). In His voluntary, atoning, and redeeming death, Jesus reached simultaneously the depth of His humiliation and the height of His gracious love for His people. It will be in proportion to how much we can begin to fathom the depth that we will fully appreciate the height. Before considering some significant statements about the death of Christ, I think it would be good to appeal again to the statement of the *Larger Catechism* for a precise synopsis of how Christ humbled Himself in His death. It really is a profound summary.

> Christ humbled himself in his death, in that having been betrayed by Judas, forsaken by his disciples, scorned and rejected by the world, condemned by Pilate, and tormented by his persecutors; having also conflicted with the terrors of death, and powers of

> darkness, felt and borne the weight of God's wrath, he laid down his life an offering for sin, enduring the painful, shameful, and cursed death of the cross. (question 49)

Christ's Death was Necessary

The fact of the matter is that "without the shedding of blood is no remission" of sins (Hebrews 9:22). This is the bottom line: Salvation is impossible without the sacrificial death of Jesus Christ. Without Christ's death, there is no gospel–no good news for sinners. God's holy justice demands that the penalty of sin be paid in full, and one way or another that penalty will be paid. God cannot let bygones be bygones when it comes to sin. Apart from the atoning death of Jesus Christ, man is left to pay his own debt to law and justice. Self-payment requires an eternity of death and unrelenting suffering. God, according to the reasoning of His grace, provided His only begotten Son to be the Savior, and His being the Savior required His death. According to the New Testament, Christ's death was the only means by which God could be both just and the justifier (Romans 3:25-26). It is on the cross of Jesus that "mercy and truth are met together" and "righteousness and peace have kissed each other" (Psalm 85:10). The Scripture forthrightly declares that if salvation were possible in any other way, then Christ died in vain–for no reason at all. "If righteousness come by the law, then Christ is dead in vain" (Galatians 2:21).

Christ's Death was Vicarious

Christ's death was a substitutionary sacrifice. We often speak of this aspect as the vicarious atonement. A vicar is simply one who fulfills the duties of another as a substitute. That Christ's death was vicarious means that He died instead of us; He died in place of us. By virtue of His perfect obedience, Jesus Christ was personally exempt from death–the consequence of disobedience. Notwithstanding His right to live, Christ assumed our guilt and fulfilled our obligation to die in payment of our sins.

This amazing truth has three notable implications. (1) It implies that the guilty party could not endure his own punishment with the remotest hope of ever satisfying justice or accomplishing reconciliation with the offended God. Man's salvation must come from a source independent of himself. (2) It implies that the person paying the penalty had no personal debt to discharge. Had Christ not been completely pure and holy before His death, He would not have been able to die for others. This is why the life of Christ is so much a vital part of the gospel. His perfect vicarious life made possible His vicarious death. (3) It implies that the offender is conscious of his guilt, his deplorable condition, and his desperate need, and that he recognizes that a substitute suffered and died in his place. Salvation does not require theological knowledge of all the theories of the atonement, but it does require the knowledge of and trust in the profoundly simple truth that "Jesus died for me."

Both the Old and the New Testaments are rich in the theology of substitutionary sacrifice. The plethora of "proof-texts" verifies this as the essence of the gospel message. To identify the Scriptures that affirm the vicarious death of Christ requires far more space than available here, but I urge you to take the time to ponder Isaiah's classic declaration. The point is pretty hard to miss.

> Surely he hath borne our griefs, and carried our sorrows. . . . he was wounded for our transgressions, he was bruised for our iniquities: the chastisement of our peace was upon him; and with his stripes we are healed. . . . the Lord hath laid on him the iniquity of us all (Isaiah 53:4-6).

Christ's Death was Successful

Every time we meditate on the cross-work of the Lord Jesus, our hearts ought to warm, overflowing with gratitude and praise for His wondrous love. To meditate on the indescribable sufferings, tortures, and agonies that our Savior endured for us should generate ever-increasing love, devotion, dedicated service, and confident assurance. This kind of subjective response to Christ is good and is an intended effect of the sufferings and death of our Lord. In fact, one of my objectives in this book is to encourage right thinking about Christ and His gospel in order to direct right living for Christ. Nevertheless, the atonement possesses an objective aspect that is vitally important, too. By objective, I mean something outside of and independent of our subjective, personal responses: something that is true regardless of feeling. So important are these objective factors that were they not true, the cross of Christ could not save us no matter what we thought about it. When we understand what the atonement did "objectively," it warrants even more "subjective" confidence, joy, and praise. There are three principal truths about the success of the death of Christ that make it a real, and not a "maybe," gospel.

Toward God

Christ's death was effective with God. This Godward effect of the atonement is called *propitiation*. Propitiation refers to the satisfaction or appeasement of God's just wrath against sin and sinners. The death of Christ satisfied the penalty of the broken law; the blood of Christ appeased the divine wrath against the sinner. The blood of Christ removed every legal impediment to man's coming to God. This fact brings us to one of the great mysteries of the cross of Jesus Christ. The crucifixion was at the same time the greatest display of God's love for sinners and the greatest display of His justice and wrath against sin. The inflexibly holy and just God poured out His infinite wrath on His dear and only Son. Because the Lord Jesus took for us the full brunt of God's wrath, there is absolutely no wrath left for us. To be in Christ is to be free from divine wrath because that wrath was appeased. God is no longer angry with those reconciled by the blood of His Son. The mystery is that the God who is justly angry at sin is the God who lovingly gave His Son "to be the propitiation for our sins" (1 John 4:10; Romans 5:8-10; 2 Corinthians 5:18-20).

Against Sin

Christ's death was effective regarding sin. This sinward effect of the atonement is called *expiation*. Expiation refers to the removal of sin and guilt, the forgiveness of sin. Christ came to "put away sin by the sacrifice of himself" (Hebrews 9:26), and this is exactly what He did. John said the purpose of Christ's coming was to "destroy the works of the devil" (1 John 3:8; cf. Hebrews 2:14). This in no way means that Christ offered Himself to Satan, but rather that His death was the ultimate bruising of the serpent's head that reversed the curse of sin (Genesis 3:15). His sacrificial death paid the penalty of sin; it provided cleansing for sin; it defeated the power of sin; it guaranteed the final escape from the very presence of sin. Through the blood of the Lord Jesus is "the forgiveness of sins, according to the riches of his grace" (Ephesians 1:7). Little wonder that Paul exclaims, "Sin shall not have dominion over you" (Romans 6:14). The old hymn answers its own question definitely. "What can wash away my sin? Nothing but the blood of Jesus."

For Man

Christ's death was effective for man. My point here is simply that the gospel works. Because the atonement satisfied God and defeated sin, it can save man. The emphasis of Scripture is on the redemption and deliverance every believer enjoys through Christ (see 1 Corinthians 7:23; Galatians 3:13; 1 Peter 1:18-19; 1 Timothy 2:6; Revelation 5:9). Believers are delivered from every curse of sin and threat of the law. Believers are assured access to God–now only spiritually, but someday completely. The death of Christ is the basis for every benefit that we enjoy in salvation: union with Christ, justification, adoption, sanctification, assurance of divine love, peace, joy, perseverance, eternal security, hope of certain resurrection, eternal glorification, and whatever else God has promised and Christ has guaranteed. The more we learn to relate every aspect of our salvation to the precious blood Christ shed for us, the more we will know and enjoy the certainty of our salvation.

Ironically, although the death of Christ successfully accomplished its eternal design, it appeared from every human perspective to mark failure. In one last humiliating gesture, the limp and lifeless body of Jesus was removed from the cross, wrapped with the spices of death, and placed in a damp, dark grave. The passive entrance of Christ to the tomb seemed to score another victory for death and the grave. Christ's being held by death seemed to end any gospel hope flowing from Him. Paradoxically, what appeared to be a place of defeat--where death kept its spoil–became the place where triumph was first revealed. He entered the tomb dead in apparent defeat; He exited the tomb alive in unmistakable triumph. "O death, where is thy sting? O grave, where is thy victory?" (1 Corinthians 15:55; see Hosea 13:14). The last place of His humiliation became the first place of His exaltation.

KEY ASPECTS OF CHRIST'S EXALTATION

Christ's humiliation was temporary, never to be repeated. His exaltation is everlasting, never to cease. Just as certainly as Philippians 2:6-8 traces the steps of Christ's voluntary humiliation, verses 9-11 set the course of His earned exaltation.

> Wherefore God also hath highly exalted him, and given him a name which is above every name: That at the name of Jesus every knee should bow, of things in heaven, and things in earth, and things under the earth; And that every tongue should confess that Jesus Christ is Lord, to the glory of God the Father.

This earned exaltation of Christ is a necessary component of the gospel. A dead Christ may testify to unselfish and sacrificing love, but a dead Christ cannot save. The good news is that Jesus Christ lives. The summary statement in the Westminster Larger Catechism isolates four specific aspects to Christ's exaltation:

> The estate of Christ's exaltation comprehendeth his resurrection, ascension, sitting at the right hand of the Father, and his coming again to judge the world. (question 51)

His Glorious Resurrection

Christ's resurrection is more than theological doctrine; it is historic fact. Every genuine Christian affirms that Jesus Christ, having been crucified on a Roman cross, bodily rose from the dead on an actual day in history. To deny the resurrection is to deny the gospel. But to believe in a resurrection that did not occur is still to perish in sins. The objective, historical certainty of the resurrection is essential to salvation (1 Corinthians 15:17). Indeed, Paul makes it clear that believing in the resurrection of Christ is worthless folly if Christ did not in truth rise from the dead. Believing it and preaching it do not make it so (see 1 Corinthians 15:14). Notwithstanding the necessary emphasis on the historicity of the resurrection, we must not ignore the equally important theology associated with it that is so wonderfully a part of our salvation. Too often it is the neglected part of the gospel.

The Resurrection Affirmed Christ's Identity

The resurrection unmistakably identified Jesus of Nazareth as the promised Messiah (Luke 24:44-46), as the true prophet of God (Matthew 12:38; John 2:18), and as the only begotten Son of God (Romans 1:4). Because the Old Testament predicted the glory that would follow the Messiah's suffering and death, the resurrection of Jesus was the powerful affirmation that He was in fact the Christ of God, the only Redeemer. His resurrection verified and validated every claim the Scripture made concerning the Messiah and that Christ made about Himself. In His earthly preaching, Jesus staked His whole prophetic authority on the prediction that He would rise from the dead (the sign of Jonah–Matthew 12:39-40; and building the temple in three days–John 12:19, 21). The resurrection set a seal on all His instructions and promises; it powerfully affirmed every other word–whether words of grace or warnings of judgment. The implications are significant: If He was right concerning this astounding prophecy, then everything else He said deserves careful hearing and obedience.

The Resurrection Accredited Christ's Atonement

Romans 4:25 is a pivotal verse: "Who was delivered for our offenses, and was raised again for our justification." The word "for" more specifically means "because." Consider the logic of the verse: Because of our justification, Christ was raised. His resurrection is the sign and the guarantee that God received His sacrifice as the full satisfaction of the Father's wrath against sin, the full payment for sin's penalty. Significantly, in this connection most of the references to the resurrection focus on God's activity in raising up Christ. Although it is true that Christ arose, it is theologically vital that we understand and believe that He was raised by the power of God's Spirit. This was the great stamp of approval on a mission accomplished. Christ's active and passive obedience secured our justification; His resurrection assures us of that fact. His death showed His willingness to save; His resurrection showed His power to save. It is only because Jesus lives that we can know that the ransom was sufficient, that the sacrifice was accepted, and that we are purchased.

The Resurrection Acclaimed Christ's Authority

Acts 2:32-36 is an important text to establish this principle: "This Jesus hath God raised up, whereof we all are witnesses . . . therefore, let all the house of Israel know assuredly, that God hath made that same Jesus, whom ye have crucified, both Lord and Christ." This passage suggests two thoughts. First, He is the Head over all things to His church; He is the *mediatorial ruler* (Ephesians 1:20-22). The resurrection acclaims or declares His right to rule and to be the absolute Lord of all. Our confidence in His enthronement flows from our belief in His rising from the dead. A Christ held prisoner to the grave would be no different from any other person who dies and He would, therefore, have no authority to rule. But that Christ does live after death and that He is consequently Lord of all are fundamental tenets of Christianity. Because He rules, believers ought to be encouraged, and sinners ought to be warned since the right to rule confers the right to judge. Second, His continuing life–the consequence of His resurrection–gives Him the uniquely special authority to be the *mediatorial representative* of His people. (Hebrews 7:25; Romans 8:34). As the successful High Priest, He conspicuously bears our names before God. The resurrection is the bedrock for His session work–itself a distinct feature of His exaltation.

The Resurrection Achieved our Salvation

The Scripture links the new birth directly to the operation of the resurrection: We have been begotten "again unto a lively hope by the resurrection of Jesus Christ from the dead" (1 Peter 1:3). Similarly, the Bible defines full salvation in terms of the Savior's life following His death: "For if, when we were enemies, we were reconciled to God by the death of his Son, much more, being reconciled, we shall be saved by his life" (Romans 5:10). If by His death Christ fulfilled every condition to purchase life for those united to Him, then those united to Him will be certainly saved in and by His life. In fact, the resurrection of Christ stands as the great guarantee of the success of His whole mission.

Paul's great defense of the believer's resurrection in 1 Corinthians 15 includes two far-reaching statements that asseverate the virtual impossibility of salvation without the resurrection. First, if Christ is still dead, then the gospel is worthless (15:14, 17). Paul compares the message of the gospel to a shell without a nut: It is empty, full of nothing. Without a resurrection, any faith in Christ is useless. After all, the object of faith determines the value of faith. Faith in a dead Christ is worthless. Second, if Christ is still dead, then believers will perish. A dead Christ cannot do anything for anyone. Intensity or sincerity of faith in Him does not infuse Him with saving power. A Christ who lives in the heart is good, but if the heart is only place He lives, there is no salvation. Believing doesn't make the resurrection true. Christianity is not make-believe. It is belief based in real, historic facts. Therefore, because the resurrection is true, believing it is salvation.

The Resurrection Assures our Immortality

Christ's life after death not only revealed the destiny of believers but also guarantees the life of every believer. Jesus said, "Because I live, ye shall live also" (John 14:19). His simple cause-effect logic is irrefutable. The logic of 1 Corinthians 15:20-23 is equally impeccable. That Christ is the "firstfruits of them that slept" means simply that others are going to follow Him out of death into life. Christ's resurrection powerfully and infallibly holds ours in tow. It is impossible for those in Christ to perish. Spiritual union with Christ assures and necessitates everlasting life. It is the indisputable fact that in Adam all must die; so in Christ all must live (1 Corinthians 15:21-22). As the first dying Adam took his natural descendants into death with him, so the second rising Adam takes His spiritual seed to life with Him. Christ redeemed us completely, and not one part of redeemed man will ever perish, not even the body. By His resurrection, Christ "hath abolished death, and hath brought life and immortality to light through the gospel" (2 Timothy 1:10).

His Glorious Ascension

Although not many texts focus directly on this single event, it is nonetheless important. Luke records the historic fact of Christ's having been taken up into heaven (Luke 24:51; Acts 1:9,11). Hebrews speaks of our great high priest "that is passed into the heavens" (4:14). This could be rendered more literally "a great high priest, that had gone through the heavens." The bodily ascension of the Lord Jesus testifies to His finished work, which earned His entrance to glory and commenced a new, intensified, manifest ministry of the Holy Spirit (John 16:7-17). In one sense, Christ's return to heaven was to be expected. He Himself said, "I came forth from the Father, and am come into the world: again, I leave the world, and go to the Father" (John 16:28). As the Son of God, He had every right to reside in His eternal glory. What made the ascension theologically special was the entering into glory of the Son of Man. The inspired apostle recognized the significance of this when he applied Psalm 8 directly and uniquely to Christ: "What is man, that thou art mindful of him? or the son of man, that thou visitest him? Thou madest him a little lower than the angels; thou crownedst him with glory and honour, and didst set him over the works of thy hands" (Hebrews 2:6-7). For a little while the Son of Man was being perfected through sufferings, but because of His perfect life He earned everlasting glory as the Ideal Man. In the person of Jesus Christ, man achieved heaven. His entrance prepared the way for all of His followers. Speaking of

Christ's entering within the veil, the most holy place of heaven itself, Hebrews plainly says, "Whither the forerunner is for us entered, even Jesus" (6:20). Christ is the pioneer who has blazed the trail for His people to enter fully into His glory. Heaven is ours because Heaven is Christ's. That is good news. Not only does His ascension foreshadow the entrance of His people into glory, but it marks the beginning of a vital part of His present ministry in behalf of His temporarily earth-bound people.

His Glorious Session

Theologians refer to the exalted status and station at the right hand of God as the *Session of Christ*. Hebrews says plainly that Christ has entered into heaven "now to appear in the presence of God for us" (9:24). As there was nothing passive about His first coming, there is nothing passive or inactive about His present position at God's right hand. Although He is sitting there, He is not idle. It is a huge mistake to assume that Christ is just sitting around heaven waiting for the Father to tell Him the time for His Second Coming. Christ is currently, constantly, and wonderfully active for His people. The two principal works of Christ between His advents are His intercession and His administration.

In His exalted session work, the Lord Jesus continues to exercise His mediatorial operations. As Prophet, He sends His Spirit to "reprove the world of sin, and of righteousness, and of judgment" (John 16:8). As Priest, He constantly intercedes for His people. As King, He administers the affairs of His kingdom, particularly His church. The *Westminster Larger Catechism* gives a clear synopsis of this work.

> Christ is exalted in his sitting at the right hand of God, in that as God-man he is advanced to the highest favor with God the Father, with all fullness of joy, glory, and power over all things in heaven and earth; and doth gather and defend his church, and subdue their enemies; furnisheth his ministers and people with gifts and graces, and maketh intercession for them. (question 54)

Prophetic Administration

His prophetic work is primarily mediate. This means He works indirectly, but He works nonetheless. Interestingly, Paul links Christ's prophetic administration to His ascension. Ephesians 4:9-10 is an interesting passage that is often misunderstood: "Now that he ascended, what is it but that he also descended first into the lower parts of the earth? He that descended is the same also that ascended up far above all the heavens, that he might fill all things." Let us be careful to follow Paul's logic. There is no question that he is referring to Christ's ascension into heaven. This ascension from earth to heaven is possible only because Christ first descended from heaven to earth. Paul's reference to lower parts is in contrast to heaven, not some lower region inside the earth. The word "earth" stands in an appositive relationship to "lower parts." In other words, "earth" identifies what the "lower parts" are. The descending refers to His Incarnation; the ascending refers to His glorious entrance to heaven. On the basis of this ascension, Paul declares that Christ "gave gifts unto men" (Ephesians 4:8). Included in this gift distribution were some "apostles; and some, prophets; and some, evangelists; and some pastors and teachers; For the perfecting of the saints, for the work of the ministry, for the edifying of the body of Christ" (Ephesians 4:11-12). Even while in heaven, Christ has not left His people without a Word.

Priestly Intercession

Christ's priestly work, on the other hand, is immediate. We are given the amazing privilege of listening in on Christ's great intercessory prayer just prior to His sacrifice on Calvary (John 17). One thing we can learn from that recorded prayer is that Christ prays with His people on His heart. He prayed both for His disciples and for every believer in every generation to follow: "I pray for them: I pray not for the world, but for them which thou hast given me; for they are thine. . . . Neither pray I for these alone, but for them also which shall believe on me through their word" (John 17:9, 20).

What He prayed on earth, He continues to pray in heaven. Although John does not again record the actual words of Christ's intercession, he assures us that "we have an advocate with the Father, Jesus Christ the righteous." The word "advocate" is *paraclete*, that one who is called alongside. Christ is the one near to the Father and near to us to intercede for us with the Father. Although we do not know His exact words as He intercedes for us, we do know the basis of His argument. That John immediately identifies the Lord as our propitiation suggests that He pleads His own blood (1 John 2:2-3). God is forever satisfied with His Son and forever satisfied with His sacrifice. None who have been saved by the blood can ever be the object of God's wrath. This intercessory work is our guarantee of the irrevocable application of the blood of Christ to save us and keep us saved forever. We will never comprehend how much we owe to the successful intercession of Christ in our behalf. The very thought ought to stop us short and move us to grateful praise for His faithfulness and effective representation of us at God's right hand. The statement of the *Westminster Larger Catechism* about Christ's intercession warrants our contemplation:

> Christ maketh intercession, by his appearing in our nature continually before the Father in heaven, in the merit of his obedience and sacrifice on earth; declaring his will to have it applied to all believers; answering all accusations against them; and procuring for them quiet of conscience, notwithstanding daily failings, access with boldness to the throne of grace, and acceptance of their persons and services. (question 55)

There is no book in the New Testament that more thoroughly instructs us concerning Christ's priestly intercession than the book of Hebrews. Although the apostle does not record the words of any heavenly prayer, two things emerge as remarkably clear from Hebrews: Christ constantly intercedes for us, and nobody can do so like Him. Hebrews 7:25 says, "Wherefore he is able also to save them to the uttermost that come unto God by him, seeing he ever liveth to make intercession for them." "To the uttermost" means completely, entirely, or perfectly. Salvation begun is always salvation finished. Hebrews 7:24 proclaims, "This man, because he continueth ever, hath an unchangeable priesthood." The word "unchangeable" means untransferrable. His priesthood cannot be passed on to anyone else. Only He has the credentials; only He has the heart to pray as He does for His people.

Kingly Administration

The kingly work of Christ is administrative, especially relating to His church. Once again we appeal to the evidence of the apostle Paul. In Ephesians 1 Paul first links Christ's resurrection to His session at God's right hand, alluding to Psalm 110. He equates the regenerating power of the Holy Spirit in the heart of believers with the same power "he wrought in Christ, when he raised him from the dead, and set him at his own right hand in the heavenly places" (Ephesians 1:20). The corollary to Christ's sitting down in heaven is that God "put all things under his feet, and gave him to be the head over all things to the church" (Ephesians 1:22). During His session Christ rules His kingdom.

John's initial apocalyptic vision of the exalted Lord illustrates the reality of Christ's superintendence of His church. When John turned to see who was speaking to him, he saw "one like unto the Son of man" in the middle of the lamp stands, having seven stars in His hand (Revelation 1:13, 16). Happily, the vision interprets itself for us. The lamp stands represent the churches, and the stars represent the ministers of those churches (Revelation 1:20). The point is beautifully obvious. Although John was exiled because of the gospel and the church was being persecuted, Christ was with them, holding tightly in His hand those whom He had appointed to lead, pastor, and teach His church. Everything was under control.

If the New Testament is clear about anything, it is clear that Christ is now at work for His people and that His work flows necessarily from His work of redemption. He accomplished a wonderful work at His first advent and will do so again at His second, but He is now active for the good of His kingdom. Our salvation is as much a present experience as it is a future eternity.

His Glorious Return

Discussions about the Second Coming concern that area of theology called eschatology, the doctrine of last things. Sadly, many today get so taken up with trying to figure out the timing and sequence of predictive details that they miss the main message. Even more sadly, many become so confident and dogmatic in their sequential schemes that they deny the orthodoxy and almost the Christianity of any who interpret differently. Let's be certain that the main theme of eschatology is not events but Christ. As believers, even if we cannot agree on the sequence of events, we ought to be able to rejoice in the knowledge of a soon-coming Christ. Jesus is coming again–personally, visibly, bodily, gloriously, really and truly. His glorious return marks the beginning of our glorious never-ending end.

Hebrews 9:28 plainly says that Christ will "appear the second time without sin unto salvation." Whereas His first advent dealt with the sin problem for His people, His Second Advent will bring the full consummation of the salvation of His people. He will change our vile bodies to become like his glorious body (Philippians 3:21). Every vestige of sin and corruption will be gone, and we will be forever with Him. What a day that will be when faith gives way to sight, and "we shall see him as he is" (1 John 3:2). Being saved is good now, but the best is yet to be.

Admittedly, I have barely scratched the surface of all that Christ has done, is doing, and will do for the full and complete salvation of His people. How can one begin to say enough or ever finish speaking about the blessed Savior and what He should mean to every Christian? Jesus Christ is the central, predominant theme of the whole Scripture and the foundation of all of Christian life and living. When Paul testifies that he determined to know nothing else except Jesus Christ and Him crucified (1 Corinthians 2:2), he models what should be the mindset of every believer. For Paul, the gospel of Jesus Christ interfered with everything in life. The gospel of Christ stood in the way of every sin and pointed the way to life and holiness. Paul himself never got over the saving and transforming power of Christ, and it is just as imperative for us to remember and to live practically in the light and the power of the complete salvation that we have in Jesus Christ. Successful Christian living in this present evil age will be in proportion to the degree that we see Christ and our place in Him. May we confess individually and confidently that "I know whom I have believed, and am persuaded that he is able to keep that which I have committed unto him against that day" (2 Timothy 1:12). We are complete in Him.

CHAPTER 3

Conversion: The Response to the Gospel

"What must I do to be saved?" That is a good question, and one's eternal destiny depends on its answer. How the needy sinner responds to the gospel of Jesus Christ is a matter of life and death. Jesus Christ is the only way, only truth, and only life (John 14:6). There is no salvation apart from Christ; indeed, His is the only "name under heaven given among men, whereby we must be saved" (Acts 4:12). But it is not the simple fact of Christ or the gospel that saves, or else salvation would be universal and evangelism unnecessary. Sinners must meet the terms and conditions of the gospel if they are to enjoy personally the benefits of Christ. These conditions of a saving response to the gospel are clear. The Lord Jesus, the Gospel Incarnate, reiterated the evangelistic message of the Old Testament (e.g., Isaiah 55:7; Ezekiel 33:11) and marked the course for New Testament preaching as He set the imperative conditions for salvation at the beginning of His earthly ministry: "Repent ye, and believe the gospel" (Mark 1:15). Similarly, Paul's answer to the Philippian jailer's question, "What must I do to be saved?" echoes Christ's command in a timeless injunction: "Believe on the Lord Jesus Christ, and thou shalt be saved" (Acts 16:30-31). This saving response to the gospel, which consists of faith and repentance, is called *conversion*.

Before we look at the issues of conversion, I need to explain why I am discussing it at this point in our survey of the gospel. I am aware that this chapter is out of theological order–at least as I understand the Scripture. It will become clear in the chapter on regeneration that I believe the Bible teaches that regeneration precedes and gives impetus to saving faith and repentance. I have already established the inviolable theological rule that nature determines behavior: we do what we do because we are what we are. How men respond to the gospel bears witness to their spiritual condition and nature. Men are naturally insensitive and unresponsive to the claims of the gospel and Christ's offer because they are spiritually dead. The Bible's pronouncement on this is quite clear: "The natural man receiveth not the things of the Spirit of God" (1 Corinthians 2:14; Colossians 2:13). Rejecting the gospel affirms spiritual death. Conversely, responding positively by accepting the gospel evinces spiritual life. Such affirmative understanding of the gospel is not natural to man; rather, it requires the intervention of the Holy Spirit. The Bible is equally clear on this point: "We have received…the spirit which is of God; that we might know the things that are freely given to us of God" (1 Corinthians 2:12). Accepting the gospel is necessary for salvation, and grace supplies everything necessary for salvation–even faith and repentance. The old creeds emphasize these truths about both faith and repentance. Notice, for instance, what they say about faith.

> The grace of faith, whereby the elect are enabled to believe to the saving of their souls is the work of the Spirit of Christ in their hearts, and is ordinarily wrought by the ministry of the Word. . . . (*The Baptist Confession of Faith*, chapter 14, section 1)

> Justifying faith is a saving grace, wrought in the heart of a sinner by the Spirit and word of God. . . . (*Westminster Larger Catechism*, question 72)

I want you to see that this is not just my theological reasoning based on some preconceived notions or even historic orthodox doctrine. It is divine revelation. Consider some of these express statements from Scripture, in which I have boldfaced the relevant words that establish this vital truth. "The God of our fathers raised up Jesus, whom ye slew and hanged on a tree . . . for **to give repentance** to Israel"(Acts 5:30-31). "Then hath God also to the Gentiles **granted repentance** unto life" (Acts 11:18). As a result of God's **opening her heart**, Lydia "attended unto the things which were spoken of Paul"(Acts 16:14). The saints in Achaia are described as those "which had **believed through grace**" (Acts

18:27). Saints are those "who **believe, according to the working of his mighty power**, Which he wrought in Christ, when he raised him from the dead" (Ephesians 1:19-20). "For by grace are ye saved through faith; and that not of yourselves: it is **the gift of God**" (Ephesians 2:8). "For unto you **it is given in the behalf of Christ, not only to believe** on him, but also to suffer for his sake" (Philippians 1:29). Ministers are to conduct themselves "In meekness instructing those who oppose themselves; if God peradventure will **give them repentance** to the acknowledging of the truth" (2 Timothy 2:25). I confess that I cannot understand or explain all of this, but neither do I want to explain it away.

I don't base my theological conclusions on hymns, but some hymns express some pretty good theology. I wonder sometimes if we ever really pay enough attention to what we sing. Listen to the words of this often-sung hymn: "I know not how **this saving faith to me He did impart**, nor how believing in His word wrought peace within my heart." The next verse is just as sound: "I know not how the Spirit moves, convincing men of sin, revealing Jesus through the Word, **creating faith in Him**."

Although regeneration is the theological and logical antecedent to conversion, conversion remains the first spiritually conscious act of the sinner. Perhaps we can make a distinction between the *theological* and *evangelistic* order. Preaching the gospel always addresses man's consciousness. Repentance is commanded to "all men every where" (Acts 17:30), and the gracious promise is that "whosoever shall call upon the name of the Lord shall be saved" (Romans 10:13). This saving faith comes only by hearing the Word of God (Romans 10:17). Therefore, the evangelistic invitation ought to be sounded far and wide to every man, because hearing the gospel is prerequisite to believing the gospel (Romans 10:14-15). Sinners are nowhere commanded to wait for regeneration; they are commanded to repent and believe. This evangelistic order is a bona fide guarantee that any sinner who comes to Christ will be saved (John 6:37). This is no maybe gospel.

The theological order, on the other hand, should be a source of great blessing to those who have been converted. Recognizing regeneration to be antecedent to conversion assures the believer that his believing is not just something that he himself has worked up; it is the gracious gift of God. Grace is always better than will power. Although not as familiar as "I Know Whom I Have Believed," another old hymn expresses this thought accurately: "I sought the Lord, and afterward I knew He moved my soul to seek Him seeking me." That's sound doctrine.

Let me issue a warning here, because some people while affirming a particular truth abuse the truth with their applications. Here is the potential problem. Some appeal to the theological order of salvation to justify what are totally unscriptural evangelistic practices. They either hesitate to offer the gospel to sinners indiscriminately or else couch the invitation of the gospel in such guarded terms that the sinner is constantly looking inside himself for signs of grace rather than looking outside himself to Christ. That conversion follows regeneration should not be a hindrance to evangelism or an obstacle in coming to Christ. If it is, the truth is being perverted by its misuse. I want to be very clear on this point: **Any understanding of the gospel that prevents its free offer to sinners manifests a gross misunderstanding**. Unhappily, too many refute the misuse by directing their attacks to the doctrine rather than to the abusers. Never abandon truth just because some misapply the truth. Remember that Jonah's excuse for not preaching in Nineveh was that he knew God was gracious, merciful, slow to anger, and abundantly kind, and that God would withhold His judgment from those who repented (Jonah 4:2). How can you dispute that orthodox confession? What was to blame? Jonah's creed or Jonah's heart? I strongly urge you to beware of and to avoid the misuse of truth.

All of the above should, therefore, explain why I have decided to begin our study of the components of salvation with conversion. Conversion is where the salvation experience starts for us in time; it is where our spiritual awareness begins. We have to start thinking correctly about the gospel right from the beginning. In this chapter I want to define conversion both in its whole and in its constituents parts. Conversion, the saving response to the gospel, finds its focus in Christ. This will be our constant theme: No part of salvation exists without reference to Jesus Christ.

THE COMPONENTS OF CONVERSION

The very word *conversion* implies change. Evangelical conversion means that the sinner is no longer what he was and that he becomes something he was not. Although true conversion always involves both aspects of change, it is possible to isolate them for the sake of analysis. Faith and repentance are the two essential components of genuine conversion. Faith is the positive operation, and repentance is the negative. Together they constitute conversion. I am not particularly happy about referring to repentance as negative because of the obvious negative connotations of the word itself. Saving repentance is every bit as positive as faith; it just provides a different perspective of conversion.

I often use the analogy that conversion is like a coin with two sides. One side of the coin is faith; the other side is repentance. Although they are distinct, one does not exist without the other. Unless a coin is counterfeit or bogus, it will always have both heads and tails. So it is that genuine conversion will always involve both faith and repentance. Sometimes, however, even the Scripture shows us only one side of the coin.

The book of Acts illustrates this. Some passages mention only the necessity of repentance: Acts 2:37-38; 3:19; 5:31; 11:18; 17:30. Others require only faith: Acts 8:12-13; 10:43; 11:17; 13:39; 16:30-31. But here is the key point. Even when the Scripture mentions only one or the other, the unnamed element is always assumed. Otherwise, the Scripture would be requiring different things for different people. The Bible explicitly states that God is no respecter of persons (Romans 2:11) and that He as "the same Lord over all is rich unto all that call upon him" (Romans 10:12). The terms of the gospel are timeless and universal. All of this must be understood in the light of Christ's full and normative statement: "Repent ye, and believe the gospel" (Mark 1:15).

But once again, I need to insert a caution before we can proceed. Failing to keep faith and repentance together has led to dangerous errors that jeopardize the gospel message. It is not within the scope of this study nor is it my desire to refute every theological error that perverts the gospel. Yet one of the motivating factors in my writing this book is that I have seen so many of the effects of bad gospel theology. Thus, without offering a full exposé, I want to identify two extreme positions that must be avoided. Interestingly, although these two aberrant teachings are poles apart, they commit the same theological and exegetical error: They both separate faith and repentance.

On the one hand, a view of the gospel referred to as "easy believism" rejects repentance as an essential part of conversion, making it an optional postscript for those Christians who want to become dedicated disciples of Christ or to experience real fellowship with God. At best, repentance simply becomes the mental decision to believe the gospel, nothing more than changing the mind. Some so-called hyper-Calvinists, on the other hand, separate repentance from faith by making it a necessary prerequisite to saving faith. They claim that a certain amount of repentance is required before faith is possible. This leads to struggles of submission that are never sufficient to lead to the certain knowledge of faith. I submit that both views are heretical–a term that I do not use lightly or carelessly. The one generates a carnal security that has no biblical warrant or spiritual evidence. The other precludes the possibility of ever arriving at an assurance of salvation. Although the seriousness and prevalence of these errors demand fuller analysis, I will resist the temptation of going into more details concerning the corollary errors associated with both views. I simply urge you to exercise caution and avoid any preaching or teaching that either adds to or subtracts from the gospel. Either equation changes the gospel.

THE POSITIVE SIDE OF CONVERSION

Faith is the positive side of conversion. It includes knowledge of the truth, assent to the truth, and trust in the truth. Theologians sometimes use the Latin terms *notitia*, *assensus*, and *fiducia*, but I think the English will work well enough. Whether we use Latin or English, saving faith always find its focus in the truth of Christ and the grace freely offered in the gospel. Without such faith, pleasing God and salvation are impossibilities (Hebrews 11:6). Therefore, putting faith in its proper place and understanding what it is are vitally important.

Key Terms for Faith

The Scripture employs several words and images when referring to faith, but three words in particular seem to sum up the three essential components of knowledge, assent, and trust.

First is the word used for Abraham's justifying faith: "And he believed in the Lord" (Genesis 15:6). This word "believe" (*'aman*) expresses the conviction that what is known is true and reliable. On the basis of that conviction, the believer declares the object of his faith to be true, acquiesces to the truth, and commits himself to it.

The second word is typically translated in the Authorized Version as "trust" (*batach*). This word emphasizes the sense of safety and security generated from the confident trust the believer places in the object of his faith. The Psalmist vividly conveys this factor: "I will say of the Lord, He is my refuge and my fortress: my God, in him will I trust" (91:2).

The New Testament word "believe" (*pisteuo*) expresses both the convinced persuasion that the gospel is true and the consequent reliance in the object upon which the conviction is based. Paul's personal testimony is a classic articulation of saving faith: "For I know whom I have believed, and am persuaded that he is able to keep that which I have committed unto him against that day" (2 Timothy 1:12).

All the words and images for faith have one key thing in common: They are all oriented toward the object. As we will soon see, the objectivity of faith underscores what is perhaps its most important component. Significantly, the confessional standards follow closely the lexical evidence of the key words.

> By this faith a Christian believeth to be true whatsoever is revealed in the Word for the authority of God himself, and also apprehendeth an excellency therein above all other writings and all things in the world, as it bears forth the glory of God in his attributes, the excellency of Christ in his nature and offices, and the power and fulness of the Holy Spirit in his workings and operations: and so is enabled to cast his soul upon the truth thus believed...but the principal acts of saving faith have immediate relation to Christ, accepting, receiving, and resting upon him alone. . . . (*Baptist Confession of Faith*, chapter 14, section 2; see also the *Westminster Confession of Faith*, chapter 14, section 2)

The Role of Faith

The Scripture is clear that believing the gospel is essential to salvation. The gospel is "the power of God unto salvation **to every one that believeth**" (Romans 1:16) and "Christ is the end of the law for righteousness **to every one that believeth**" (Romans 10:4). What I call the ethical dative or dative of personal interest ("to everyone that believeth") limits the application of the gospel's divine power and benefits of Christ's work to believers. Since believing is essential, knowing its function or role in salvation will help us in our overall understanding of the gospel.

Let's begin with the Scripture. "For by grace are ye saved through faith; and that not of yourselves: it is the gift of God: Not of works, lest any man should boast" (Ephesians 2:8-9). This is a key text that declares the logic of salvation. Although I see no problem with the translation "by grace," the grammatical construction could also express cause: "For because of grace are ye saved." Compare this with the great transition statement of verse 4 that highlights the mercy of God as the cause of our regeneration: "But God, because He is rich in mercy . . ." (my translation). Consequently, I prefer seeing the causal idea maintained in verse 8 as well. The translation "through faith" is well expressed. The preposition "through" in this grammatical structure designates agency or instrumentality. Here is the logic: Because of grace, we are saved by means of faith. Just in case we miss the implications of the logic, Paul explicitly explains that this faith has neither personal origination nor meritorious worth: It is God's gift making it impossible for the sinner to work it up or to take credit for it. The originating cause of salvation is sovereign grace; the meritorious cause of salvation is Christ and His work; the effectual means of salvation is faith.

This is the uniform teaching of Scripture. Paul begins his classic exposition of the gospel by making it clear that the gospel is a matter of faith. "For therein [the gospel of Christ] is the righteousness of God revealed from faith to faith: as it is written, The just shall live by faith" (Romans 1:17). The preposition "by" is different from the one used in Ephesians 2:8, but it also conveys the idea of means or instrumentality. This is clear not only from the usage of the preposition itself, but also from the original intent of the prophet Habakkuk whom Paul quotes (see Habakkuk 2:4). The Hebrew preposition translated "by" demands the notion of agency.

The implications of recognizing faith as the means of salvation are practical and weighty. If faith were the meritorious cause of our salvation, the pressure on us would be insurmountable to make sure that everything about the exercise of faith was just right to achieve the necessary merit. We would be under a constant cloud of doubt, wondering if we were doing it just right. I have seen far too many Christians beclouded by that kind of doubt, and I confess that I have been there myself. The tendency is constantly to evaluate the quality of faith. Questions of "enough" harass the mind–sincere enough, fervent enough, honest enough, heartfelt enough, or just plain enough. We make imperceptible distinctions between believing the gospel and really believing the gospel and then wonder if we have really believed.

Thankfully, the Bible never designates the amount of faith or level of sincerity required for saving faith. Christ informs us concerning how much faith we need to move mountains, but He never qualifies how much faith we need to be saved, just that we need faith. "He that believeth on him is not condemned: but he that believeth not is condemned" (John 3:18). We must learn that saving faith is not simply subjective efforts of make-believe. Here is the vital point to which I alluded earlier: Saving faith is objective. I will repeat it again and again. The object of faith determines the value of faith. Jeremiah illustrates this principle when he contrasts the cursed man and the blessed man. "Cursed be the man that trusteth in man" (Jeremiah 17:5), but "Blessed is the man that trusteth in the Lord" (17:7). The prophet uses the same word for trust in both verses; that is, the cursed man and the blessed man are doing the same thing. The difference is not the fact of trust, but the object of trust. The object makes all the difference. Similarly, in his famous Temple Sermon, Jeremiah warned religious sinners not to trust in lying words (Jeremiah 7:4, 8). Lying words are unsubstantial, empty words of deception. To trust nothingness is vain trust.

What an important lesson this is. Saving faith saves not because we believe, but because of what we believe. All the merit, virtue, and worth is in Christ. Therefore, even if faith in Christ is weak and imperfect (and it always will be), it receives full and complete salvation because Christ is strong and perfect. God accepts our faith not for the merit of its exercise but for the merit of Christ in whom we believe. No analogy is perfect, but I suggest that faith is like a straw through which we enjoy a refreshing cool drink. The benefits of drinking come not from the size or the quality of the straw, but from where the straw is placed and what flows up the straw. Realizing that faith is the means of appropriating the benefits of the gospel rather than the merit for which we receive reward will keep us focused on Christ rather than on ourselves. So quit taking your "spiritual temperature" to measure how your faith is doing. You will never be satisfied with what you see inside. Look to Christ and your faith will do fine. He is what gives value to your faith. Ironically, the more we look away from self to Christ, the more our faith will grow.

The Organ of Faith

The Bible makes saving faith a matter of the heart. "That if thou shalt confess with thy mouth the Lord Jesus, and shalt believe **in thine heart** that God hath raised him from the dead, thou shalt be saved. For **with the heart** man believeth unto righteousness; and with the mouth confession is made unto salvation" (Romans 10:9-10). Remember that throughout the Scripture, the heart refers to the entirety of the inner man–the mind, the emotions, and the will. Genuine saving faith engages each of these components of man's being.

First, faith is a matter of the head. Faith cannot occur in a mental vacuum. You cannot believe what you do not know. The message of the gospel is a matter of revelation, not speculation. Faith, contrary to natural reasoning, is not a leap in the dark; rather, it is stepping out into the light of the sure promises of God offered in the gospel of Christ. It is the special operation of the Holy Spirit to illumine our minds so "that we might know the things that are freely given to us of God" (1 Corinthians 2:12). Truth is central to faith. How much we know, however, is not the issue; whom we know is crucial. Saving knowledge uniquely focuses on Christ because He is the way, the truth, and the life (John 14:6). Isaiah, in his great gospel message of the Suffering Servant, stressed the knowledge part of justifying faith: "By his knowledge shall my righteous servant justify many" (Isaiah 53:11). The syntax literally reads, "by the knowledge of him," and according to grammatical jargon it expresses an objective genitive. In other words, it is by means of knowing Him that sinners are justified. The Lord Jesus also defined eternal life in terms of that personal knowledge of Him: "And this is life eternal, that they might know thee the only true God, and Jesus Christ, whom thou hast sent" (John 17:3). Thankfully, there are no theological entrance exams to heaven. We can even be wrong on some of our theological interpretations and ignorant of all the theories of the atonement. But saving faith is never wrong on who the Savior is or ignorant of what He has done to save us. Saving faith knows the fundamental message of the gospel that Jesus died and rose again. As knowledge increases, so can the enjoyment and assurance of faith.

Second, faith is a matter of the emotion. Emotion refers to that state of inner consciousness that is influenced by external stimuli capable of producing all kinds of feelings (fear, happiness, sorrow, love, hate, etc). Saving faith feels the gospel. The truth of the gospel applied in the heart by the Holy Spirit, whose ministry is to reprove and convict (John 16:8-9), serves as a most effective stimulus to persuade the sinner of his personal need for the gospel. This is exactly what happened when Peter preached the gospel on the day of Pentecost. "Now when they heard this, they were pricked in their heart, and said…what shall we do?" (Acts 2:37). That's what happens every time saving faith operates. Intellectually we know that Jesus died; emotionally we are convinced that Jesus died for us personally and we humbly yield to the truth. However, don't confuse the emotional aspect of faith with outward displays, since it is personality that affects the outward displays. The Holy Spirit stirs the conviction that there is no alternative but Christ. Listen to Peter's confession. "Lord, to whom shall we go? thou hast the words of eternal life. And we believe and are sure that thou are that Christ, the Son of the living God" (John 6:68-69).

Third, faith is a matter of the will. The will or volition is that part of our inner being that acts upon knowledge and feeling. Man's will always operates within the sphere of his disposition, inclinations, biases, and desires; he chooses to do what he wants to do. Prior to conversion, the depraved will choose behavior within the sphere of spiritual death and corruption. The Bible is clear that before God's gracious work of regeneration, "we all had our conversation [manner of living] in times past in the lusts of our flesh, fulfilling the desires of the flesh and of the mind" (Ephesians 2:3). Salvation requires the conscious and willful decision to choose Christ. In fact, that the Scripture commands men to believe places the matter of salvation squarely before the will. Imperatives are always addressed directly to the volition. Everyone chooses either to obey or not. Thankfully, the power in the gospel can change the whole heart–our minds, our emotions, and our wills. With a new disposition come all the new inclinations, biases and desires. Saving faith includes the conscious choice to abandon every other hope and to entrust one's eternal soul and destiny to Christ by adhering to His claims, relying on His atoning work, and cleaving to Him.

It is impossible to overemphasize the necessity of heart faith. Saving faith is the operation of the whole heart. Intellectual understanding of truth is vital, but not sufficient (see James 2:19). Feeling need is vital, but not sufficient (see 2 Corinthians 7:10). The resolute laying hold of Christ as He is offered freely in the gospel brings it all together. I'm afraid we get a bit careless sometimes in our use of biblical language. I have no problem with the common explanation of faith as "asking Jesus to come into the heart," since it is Christ in us that is our hope of glory (Colossians 1:27). But we need to understand that Christ in the heart involves a completely new way of thinking, feeling, and choosing. In this context, another hymn comes to mind: "What a wonderful change in my life has been wrought since Jesus came into my heart! I have light in my soul for which long I have sought, since Jesus came into my heart!"

Factors of Faith

Saving faith recognizes that there is no hope apart from Christ, rests completely on Christ and His total sufficiency, and remains because it is a spiritual work. The statement of the *Westminster Shorter Catechism* sums up nicely the key factors of saving faith: "Faith in Jesus Christ is a saving grace, whereby we receive and rest upon him alone for salvation, as he is offered in the gospel" (question 86).

Receiving Christ

Receiving Christ means that we appropriate Him to ourselves by taking into our possession all that He is and all that He has purchased for us. This is the language of Scripture. "But as many as received him, to them gave he power to become the sons of God, even to them that believe on his name" (John 1:12). Colossians also refers to believers as those who "received Christ Jesus the Lord" (2:6). The act of receiving implies a sort of passive inactivity. It is not a trade or exchange, for there is nothing that we can offer Him to match or deserve what He offers us. It is a gift to receive: "The gift of God is eternal life through Jesus Christ our Lord" (Romans 6:23). As Toplady eloquently expressed it, "Nothing in my hand I bring, simply to Thy cross I cling."

The act of receiving also precludes any negotiations or selective acceptance. Saving faith does not pick and choose what part of the gospel to believe or what truth about Christ to accept. Salvation is defined in terms of having Christ, not in terms of accepting one or another or some combination of His offices: "He that hath the Son hath life" (1 John 5:12). Faith lays hold of Christ as He is offered. Colossians 2:6 sums up what must be received for salvation: "Christ Jesus the Lord."

I often emphasize that we must not gloss over the way the Bible refers to the Lord. The names of God and the designations of Christ are never haphazard. Observe the significance. *To receive Christ* means that we are accepting Him as the one and only Mediator between God and men. We accept Him as the ideal Prophet who perfectly represents God and reveals the will of God for our salvation. We accept Him as the ideal Priest who perfectly represents us before God, having offered Himself as the perfect sacrifice and atonement for our sins. We accept Him as the ideal King who, having conquered us by His grace, owns us, commands us, and protects us. *To receive Jesus* means that we are accepting Him as the Incarnate Son of God who came to this world for the sole purpose of saving His people from their sins. *To receive the Lord* means that we accept Him as our absolute sovereign Master to whom we happily and willfully submit our lives. This does not mean that we must somehow attain sinlessness before receiving Christ, but it does mean that in coming to Christ we must exhibit the willingness to surrender every known sin. The gospel does not require that we must be perfect subjects in Christ's kingdom, but it does require that we acknowledge Him as the perfect Master. We must receive Him without reservation. It is impossible to separate His Saviorhood from His Lordship. We must receive Christ as He is. He will not be received otherwise.

Resting on Christ

Resting on Christ means that we have ceased from all of our self-efforts and that we rely on Him completely to save us. I have already referred to Jeremiah's contrast between the cursed man and blessed man (Jeremiah 17:5-8), but let me direct your attention to it again. The prophet makes it plain that trusting self and trusting the Lord are mutually exclusive. The cursed man who trusts in himself and his abilities is following his own deceitful heart in departing from the Lord (17:3). Contrarily, the blessed man abandons self and trusts the Lord, finding in Him his only hope (17:7). Resting on Christ means that we have come to the realization that Christ and nothing else and no one else can save. It is the essence of trust and personal commitment. By faith we entrust our eternal souls to Christ, believing wholeheartedly the truths of the gospel. Resting on Christ means that we solemnly acknowledge that no hope exists apart from Him and that trusting Him conveys us into the experience of all that grace supplies. Every true believer asks Peter's question and answers it the same way: "Lord, to whom shall we go? thou hast the words of eternal life" (John 6:68). "Jesus, I am resting, resting, in the joy of what Thou art." This pleasant sentiment gains in its loveliness when sung as the testimony of a heart truly at peace.

This part of faith is the most enjoyable, yet ironically the joy part often proves elusive to believers. To be resting on Christ is the safest refuge conceivable either to God or to man. Unfortunately, we can actually be secure in that refuge without enjoying an accompanying peace of mind. Too often Christians tend to rest in Christ the way I sit on airplanes. I am not a good flier. Not understanding how the massive weight of the plane defies gravity, and being prohibited from having any input or control in the plane's operation, I tend never to put my full weight in the little seat. So far, notwithstanding the pressure on my elbows and the whiteness of my knuckles, the planes I have been on have never "let me down." They have carried my full weight even though I have never sat down all the way. The operation of the plane did not depend on my comfort level. Again, no illustration is perfect, but I hope you get the point. The security of resting on Christ depends on Christ and not on how well we rest. The secret to happy resting is confident attention to the unfailing Savior. The enjoyment of trusting Christ will be in proportion to our conscious thinking about Him. "Thou wilt keep him in perfect peace, whose mind is stayed on thee: because he trusteth in thee" (Isaiah 26:3).

Remaining in Christ

There is one final factor of saving faith: It persists. Saving faith is not just a momentary, historic, crisis decision. The issue is not whether or not we believed the gospel, but whether or not we are believing the gospel. Genuine faith always believes; it never gives up on Christ. A peculiarity of Greek grammar makes this point often in the New Testament. I will avoid technicalities, but I do want you to apprehend the significance. The tense of the verb in Greek functions beyond simple designations of time as past, present, or future. It can also express how a particular action takes place. The most common tense used in the New Testament is called the aorist. I like to explain the aorist as a snapshot or still picture of the action; it captures and portrays the fact of something. Another tense called the present is more like a video recording of the movement as it is taking place. Let me put it this way. Saving faith occurs in the present tense; it is always in operation. This does not mean that it does not start; but once it starts it never stops.

John 1:12 grammatically refers to both the inception and the continuance of saving faith. I will translate it in a way that expresses the tense nuances. "But as many as received him historically and once for all, He gave to them once for all the right to become the children of God–to them who are constantly believing in His name." There must be an initial, conscious, willful decision to receive Christ; no one unconsciously evolves into salvation. Salvation is obtained at the moment of accepting Christ. In this sense, faith begins at a crisis moment. However, the certain evidence of faith begun is continuing faith. Similarly, Paul restricts the divine and saving power of the gospel "to all who are constantly believing" (Romans 1:16) and he also defines heart faith as "constantly believing" (Romans 10:10).

I don't want to get ahead of myself because I will discuss the whole issue of assurance of faith in a separate chapter (please continue to keep in mind that all these components of salvation are inseparable). But there is a crucially significant application here. Remaining faith is an important aid to the resting part of faith we were addressing above. When faith is defined simply in terms of a historic decision, a tension of doubt often develops within the soul and mind. The tendency is to strain our recollection, trying to remember all the circumstances and feelings that led to the crisis moment. Racking the brain for assurance of faith only wrecks the chances of reaching that peaceful assurance. Far too many Christians have been put in the bondage of doubt and fear by those who have told them that unless they can remember the date of their conversion, they have no legitimate claim to salvation. The solution to the doubt has been to decide again and then again and again. Assurance lasts as long as memory. I have read my Bible many times, and I have never yet read where the Holy Spirit directs the doubting heart to a past decision. Rather, the Scripture always directs faith to Christ. The day of conversion ought to be a precious and wonderful memory. But the proof of its reality rests in the continuing faith in Christ. If we are believing the gospel, there can be absolutely no question that we believed the gospel, even if all the details of our initial reception of Christ have escaped our memory. Christ is always the answer.

Faith is the necessary and saving response to the gospel. It flows from Christ and His atoning work, and it is fixed on the Person from whom it flows. May it be our testimony, "Lord, I believe." May it be our prayer, "Lord, help my unbelief."

The "Negative" Side of Conversion

God's call to life in Christ is a call to holiness (1 Thessalonians 4:7), and the Thessalonian believers illustrated the saving response to that call: They "turned to God from idols to serve the living and true God" (1 Thessalonians 1:9). Their turning to a new way of life from an old represented the essence of repentance. Saving repentance–like saving faith–begins, continues and ends in Christ. Its place in conversion is as vital as faith's, but it defines conversion from a different perspective. Whereas faith focuses on the grace of God that leads us to Christ, repentance focuses on the grace of God that leads us away from sin by turning us around to see and to follow after Christ. Habitually pursuing sin and savingly pursuing Christ are mutually exclusive. In the physical realm, it is impossible to go in two directions simultaneously or to look in two places at once. That's not hard to understand. Neither should it be hard to recognize the same principle of one-direction restrictions in the spiritual realm. Repentance starts us and keeps us on our spiritual journey. *The Baptist Confession of Faith* particularly remarks that repentance is "to be continued through the whole course of our lives" (chapter 15, section 4). Repenting from sin and believing in Christ constitute the earmarks of genuine conversion. The honest and faithful preaching of the gospel always includes both: "Repentance unto life is an evangelical grace, the doctrine whereof is to be preached by every minister of the Gospel, as well as that of faith in Christ" (*Westminster Confession of Faith*, chapter 15, section 1).

Before defining the biblical terms and highlighting the salient factors of repentance, I want you to think through the classic confessional statements. They clearly delineate the elements of repentance that the Scripture demands. I think you will see from these theological statements that repentance is not so negative after all.

> Repentance unto life is a saving grace, wrought in the heart of a sinner by the Spirit and word of God, whereby, out of the sight and sense, not only of the danger, but also of the filthiness and odiousness of his sins, and upon the apprehension of God's mercy in Christ, to such as are penitent, he so grieves for and hates his sins, as that he turns from them all to God, purposing and endeavouring constantly to walk with him in all the ways of new obedience. (*Westminster Larger Catechism*, question 76; see the similar statement in the *Westminster Confession of Faith*, chapter 15, section 2)

> This saving repentance is an evangelical grace, whereby a person, being by the Holy Spirit made sensible of the manifold evils of his sin, doth, by faith in Christ, humble himself for it with godly sor-

> row, detestation of it and self-abhorrency, praying for pardon and strength of grace, with a purpose and endeavor, by supplies of the Spirit, to walk before God unto all well-pleasing in all things. (*Baptist Confession of Faith*, chapter 15, section 3)

Key Terms for Repentance

Three words stand out in the Scripture as the principal terms designating repentance–one from the Old Testament and two from the New. Although the words on the surface appear to define repentance differently, the contexts of both converge into the same theological concept. Old and New Testament theology agree that repentance is a new way of life that reflects a new way of thinking. I am not going to present a thorough word study analysis of these terms, but I think a synopsis will help us grasp the importance of repentance as the necessary response to the gospel.

The technical term for repentance in Hebrew is *shub*. This word occurs over a thousand times in the Old Testament, not always in a context of spiritual conversion. Yet even when it does designate evangelical repentance, it is seldom translated "to repent" in the Authorized Version, which, even in obviously theological contexts, translates the word either "to turn" or "to return." But the notion of turning, particularly a *shub* kind of turning, vividly portrays the reversal of direction that is so integral to repentance. This word, while it does require an about-face, involves more than just facing a new direction. It implies movement. This is one biblical reason that the *Baptist Confession of Faith* was justified in describing repentance as that which is "to be continued through the whole course of our lives." Something moving in one direction turns around and moves in the opposite direction. It is not just a crisis turning; it sets the course for a whole new journey. The application of this to repentance is significant. The Old Testament explicitly teaches that repentance involves a turning from sin (Jeremiah 18:8) and a turning to God (Malachi 3:7). Sinners moving headlong away from God, following their natural impulses and inclinations straight to hell, turn completely around and move toward God and holiness, following their new spiritual impulses and inclinations. Once God was behind and hell was in front. Repentance puts God in front and hell forever behind.

The Septuagint, the Greek translation of the Old Testament, usually translated the Hebrew *shub* with the word *epistrepho*, which conveys the same idea of turning around. The New Testament continued to use the word to designate repentance. Like its Old Testament counterpart, it is not limited to conversion. It appears thirty-six times in the New Testament, but only half of the occurrences are theological. Most frequently, the New Testament points to the new direction of life toward God rather than the old life away from which the converted sinner has turned. Paul, nevertheless, did view the before and after directions when he referred to the Thessalonians' turning to God from their idols (1 Thessalonians 1:9). More typical is the explanation of his ministry to Agrippa. He testified that he preached the gospel to both Jew and Gentile "that they should repent and **turn** to God, and do works meet for repentance" (Acts 26:20). This text introduces the second key New Testament word.

The word translated "repent" in Acts 26:20 is the Greek word *metanoeo*, and it ultimately developed into the technical term for repentance in the New Testament. The Greek language is lexically elastic and can easily form words by combining two words into a single one. *Metanoeo* is such a compound composed of the preposition *meta*, meaning "after," and the verb *noeo*, meaning "to think." The potential linguistic danger associated with compound words is the assumption that the meaning of the compound is simply the sum of its parts. This assumption of lexical transparency has led to a narrow and consequently erroneous definition of *metanoeo* as "to change the mind."

I have instructed my Hebrew and Greek students countless times that the meaning of words is to be determined by contextual usage and not by etymological assumptions. Contextual usage reveals actual meaning, whereas etymology creates potentially artificial definitions that are imposed on the word wherever it occurs. Sometimes the consequences are lexically cute; other times, more serious. In this particular instance, limiting the meaning of this New Testament word for "repent" to a mental act has had severe consequences. Some theologians have reduced repentance to nothing more than a single crisis decision of the intellect that requires no subsequent change of life. This is a dangerous and unbiblical conclusion. To appeal to the etymological definition of a Greek word to support what in actuality I believe is an unfounded theological presupposition is grasping at straws–exegetical trickery.

I do not deny that repentance–whether viewed from the Old Testament or the New Testament–requires a change of mind. But I vehemently deny–from both theological necessity and lexical usage–that the New Testament limits repentance to the head. Just the fact that the New Testament conjoins the word *epistrepho*–"to return"–with *metanoeo*–"to repent"–indicates that reversing the course of life was included in the New Testament's theology of repentance. Even when it occurs without the defining term "to return," *metanoeo*, as the technical word for repentance, conveys and includes the necessary forsaking of sin as well as an intellectual persuasion of truth. For instance, Christ issued a sober warning to those who assumed that fatal calamities befell a certain group of Galilæans and those crushed by a falling tower because they were greater sinners than normal. He implied that the sins of those to whom He was talking were just as great and life-threatening: "I tell you, Nay: but, except he repent, ye shall all likewise perish" (Luke 13:3, 5). When we realize that repentance occupied so paramount a position in the preaching of Christ and that Christ so clearly defined what repentance entails, we should be more than cautious about redefining the concept based on either preconceived conclusions or convenient exegetical principles.

The Expressions of Repentance

Repentance, like faith, is a matter of the heart. Issuing from a divinely renewed heart, it is an operation of the heart. The prophet Jeremiah declared the Lord's direct word concerning heart repentance: "And I will give them an heart to know me, that

I am the Lord: and they shall be my people, and I will be their God: for they shall return unto me with their whole heart" (Jeremiah 24:7). In what I regard as one of Scripture's greatest invitations to salvation, the Lord says, "Turn ye even to me with all your heart" (Joel 2:12). Once again, since scriptural references to the heart include the mind, the emotion, and the will, genuine saving repentance must engage each of these components of man's being.

First, repentance is a matter of the mind. The repentant sinner understands the heinous nature of sin as an offense against God and recognizes God as the only source of mercy. The Psalmist expressed this twofold knowledge clearly. "If thou, Lord, shouldest mark iniquities, O Lord, who shall stand? But there is forgiveness with thee, that thou mayest be feared. . . . for with the Lord there is mercy, and with him is plenteous redemption" (Psalm 130:3-4, 7). The incentive and encouragement to repentance, according to Joel, is the knowledge that God is "gracious and merciful, slow to anger, and of great kindness, and repenteth him of the evil" (Joel 2:13). Don't misunderstand the last statement. The word translated "repenteth" is not the Hebrew word that refers to saving repentance as part of spiritual conversion. Any idea of that kind of repentance would be inappropriate to God; it refers instead to God's gracious relenting of judgment. The word "evil" does not refer to sin; rather, it refers to the calamity of judgment to which God has sentenced the unrepentant, guilty sinner. The wonderful truth that repenting sinners know is that God withholds His judgment from all those who with the heart turn to Him.

Second, repentance is a matter of the emotion. The repentant sinner grieves and sorrows over his sin. In repentance, the sinner offers no excuses for sin. Rather, with contrition, godly sorrow, and hatred of sin, he confesses that he has violated the law of the Lord. Until sin is felt and freely confessed, genuine conversion cannot ensue. Ezekiel describes a regenerated people as remembering their evil ways and loathing themselves because of their iniquities and abominations (36:31). Joel specifically explains what it means to turn to God with the heart by adding the requirement to turn "with fasting, and with weeping, and with mourning" (Joel 2:12). Fasting, weeping, and mourning were common outward displays of grief and sorrow in the ancient Near East. But true repentance does not consist in outward displays. Consequently, the prophet adds a most important qualifying statement: "And rend your heart, and not your garments" (2:13). The volume of tears or the loudness of audible cries does not measure repentance; it is measured by the inward abhorrence of sin. Since we are all different, we must realize that while emotional demonstration may indicate something about personality, it cannot accurately reflect inner spiritual realities. Regardless of the outward exhibition, genuine repentance flows from a broken spirit and a contrite heart. God never despises that kind of heart, promising to dwell in fellowship with all who are so broken (Psalm 51:17; Isaiah 57:15).

Third, repentance is a matter of the will. The repentant sinner obediently resolves to forsake his old ways and to seek the Lord. I think Isaiah's great gospel call expresses this demand clearly. "Seek ye the Lord while he may be found, call ye upon him while he is near: Let the wicked forsake his way, and the unrighteous man his thoughts: and let him return unto the Lord, and he will have mercy upon him; and to our God, for he will abundantly pardon" (Isaiah 55:6-7). The language is unabiguous. God puts the claims of the gospel directly to man's will by commanding sinners to seek Him and forsake their sins. It is incumbent on sinners to obey. Notice how unequivocally the Lord holds men responsible for their response to His demands.

> Repent, and turn yourselves from all your transgressions; so iniquity shall not be you ruin. Cast away from you all your transgressions, whereby ye have transgressed; and make you a new heart and a new spirit: for why will ye die, O house of Israel? For I have no pleasure in the death of him that dieth, saith the Lord God: wherefore turn yourselves, and live ye." (Ezekiel 18:30-32)

Thankfully, it is the goodness of God that leads sinners to repentance (Romans 2:4).

Human religion never affords any certainty on how men can get to God or achieve salvation. True religion, Christianity, presents a God who has not only accomplished what is necessary for salvation in the gospel of His Son, but who has graciously and clearly revealed the way to life. The message of the gospel is accessible. Listen to how Moses put it.

> For this commandment which I command thee this day, it is not hidden from thee, neither is far off. It is not in heaven, that thou shouldest say, Who shall go up for us to heaven, and bring it unto us, that we may hear it, and do it? Neither is it beyond the sea, that thou shouldest say, Who shall go over the sea for us, and bring it unto us, that we may hear it, and do it? But the word is very nigh unto thee, in thy mouth, and in thy heart, that thou mayest do it. (Deuteronomy 30:11-14)

Significantly, Paul refers to this very passage and defines it as referring to "the word of faith, which we preach" (Romans 10:6-8).

In accepting the gospel, no one is required to do the impossible. The terms of the gospel are the same for all the world of sinners. The terms do not change depending on social status or race. The promise is extended that "whosoever shall call upon the name of the Lord shall be saved" (Romans 10:13; Joel 2:32), and the assurance is guaranteed that "whosoever believeth on him shall not be ashamed" (Romans 10:11; Isaiah 28:16). Confessing with the life that Jesus is Lord while believing the gospel in the heart is the saving response to the gospel. This is basic to any further understanding or enjoyment of the gospel. May God establish and confirm us all on the indestructible, unshakable foundation of faith.

CHAPTER 4

Regeneration: New Life in the Gospel

On September 18, 1949, I was born in Ypsilanti, Michigan. I am told that it was a happy day. Although I had no input into my conception or time of birth and cannot recollect anything of that day, I have been alive ever since. One moment I did not exist. The next moment the miracle of life occurred, and I was on my way. Humanly speaking, I owe my life to my parents and ultimately to God, the Creator of life. Had I not been born I would not be alive–that is obvious. The fact that I was not conscious of my conception and do not remember my birthday is irrelevant to the issue. The fact of my life is the irrefutable evidence of my birth. Who can ultimately explain the miracle of life?

The striking parallel between the beginning of physical life and the beginning of spiritual life is illustrated vividly in God's creation of Adam. Genesis 2:7 is a key text: "And the Lord God formed man of the dust of the ground, and breathed into his nostrils the breath of life; and man became a living soul." In the first creation, Adam had no physical life until he received the special breath of God. The molded dirt may have resembled Adam's eventual appearance, but it was just a lifeless sculpture until God breathed into it. As a lifeless shape, the first man could contribute nothing to his becoming alive. But when God breathed into the lifeless form, man became alive, and he lived as proof of his having received the principle of life. Apart from that special divine breath, Adam was insensitive to paradise.

Significantly, the Scripture refers to the beginning of spiritual life in terms of creation. "Therefore if any man be in Christ, he is a new creature [creation]" (2 Corinthians 5:17). "For in Christ Jesus neither circumcision availeth any thing, nor uncircumcision, but a new creature" (Galatians 6:15). "For we are his workmanship, created in Christ Jesus" (Ephesians 2:10). In the initial process of natural creation, man was insensible to the physical world without the life-imparting breath of God; so in spiritual creation, man remains dead to anything spiritual without the life-imparting Spirit of God (see 1 Corinthians 2:14). In a most tragic sense, every sinner is dead to paradise. Just as Adam required God's breath for physical life, every sinner requires a gracious and special intervention of God to bring him to spiritual life. Consequently, the Scripture speaks of God's making dead sinners alive. "But God, who is rich in mercy, for his great love wherewith he loved us, Even when we were dead in sins, hath quickened us [made us alive] together with Christ" (Ephesians 2:4-5). "And you, being dead in your sins and the uncircumcision of your flesh, hath he quickened [made alive] together with him..." (Colossians 2:13). Adam made no contribution to his becoming alive; neither does the sinner aid God in becoming spiritually alive. Creation is always the unique and exclusive work of God. Who can explain the miracle of life?

THE DEFINITION OF NEW LIFE

This component of the gospel that concerns the inception of spiritual life is *regeneration*. Regeneration refers to the implantation of the principle of spiritual life into the heart of the sinner that results in an instantaneous, radical, and obvious change of nature affecting the whole governing disposition of life. The prophet Ezekiel explained regeneration in terms of God's giving the sinner a new heart and a new spirit: "A new heart also will I give you, and a new spirit will I put within you: and I will take away the stony heart out of your flesh, and I will give you a heart of flesh" (Ezekiel 36:26). The heart, of course, refers to man's mind, emotions, and will. The spirit refers to the impulses that direct and regulate the desires, thoughts, and conduct of life. The prophet's description of the old heart as stony portrays an inward nature that is cold, unfeeling, and hard. A petrified heart is utterly dead, incapable of functioning. It is a graphic image of the helpless condition of the sinner, void of any spiritual life or responsiveness. In regeneration, God graciously turns the heart of stone into viable flesh that responds to spiritual stimuli. This regeneration creates a revolutionary change in the way the sinner thinks, what he desires, and how he chooses to live. He has a new nature that is capable of spiritual activity. One moment the sinner was dead, the next he is alive. Consequently, "old things are passed away; behold, all things are become new" (2 Corinthians 5:17).

Regeneration is the application of spiritual life that awakens the sinner from the stupor of spiritual death, enabling him to see, to understand, and to grasp Christ as He is offered freely in the gospel. Both the *Westminster Standards* and the *Baptist Confession of Faith* define this regeneration in terms of effectual calling.

> Effectual calling is the work of God's almighty power and grace, whereby (out of his free and special love to his elect, and from nothing in them moving him thereonto) he doth, in his accepted time, invite and draw them to Jesus Christ, by his word and Spirit; savingly enlightening their minds, renewing and powerfully determining their wills, so as they (although in themselves dead in sin) are hereby made willing and able freely to answer his call, and to accept and embrace the grace offered and conveyed therein. (*Westminster Larger Catechism*, question 67)

> Effectual c alling is the work of God's Spirit, whereby, convincing us of our sin and misery, enlightening our minds in the knowledge of Christ, and renewing our wills, he doth persuade and enable us to embrace Jesus Christ, freely offered to us in the gospel. (*Westminster Shorter Catechism*, question 31)

> This effectual call is of God's free and special grace alone, not from anything at all foreseen in man, nor from any power or agency in the creature, being wholly passive therein, being dead in sins and trespasses, until being quickened and renewed by the Holy Spirit; he is thereby enabled to answer this call, and to embrace the grace offered and conveyed in it, and that by no less power than that which raised up Christ from the dead. (*Baptist Confession*, Chapter 10, section 2)

What God does so graciously and powerfully in this life-giving call to spiritual life is delineated in Christ's raising Jairus's daughter and His friend Lazarus from physical death. As Christ stood over the dead girl, He simply said, "Talitha cumi: which is being interpreted, Damsel, I say unto thee, arise" (Mark 5:41). At Christ's command, the girl immediately arose and walked (Mark 5:42). Having received life, she lived; she did not choose rather to stay dead. Standing outside the tomb of Lazarus, Jesus cried out, "Lazarus, come forth" (John 11:43). At Christ's command, Lazarus immediately emerged from the tomb (John 11:44). Lazarus likewise did not reject Christ's command, choosing to stay dead; he exhibited all the vital signs of life. Something in Christ's call both instilled life and made living irresistible.

My point is that anyone else could have said "Talitha cumi" all day long without any effect on the dead girl. Anyone else could have commanded the remains of Lazarus to come out of the grave without any effect whatsoever on the corpse. But in the command of Christ was the power to live. His call was effectual and irresistible.

So it is every time God by His Spirit through His Word brings dead sinners to spiritual life. Whereas it was the power of the Living Word that gave life to the little girl and Lazarus, it is the written Word, the Spirit-used means of grace, that speaks the life-giving command to sinners (see 1 Peter 1:23). Without that special and irresistibly effective application by the Spirit, we can command sinners all day long to live with the same ineffectiveness that we would have experienced standing outside the tomb of Lazarus.

Remember when God commanded the prophet Ezekiel to preach to the dry bones (Ezekiel 37)? Strangely enough, something about Ezekiel's preaching caused an outward transformation in the bones: They assembled and gave every appearance of being alive (37:7). Nevertheless, they were not alive (37:8). It was not until the wind (literally, the Spirit) entered the lifeless forms that they lived (37:9-10). I am well aware of the eschatological implications of this prophecy, and as a premillennialist, I rejoice in the significance this has for future Israel. Yet I am equally aware of the spiritual lesson here. Let's be careful not to let our prophetic views rob the Word of its constant relevance. The point for us now is this: What God will do in saving that future nation (as individuals) is what He does every time He brings a dead sinner to life. It is most sobering to me as a preacher of the gospel to realize that although my preaching may inspire outward results, I have no power to impart or implant spiritual life. That is uniquely the work of God. When the Spirit of God implants the principle of life within the soul, the regenerated soul will evidence all the vital signs of spiritual life.

Regeneration is good news for dead sinners. Without it, sinners remain spiritually lifeless and forever doomed. Man is in such a desperate condition that without a radical change of heart, he has no hope. His best efforts in reformation of character are folly and amount to nothing in the attainment of spiritual life. I think you have seen from the Scripture texts already cited that this link in the gospel chain–like every other link–does not exist apart from Jesus Christ. Man's spiritual death and inability are answered by God's gracious provision in the atoning death of His Son, the Lord Jesus Christ. It is only because of Christ and together with Christ that dead sinners can live. Together with Christ, we can experience *new life in the gospel.*

THE EXPOSITION OF NEW LIFE

In this chapter, I want to consider the new life that we as believers have in Jesus Christ. The gospel of Jesus Christ includes everything that we need for complete salvation. The doctrine of regeneration directs us to our most fundamental and basic need. Being dead in our trespasses and sins means that more than anything else we need life, and God graciously according to "his divine power hath given unto us all things that pertain unto life and godliness" (2 Peter 1:3). Although the Scripture uses various images to describe the essence of regeneration (e.g., circumcision–Deuteronomy 30:6; resurrection–Ephesians 2:5-6; creation–Ephesians 2:10; spiritual baptism–1 Corinthians 12:13; new covenant–Jeremiah 31:33), perhaps the most expressive is that of the new birth (see John 1:12-13; Titus 3:5; 1 Peter 1:3, 23; 1 John 5:4). Nowhere is the new birth defined in more detail and with more precision than in John 3 where the Lord Jesus explained to Nicodemus what it means to be born again. I can think of no better way to understand regeneration and the new birth than to learn from the Savior Himself.

Five important lessons summarize Christ's teaching about the new birth; these flow from two great statements of necessity: (1) you *must* be born again (3:7) and (2) the Son of man *must* be lifted up (3:14). These two necessities are inseparably linked–the possibility of the first depends on the performance of the second. Every other statement in this most famous of texts hinges on these two "musts." I want us to take our place in the night class along with Nicodemus and listen and learn from the Master Teacher as He explains through these five principles the new life that is provided in the gospel and required for entrance into the kingdom of heaven.

The Necessity of New Life

Christ makes it unmistakably clear that new life requires a new birth. As in the first birth a physical life issues from previous nonexistence, so in the second birth a formerly nonexistent spiritual life comes into being. Without a physical birth there is no physical life. Similarly, if there is no new birth, there is no salvation. The new birth, therefore, is not optional for spiritual life; it is necessary. Twice in this passage Jesus tells Nicodemus that being "born again" is indispensable to salvation (3:3, 7). That Christ demands another birth to follow natural birth makes the Authorized Version's translation "again" appropriate. However, the word translated "again" literally means "from above." This sense of the word is perhaps more pertinent to man's need because it calls special attention to the divine source of spiritual life which guarantees the necessary qualifications for entrance into the kingdom of God. We will note more about the "from above" agent of regeneration in the following sections.

The significance for now is that a new birth is necessary for salvation because the first birth does not produce the kind of life that is fit for God's kingdom. Christ's statement in verse 6 is most telling: "That which is born of the flesh is flesh." This reveals the folly of Nicodemus's comment about entering as a grown man into his mother's womb to be born again (3:4). Even if that were possible, it would neither solve man's fundamental problem nor provide the necessary qualification for citizenship in God's kingdom. A second birth from his mother's womb would produce the same sinful and corrupt flesh as the first birth. The flesh can give birth only to more flesh: Kind propagates according to its kind. Every man owns David's confession: "Behold, I was shapen in iniquity; and in sin did my mother conceive me" (Psalm 51:5). Fallen sinful flesh is unfit for glory: "So then they that are in the flesh cannot please God" (Romans 8:8). Indeed, to live after the flesh leads inevitably to death (Romans 8:13). Therefore, by Christ's definition, being born again is not just a fresh start or a second chance at life. It must be a birth of a completely different sort from the first birth. It must be a birth that changes the fleshly nature that is so naturally corrupt and bent against God. It is more than simply being born again; it must be being born from above. As we will see, "That which is born of the Spirit is spirit" (3:6).

What Christ requires is a change of nature that affects the whole man. Although the new birth will reveal itself in moral reforms and character improvements, the transformation of life flows from a new nature that innately has new desires, impulses, and inclinations. The new birth is a change from the inside out that comes from above.

The Agent of New Life

The apostle John in his opening discourse explicitly identified God as the source of the birth of the sons of God, those who believe on His name: "Which were born, not of blood, nor of the will of the flesh, nor of the will of man, but of God" (John 1:13). Likewise, Peter recognized the heavenly source of the new birth when he blessed "the God and Father of our Lord Jesus Christ" who had "begotten us again" (1 Peter 1:3). Though not using the language of birth, Titus named the Holy Spirit as the agent of regeneration (Titus 3:5). All this accords with Christ's demand for a birth from above. That God the Father through the action of the Holy Spirit issues life to sinners, bringing them forth to spiritual life, highlights the absolute grace demonstrated in this component of the gospel. No man authored his own existence in the first birth, and no man can give life to his soul in the second birth. But what man cannot do for himself, God graciously does. In this text, the Lord Jesus isolated two essential truths about the new birth that feature the special operation of the Spirit.

The New Birth is a Spiritual Work

First, Christ defined the spiritual character of the work. In verse 5 He declared emphatically, "Except a man be born of water and of the Spirit, he cannot enter into the kingdom of God." Unfortunately, many interpretations have obscured and even perverted the meaning of this statement. It is beyond my intention to refute all of the misinterpretations, but perhaps I should dismiss a couple of the more common ones. The interpretation that equates the water birth with baptism certainly must be rejected on the grounds that it leads to the heresy of baptismal regeneration. As important as water baptism is for the Christian, it is not a requirement for entering God's kingdom. Water baptism has no power to generate spiritual life. Further, the interpretation that equates the water birth with the first birth should be rejected on the grounds that it would be stating the obvious. Of course, the first birth that brought us into the human race precedes any possibility of a second birth. But it misses the point to say simply that natural life is a prerequisite to spiritual life. That Christ addresses this requirement to "man" assumes the first birth. I think this interpretation, while it may not be heretical, plays too much on the translation "born again."

I suggest, rather, that the explanation must focus on the primary notion of being born "from above." The grammatical construction of verse 5 provides the best interpretation. The translation in the Authorized Version is quite literal, except that no definite article governs the word "spirit." The problem is not so much with the translation as with the common failure to recognize the figure of speech that Christ uses. I will try not to get technical, but I love Greek grammar almost as much as Hebrew. This figure of speech, however, is not unique to Greek or Hebrew. The linking of "water and spirit" is a literary device called *hendiadys*. This is itself a Greek word that means "one through two." It refers to the linking of two nouns by the conjunction "and" to express one complex idea that would normally be expressed by an adjective modifying a noun. Being born "of water and of spirit" refers, consequently, to *spiritual water*, which pertains ultimately to *spiritual cleansing*.

By defining the new birth in terms of a necessary spiritual cleansing, Jesus links His exposition of regeneration to other Scripture. Ezekiel, immediately before citing the Lord's promise to give a new heart and new spirit (regeneration), communicated the Lord's promise that He would "sprinkle clean water upon you" (Ezekiel 36:25-26). Recognizing this obvious link to Ezekiel explains for us Christ's query to Nicodemus, "Art thou a master [teacher] of Israel, and knowest not these things?" (3:10). I believe that Christ was simply asking Nicodemus if he had ever read Ezekiel 36. He should have known the theology of the regeneration: It was Old Testament theology as well as New. Similarly, Titus spoke of the "the washing of regeneration, and renewing of the Holy Ghost" (3:5). Thus, Christ is teaching that the new birth involves an inward cleansing from the filthiness and pollution that preclude entrance into heaven. Such a cleansing is spiritual work because man is absolutely incapable of cleansing himself (see Jeremiah 2:22).

Second, Christ affirms the success of this spiritual cleansing: "That which is born of the Spirit is spirit" (3:6). As certainly as flesh begets flesh, so the Spirit begets spirit. This certain offspring parallels Ezekiel's declaration that when God promises to sprinkle clean water on you, the certain consequence is that you will be clean (36:25). Because the source of the new birth is from above and because the agent of the new birth is the Holy Spirit, there is never a miscarriage. The new birth always works; it always fits the sinner for the kingdom.

The New Birth is a Sovereign Work

Life is mysterious. Its origin and perpetuation are beyond human comprehension. As inexplicable as natural life is, the mystery of spiritual life is infinitely more unfathomable. The application of the new birth by the Holy Spirit is the sovereign work of God. Its execution is according to God's gracious good pleasure, and it defies human explanation. But we should not stumble over what we cannot explain. Although the mechanics and the administration of this gracious work may be mysterious, sovereign, and incomprehensible, its effects are always evident.

The Lord Jesus compared the efficacious operation of the Holy Spirit in the new birth to the blowing of the wind. "The wind bloweth where it listeth, and thou hearest the sound thereof, but canst not tell whence it cometh, and whither it goeth: so is every one that is born of the Spirit" (3:8). This is a most vivid analogy because the Greek terms for "wind" and "spirit" are exactly the same word. We may not be able to control the wind's direction or force, but it always makes its presence known. To one degree or another, we can hear it and feel it.

So it is with the life-giving operation of the Holy Spirit. Why He moves as He does and where He moves is beyond our knowledge and beyond our control, but His movements are always discernible. The new birth is the consequence of the Spirit's breathing that cannot be hidden. The hymn writer expressed well the theology of Christ's wind/spirit analogy: "I know not how the Spirit moves, convincing men of sin, revealing Jesus through the Word, creating faith in Him." But the evidence of that working is obvious: "But I know whom I have believed, and am persuaded that He is able to keep that which I've committed unto Him against that day." The sovereign act of the new birth always issues forth in spiritual life that lays hold of Christ in faith. When we are born of the Spirit, we will know it.

The Provision for New Life

New life via new birth is necessary for salvation. That is fact, but it is hardly good news. Commanding a dead man to live is futile: Death cannot generate life. Spiritual life must come from above, not within. The gospel, the good news, is that God has provided the means and the way whereby dead, spiritually oblivious sinners can receive the necessary life. Grace provides what the requirement for life demands. Grace makes possible what is humanly impossible. In His discourse to Nicodemus, the Lord Jesus made two astounding statements concerning the provision for new life.

Based in the Love of God

The provision for new life, spiritual and eternal, flows from God's wondrous, incomprehensible, and mysterious love. Christ declared this amazing love in what is without doubt the most famous and most frequently quoted verse in the Bible: "For God so loved the world, that he gave his only begotten Son, that whosoever believeth in him should not perish, but have everlasting life" (3:16). Who in the world cannot find hope in this astounding declaration?

Although this wondrous statement can stand by itself in its unparalleled clarity, let me make some observations to boldface the full significance of this divine love that expressed itself in the giving of Christ and applies itself in the giving of new life. The word "love," of course, is that great New Testament word that finds its most expressive definition in God Himself, who is love (1 John 4:8). Its stimulus is within God who loves and not in the world which is loved. Humanly speaking, God's love for the world makes no sense since the world consists of sinners who are highly repulsive and unworthy of love. Why God loves us is answered only within the sovereign will and good pleasure of God. God loves because He loves (Deuteronomy 7:7-8); love, therefore, is a word of grace. "Amazing love! How can it be that Thou my God, shouldst die for me?" What more can I say?

The word "so" designates not the degree to which God loves but the way in which God demonstrated His love for the world. The two "that" statements (different words in the Greek text) define the way in terms of consequence and purpose. The *conse-*

quence of the divine love is that He gave His own eternal Son. Because He loved, He gave. Although the world is filled with sinners who are unlovely, unresponsive, and ungrateful, yet for His own sake He loved them. Given that the supreme and eternal object of the Father's love is His only begotten Son (John 17:23-24), the sacrificial giving of the Son heightens the magnitude of God's love for the world. What an unspeakable gift to a lost and dying world (2 Corinthians 9:15)! The *purpose* of His having given the Son is to rescue the perishing by providing the necessary new, spiritual, and everlasting life. Notice how the apostle Paul similarly and pointedly links God's love with the work of regeneration: "But God, who is rich in mercy, for his great love wherewith he loved us, even when we were dead in sins, hath quickened us together with Christ" (Ephesians 2:4-5).

God did not give His Son in vain; God's purpose always translates to reality. In His love God gave His Son to provide life for dead sinners, and Christ fulfilled that purpose. New life is in Christ, and being in Christ is the only way to know and experience God's love. The apostle John makes this point in what seems to be his inspired commentary on John 3:16. "God hath given to us eternal life, and this life is in his Son. He that hath the Son hath life" (1 John 5:11-12). "In this was manifested the love of God toward us, because that God sent his only begotten Son into the world, that we might live through him" (1 John 4:9). God's love is the sinner's only hope.

Purchased by Christ's Atoning Death

Although God's love is the basis of the sinner's hope, the sinner's salvation is that God's love moved Him to give Christ to die and thereby to purchase every element of salvation, including the new birth. "Herein is love, not that we loved God, but that he loved us, and sent his Son to be the propitiation for our sins" (1 John 4:10). Again we see that no part of the gospel message is ever very far from the cross of Jesus Christ. Significantly, the Lord Jesus coupled "ye must be born again" (3:7) with "even so must the Son of man be lifted up" (3:14). The unfailing purpose of His being lifted up was that believers "should not perish, but have eternal life" (3:15).

Christ compared His being lifted up on the cross with Moses's lifting up the serpent in the wilderness (see Numbers 21:9). The parallels between that ancient action and Christ's eternally efficacious act are obvious and instructive. The only cure for those suffering the curse from the deadly venom of the fiery serpents was for them to look in faith to the emblem of curse itself. The emblem of destruction was at the same time the emblem of healing. So the only remedy for those under the curse of sin is to look in faith to the cross work of Jesus. Christ purchased the remedy from the curse by becoming the curse: He who knew no sin became sin. Christ's being lifted up reveals and declares both the wrath of God in the condemnation of sinners and the love of God in the pardon of all those who believe. His death is the believer's life. His cross is the believer's title to God's kingdom. His being lifted up is the believer's ladder to heaven.

The "must" of the new birth is possible because of the "must" of the cross. It is because God loved us and Christ died for us that the Holy Spirit imparts to us new life through the new birth. From plan to execution to application, salvation is of the Lord.

The Appropriation of New Life

Sinners appropriate new life by way of the new birth by means of faith. Throughout this discourse Christ limited the benefits of the new birth to those who believe. In the historic context of the Old Testament picture prophecy of Moses's lifting up the serpent, every Israelite who looked to the poled serpent was healed. So it is that whoever in the world looks to Christ is saved. "Look unto me, and be ye saved, all the ends of the earth: for I am God, and there is none else" (Isaiah 45:22). The old hymn faithfully expresses this theology: "Look and live, O sinner live, Look to Jesus now and live; 'Tis recorded in His word, Hallelujah! It is only that you look and live." The Son of man had to be lifted up "that whosoever believeth in him should not perish, but have everlasting life" (3:15). God so loved the world and gave His Son "that whosoever believeth in him should not perish, but have everlasting life" (3:16). The infallible promise is that "he that believeth on him is not condemned" (3:18).

Nothing apart from faith can secure interest in Christ and His atoning death. But this raises a serious question: How can a sinner who is dead in trespasses and sin, blind and insensitive to spiritual matters, exercise faith, which is obviously a spiritual act? Every orthodox theologian agrees that both faith and regeneration are necessary for the experience of new, spiritual life. Without the new birth there is no salvation; without faith there is no salvation. I am well aware (by personal experience) of the oftentimes heated theological controversy that offers conflicting answers to this question. Some theologians argue that faith is the necessary prerequisite to the new birth: Faith precedes regeneration. Others argue that the new birth is the prerequisite to faith: Regeneration precedes faith.

It is not my purpose in this practical exposition to enter the controversy by defending or refuting the issues in this debate. However, it is impossible for me to say anything without revealing my interpretation. So let me quickly lay it on the table. I believe that biblically, theologically, logically, and temporally, regeneration precedes the exercise of faith. The new birth is the work of the Holy Spirit; saving faith is the evidence of the new life. In regeneration, the Holy Spirit changes our nature and secures for us and in us the holy exercise of a new disposition, thereby enabling us and inciting within us the desire to repent from our sins and believe the gospel. Although the fact of the new birth precedes faith, the consciousness of it follows. Awareness of life exists only after life. I know I was born the first time because I am now alive and do the stuff that living people do. I know I was born again because I now am spiritually alive and do what spiritually alive people do–not the least of which is believing the gospel. Just as my breathing is the indication and not the cause of life, so my believing is the evidence of spiritual life, not the cause of it.

Perhaps some Christians reason that faith leads to life rather than proceeds from life because faith is the first conscious act of the sinner who believes the gospel. I do believe that conversion (the exercise of faith and repentance) occurs instantaneously at regeneration. Life and death are mutually exclusive. Death does not exist where there is life, and life does not exist where death is. That would seem to be self-evidently logical. I had a student explain to me one time, however, that being spiritually dead was analogous to a dead car battery. There is not enough "juice" to start the car and keep it running, but, he maintained, there is enough "juice" to turn the lights on. His contention was that man, although "dead," has enough "life" in him to believe (turn the lights on). God then responds to that exercise of faith by giving the regenerating Spirit. That was his way of arguing that faith precedes regeneration. My guess is that Paul had no clue about any latent power in a dead battery, but that he knew a dead donkey when he saw one. Dead is dead. The only way I can explain that is to stress the total absence of life. Therefore, the ability and desire to believe are the gracious gifts of God. With the new life come the operations of new life.

However, I must issue a word of caution and encourage us to stick to the language and logic of Scripture. In His conversation with Nicodemus, Christ did not make the new birth a matter of introversive speculation. Christ, while addressing the necessity of being born again, focused His application on its evidence, the necessity of belief. Nowhere does the Scripture instruct the sinner to examine himself for a spark of life to explain or justify his accepting Christ's invitation or his obeying the command to believe. The commands of Scripture are always addressed to man's consciousness, to where he is. It is not for us to wonder if God loved us and Christ died for us; it is for us to believe the gospel with the heart and confess with the mouth that Jesus is Lord (Romans 10:9-10). Christ, the Living Word and the whole of the written Word, offers the gospel of new life to any and all in the world of sinners. The guarantee of the whole Scripture is that those who so believe are indeed born again. To be part of the "whosoever" that believes and calls on the Lord for salvation is to be guaranteed the promised everlasting life. This ought to furnish us the assurance that saving faith is not self-generated, but is rather the irrefutable evidence of the regenerating work of the Holy Spirit of God.

The Forfeiture of the New Life

Christ, having just announced God's gracious love in sending Him to die, declares as emphatically that apart from Him sinners will experience nothing of that divine love. Jesus concluded His lesson to Nicodemus about the new birth with a solemn warning to those who refuse to believe. Sinners forfeit life when they refuse to believe in Jesus Christ. Eternal destiny is defined and determined ultimately by one's relationship to the Lord Jesus Christ. He that is condemned is condemned "because he hath not believed in the name of the only begotten Son of God" (3:18). It is that simple. What Christ said to Nicodemus in this text parallels closely what He said as the Wisdom of God: "For whoso findeth me findeth life, and shall obtain favour of the Lord. But he that sinneth against me wrongeth his own soul: all they that hate [reject] me love [choose] death" (Proverbs 8: 35-36).

The Savior's condemnation of unbelievers emphasizes why the new birth is so essential. The Lord's warning underscores the depth of spiritual death and blindness that keeps sinners willfully in darkness even in the presence of the light: "And this is the condemnation, that light is come into the world, and men loved darkness rather than light, because their deeds were evil. For every one that doeth evil hateth the light, neither cometh to the light, lest his deeds should be reproved" (3:19-20). Man left to himself relentlessly follows his own natural inclinations and always chooses the way of darkness and death. Choosing the way of light and life, on the other hand, is the evidence of doing those things that are wrought by God (3:21). Condemnation is always earned, but salvation is always of grace. That is always the message of the gospel.

The new birth cannot be experienced without faith in Jesus Christ. As we seek to understand and enjoy regeneration, we have to direct our thinking to Christ. As believers we ought to rejoice in the life that we have in, through, and because of Christ. We don't have to understand the mysterious mechanics of how the new birth operates or even be right in our understanding of the order of salvation, but we must understand that "he that hath the Son hath life" (1 John 5:12). It doesn't matter what else we have or do not have; we have to have Christ to have life. Heaven may be gained without money, education, fame, and many other things, but heaven cannot be gained without the new birth made possible by the atoning death of God's only begotten Son. Regeneration, like every other component of the gospel, exists only in terms of Christ. We are, indeed, complete in Him.

CHAPTER 5

UNION WITH CHRIST: THE SECURITY OF THE GOSPEL

"Muscular" and "brawny" have never been adjectives used to describe me. I have been both fat and skinny at various stages of life, but never strong. As a boy, I was often an easy target for the school bullies. I remember once in junior high that I foolishly became bold enough to challenge a school-bus bully who had repeatedly knocked my books out of my hands as I passed him on the way to my seat. In the one and only fistfight of my life, I took him on. I remember quite an adrenaline rush as several busloads of students formed a ring around us outside the school to witness the bully's getting what everyone knew he deserved. As I recall, I caused significant damage to his knuckles when his punch followed through to my teeth after fattening my lip. I decided from that point on to rely on my logic and my wit, both of which far exceeded my brawn. Logically–via my wit–I secured the friendship of some of the school athletes, who accepted me regardless of the fact that I was a trombone-playing debater–atypical proficiencies for the in-crowd. Notwithstanding my personal weakness, I felt fairly safe when I stuck with the big boys–even when the bullies were around. My security was in my associations. As time passed, there were other advantages as well. On the merit and reputation of the guys I was with, I enjoyed benefits that on my own I would not have known. Although I fit the classic profile of a nerd, I was an accepted part of school society.

No analogy or illustration is ever perfect, but this reminiscence suggests an essential and most wonderful component of the gospel: union with Christ. When I was a kid, my safety and acceptance among my peers depended on my association with the popular athletes. Infinitely more importantly, the believer's security and acceptance with God depend on his association–indeed, his union–with Jesus Christ. Because believers and Christ are mutually united–believers in Christ (Colossians 3:3) and Christ in believers (Colossians 1:27; see also 1 John 3:24 and 4:13)–all the merit and infinite worth of Jesus Christ become the shared experience and possession of every believer. This is mind-boggling when we realize that in Christ dwells "all the fulness of the Godhead bodily" and that believers are complete in Him (Colossians 2:9-10).

As a kid, I took advantage of my corporate security and acceptance and consequently enjoyed a relatively happy adolescence. Tragically, too many Christians, who are in fact united to Christ, do not consciously and deliberately take advantage of what that union means and all it guarantees for a happy Christian life. As a result, these Christians struggle with doubt, intimidation, and fear, facing the issues of life and death as though they were alone. Many genuine and sincere believers, desiring with all of their hearts to serve the Lord and do what pleases Him, live under the constant burden of guilt. They realize correctly that all of their best efforts are tainted with sin and imperfection, but under that load of guilt, they constantly search for more and more issues in their lives that they can surrender to salve their consciences for awhile. Why can we not learn that living and serving the Lord under guilt betrays the gospel?

Would to God that every one of us who knows the Lord Jesus as his Savior would learn to live in the reality of our union with Him. If only we would realize that regardless of our personal failures, imperfections, and sins, the merit of Jesus Christ encompasses and subsumes all of our service to Him. What we do personally cannot increase or decrease God's acceptance of us. What we do as believers is pleasing and acceptable to God because He always sees us together with His Son, His dearly Beloved. When I was kid, others accepted me on the merits of my friends; infinitely more so, because I am a Christian, God accepts me on the merits of my Savior. Sadly, the reality of the believer's union with Christ, which is so much a part of gospel theology, is so little a part of modern Christianity. I don't know how many times in my teaching career I have addressed this particular theme only to find students supposing it to be some new doctrine. They have often asked me, "Why haven't we ever heard this before?" I could never answer that question.

Let me, however, add this caution. Do not take this truth in the wrong direction, and beware of those who do. The fact that our personal behavior neither adds to nor distracts from our acceptance before God in Christ is not license to sin or reason to abandon the pursuit of personal purity. Rather, it is faith in the reality of our union with Christ that leads to the proper obedience of God's laws for holiness. Again, my premise directly applies: Right thinking about the gospel produces right living in the gospel, not wrong or careless living. Fixing our minds on the amazing truth that we are united to Christ will profoundly impact the way we live. It will give us boldness and motivation for life and confidence for death. It is as we learn to take advantage of everything that we are and have in Christ that we will experience all the benefits of our completeness in Him. I think that one of the greatest advantages that union with Christ provides us is the profound sense of assurance and security flowing from the knowledge that God deals with us only and always in terms of Christ. What is true about Christ is true for those in Christ. For instance, compare what Isaiah said about the coming Christ with what Paul says about believers. Just as there were none that could successfully accuse or condemn Christ (Isaiah 50:8-9), neither can any accuse or condemn those that God has justified in Christ (Romans 8:33-34). This is why I say summarily that union with Christ is our *security in the gospel*.

Union with Christ–this nexus in the gospel–itself is multifaceted. The Scripture reveals this essential doctrine from different perspectives, each of which has its own application and all of which coalesce to form one glorious and indissoluble union with the Savior.

UNITED TO CHRIST REPRESENTATIVELY

That Christ is the federal, covenant or representative Head of His people is the beginning point for any consideration of the believer's union with Christ. In this context these terms (federal, covenant, and representative) can be used interchangeably. This aspect of our union primarily concerns our legal standing before God. One essential reason I can say God only and always deals with us as He deals with Christ is that Christ stands as our legal representative before God. When God sees Christ, He sees us. Notwithstanding the primary significance of this aspect of our union, I am going to be cursory in my comments at this point because we have already examined some of its implications and will do so further, particularly in the chapter on justification.

In chapter 1 we considered the relationship between Adam's sin and our guilt. Because God had ordained Adam to be a public or representative man, his obedience or disobedience to the terms of the probation (Genesis 2:16-17) would affect the entire human race that was in him as the first man. When he sinned, he earned death both for himself personally and for the entire human race corporately united to him. The Scripture is emphatically clear: "In Adam all die" (1 Corinthians 15:22). In addition to placing humanity under the death penalty, Adam plunged the human race into such inherent and individually deserved guilt and corruption that successfully earning salvation became absolutely and totally impossible. Adam's first sin justly counted as ours. Man's just condemnation is why the gospel is necessary.

God's matchless, infinite grace is why there is a gospel. Man needed a new representative who could and would fulfill the requirements for life. God appointed His Son to that position. The Lord Jesus Christ is the only One divinely chosen and qualified to be the Savior of sinners. As the Scripture declares: "In Christ shall all be made alive" (1 Corinthians 15:22). Whereas by nature, all men in Adam are under the sentence of death, by grace, all believers in Christ are alive. The representative to whom we are united determines our eternal destiny. Christ, like Adam, was ordained to be a public or representative man. In order for the Son of God to be our representative, He had to become the Son of Man. In His Incarnation, the eternal Son of God partook of the same flesh and blood as those He came to represent–His brethren, the children given to Him (Hebrews 2:11-14). The Incarnation was Christ's identifying Himself with us.

Three key texts stand out that contrast Christ's success as the second man with the first man's failure–Psalm 8, Romans 5, and 1 Corinthians 15. Indeed, I believe that the Old Testament text was the foundation for the New Testament's development. Psalm 8 is a messianic song highlighting the greatness and grace of God and pointing to the Lord Jesus as the only means by which fallen man can come to the enjoyment and experience of the privileged rank God assigned to man in creation. In *Beginning at Moses*, I give a full synopsis of the Psalm, establishing its messianic content and significance (pp. 304-307). For now, I want to focus attention on verses 4-6, the principal messianic statements. Having considered the vastness of creation, David raised the question as to why God would give such special attention to man, particularly since man had so tragically fallen from his original glory. He used two terms for man that contrast the diminutiveness of man with the vastness of creation. "What is man, that thou are mindful of him? And the son of man, that thou visitest him?" The first word for "man" emphasizes man's frailty and mortality. The second expression, "son of man (*adam*)," also underscores man's inherent weakness and insignificance as earthy. This is why, I think, in one of the key New Testament commentaries on this "man theology" Paul said, "The first man is of the earth, earthy" (1 Corinthians 15:47).

According to Paul, whereas the first man was of the earth, the second man is "the Lord from heaven" (1 Corinthians 15:45-47). David's description of the ideal man in verses 5 and 6, though not as explicit, matches Paul's. The apostle speaks of a man ("the last Adam," "the second man") who, unlike the first man, honorably and unfailingly fulfilled the high station God intended for mankind. In His condescending and humiliating

Incarnation, the Second Person of the Eternal Trinity was temporarily diminished to a position lower than that of the angels in order to perform the necessary obedience to merit and restore life to the race of which He was the Head. He was the Ideal Man. Having fulfilled the necessary requirements to satisfy God's demands, He was then crowned with glory and honor. Christ's commissioned humiliation led to His earned exaltation, whereas Adam's created exaltation crashed into deserved humiliation. Everything the first Adam lost, the second Adam regained.

Paul effectively demonstrates that what Christ did in fulfilling the requirements of life and regaining Paradise, He did as a public figure. There is a remarkable connection between our representative and us. Just as in Adam "we have borne the image of the earthy," in Christ "we shall also bear the image of the heavenly" (1 Corinthians 15:49). Romans 5:12-19 is unquestionably the most explicit biblical exposition contrasting the corporate effect of Adam's disobedience with the corporate effect of Christ's obedience. In chapter 6 ("Justification: The Legality of the Gospel") I will develop the implications of Christ's vicarious active and passive obedience in some detail. In our place and as our representative, Christ fulfilled every demand of God's righteous law. He worked so that we might receive grace. I do not here want to anticipate everything that we will learn about our justification through faith in Christ, but I do want us to understand the connection between our justification and our representative union with Christ. God's just imputation of our guilt to Christ and His equally just imputation of Christ's righteousness to us are righteously legal acts because Christ is our covenant Head, our representative. Accordingly, the prophet Isaiah in one of his famous Servant Songs records God's word to His Servant that identifies Him in terms of the covenant: "I will preserve thee, and give thee for a covenant of the people" (Isaiah 49:8; see also Isaiah 42:6).

All of this deals with the issues of legality. As our representative, Christ accepted our liabilities, and His merit accrues to us. In chapter 1, I asked the question, "If Adam did it, how come I'm guilty?" I can now ask this question, "If Christ did it, how come

I'm innocent?" If it was a just thing for God to condemn us in Adam because he was the head of the whole human race, it is a just thing for God to justify us in Christ because He is the Head of the redeemed race. Christ's righteousness counts for us. Therefore, there is no condemnation to those who are "in" Christ Jesus (Romans 8:1). We are graciously accepted by God in Christ, the Beloved (Ephesians 1:6). To be thus united to Christ is to be in the safest place possible. Here is the real security of the gospel.

United to Christ Mystically

The believer's union with Christ is mystical. Don't be afraid of this word. Theologically, "mystical" refers to spiritual truth that surpasses human comprehension because of the transcendence of its nature and significance, and thus, it is a most appropriate word to designate our union with Jesus Christ. This mystical union is a truth that, notwithstanding its reality, defies explanation. If I may, let me put it in these terms: Union with Christ is so profound, it is almost too good to be true. Yet it *is* true, and we must believe it on the authority of God's certain revelation and learn to live in its reality.

Being in union with Christ goes beyond enjoying His legal representation or even His constant company. The Lord Jesus promised that He would be with us, even to the end of the world (Matthew 28:20). The inspired apostle assures us that the Lord will never leave us or forsake us, giving us the boldness to affirm, "The Lord is my helper, and I will not fear what man shall do unto me" (Hebrews 13:5-6). If that uninterrupted companionship were the only level of our association with Christ, it would be wonderful and far beyond what we deserve. The witness of Scripture, however, is not just that Christ is with us but that we are in Him. Read particularly the books of Ephesians and Colossians and just count the number of times we are actually said to be in Christ. It is astounding. We are not just experiencing His presence nor are we somehow appended or attached to him; we are actually in Him. How can I explain that? I can't. It is a mystical union. Yet there are two things about this union that I do want us to think about.

A Spiritual Union

Although believers consciously enter into union with Christ through faith (Ephesians 3:17; Colossians 2:12), the execution of the union and the attestation to its reality are the operations of the Holy Spirit. In Ephesians 2:20-22, Paul used the analogy of a building to explain the believer's union with Christ.

> And are built upon the foundation of the apostles and prophets, Jesus Christ himself being the chief corner stone; In whom all the building fitly framed together groweth unto an holy temple in the Lord: In whom ye also are builded together for an habitation of God through the Spirit.

Not only does he make it clear that Christ, as the foundation and cornerstone, is essential to the building's existence, but he also explains that the components of the superstructure–i.e., believers–are put into place through the agency of the Holy Spirit. In 1 Corinthians 12, the apostle uses another analogy, describing the church as the body of Christ. Although his focus of application is on the unity that all the individual members have in the body, he does make a significant statement revealing how believers become part of this body of Christ: "For by one Spirit are we all baptized into one body" (12:13). Obviously, Paul is not referring to water baptism, which is a visible sign administered by an ordained minister that publicly identifies an individual as a member of the church. But water baptism, regardless of its great importance, does not and cannot save. Rather, Paul is speaking of that spiritual baptism whereby the Holy Spirit of God actually accomplishes and effects a real and spiritual union with the Savior. By some divine and inexplicable means, the Holy Spirit places us in Christ.

The beauty of this action's being a spiritual work is that the Holy Spirit, just like the Father and the Son, never fails in what He does. Thankfully, we are not left to ourselves to figure out how to achieve or attain this necessary element of our salvation.

It is a divine work, requiring no contribution from us. Although we cannot comprehend how this spiritual union occurs, the Holy Spirit has given to us an internal witness that assures us that He has done His job. As evidence that we are in Christ, we have the Spirit of Christ in us: "If any man have not the Spirit of Christ, he is none of his" (Romans 8:9). As evidence that we have the Spirit of Christ, the Holy Spirit bears witness with our spirit not only that we are the children of God, but also that we share with Christ everything from His sufferings to His glorification (Romans 8:16-17).

A Spiritual Communion

Being in union with Christ means that every believer jointly participates and shares in the work of the Lord Jesus. This particular truth really staggers the mind. In a way that we cannot fathom, in Christ–and therefore together *with* Christ–believers partake in all Christ did to accomplish redemption, and they share jointly in the success of His work. Once again, I'm glad that truth is not limited within the bounds of my comprehension. Nevertheless, to encourage our contemplation of this aspect of our union, I want to discuss just some of the things that the Bible reveals we experience with Christ.

Union with Christ's Death

In union with Christ, believers died with their Savior. Consider these astounding statements that declare the believer's communion with the death of Christ. "I am crucified with Christ" (Galatians 2:20). "We are buried with him by baptism into death" (Romans 6:4; also Colossians 2:12). "Our old man is crucified with him" (Romans 6:6). "If one died for all, then were all dead [i.e. all died]" (2 Corinthians 5:14). Obviously, we did not hang on the cross along with Christ to suffer all of the physical agony and torment that He endured in both body and soul. In the physical sense, Christ suffered and died alone as the substitute for His people. He bore our penalty and exempted us from ever having to pay the price of our sin. Yet mystically we were united to Him.

When Christ died, all of His people died with Him. God counted believers as being in His Son.

This union guarantees that everything our Lord purchased on the cross is the certain possession of all those united to Him. When Christ was crucified, He satisfied God's righteousness, secured the forgiveness of sin, and severed the connection to sin's doom and dominion. So if we died with Him, God's law has no more claim against us–justice has been served. If we died with Him, we have received pardon from guilt and forgiveness for all our sins. We have every right to face our sins and claim the blood of Christ to keep on cleansing us every time we need forgiving (1 John 1:7). If we died with Him, we have been freed from sin's dominating power over us (Romans 6:14). In Christ, we possess definitely the power to be free from the whole oppressive burden of sin.

Union with His death not only provides certain security in our knowing that we are the partakers of all He purchased, but it also generates both the motive and the power for holy living. A united life leads to a transformed life. This is clearly Paul's logic in Colossians 3. Paul first declares the united life: "For ye are dead, and your life is hid with Christ in God" (3:3). Note carefully the verb tenses. The expression "ye are dead" does not refer to being in a condition or state of death; rather, it refers to a past act–that time when the believer died with Christ–and could be translated "you died." The next statement could be translated "your life has been hidden with Christ." This particular tense expresses a past-completed act that has continuing consequences. Here is the idea: When we died with Christ, we were at that very time placed in Christ, and there we constantly remain.

Paul next defines the transformed life. The apostolic application of this gospel is simply that we are to quit sinning: "Mortify therefore your members which are upon the earth. . . . Put on the new man" (3:5, 10). This dying to sin and living to righteousness becomes normal behavior in the light of Christ's being "all, and in all" (3:11). Paul reasons the same way in Romans: "Knowing this, that our old man is crucified with him, that the body of sin might be destroyed, that henceforth we should not serve sin"

(6:6). Here is part of the secret to victorious living. We must learn to look down on sin from the vantage point of the cross, for we indeed were crucified with Christ. The sin that is so alluring when in our face will lose its appeal from the perspective of the old rugged cross.

Union with Christ's Resurrection

In union with Christ, believers have been raised from spiritual death to spiritual life and have the certain prospect of the bodily resurrection as well. By His death, our Savior "abolished death, and hath brought life and immortality to light through the gospel" (2 Timothy 1:10). When Christ rose from the dead, we rose from the dead with Him. I might on my own authority hesitate to say that, but again the Scripture is explicit in what it teaches. "Even when we were dead in sins, hath quickened us together with Christ…and hath raised us up together" (Ephesians 2:5-6). "For if [since] we have been planted together in the likeness of his death, we shall be also in the likeness of his resurrection" (Romans 6:5). "Now if [since] we be dead [died] with Christ, we believe that we shall also live with him" (Romans 6:8). "Ye are risen with him through the faith of the operation of God, who hath raised him from the dead. And you, being dead in your sins and the uncircumcision of your flesh, hath he quickened together with him" (Colossians 2:12-13). "If [since] ye then be risen with Christ, seek those things which are above" (Colossians 3:1). Christ Himself assures us that because He lives, we will live also (John 14:19). In the immediate context of that promise, the Lord Jesus defined that mutual life as evidence of union with Him: "At that day ye shall know that I am in my Father, and ye in me, and I in you" (John 14:20).

Communion with the death of Christ necessarily means communion with His resurrection and life. It is impossible to be united to His death without being united to His life. "It is a faithful saying: For if we be dead with him, we shall also live with him" (2 Timothy 2:11). Just as certainly as believers partake of what Christ achieved by His atoning death, so they partake of all the victory of His glorious resurrection. This shared life includes the spiritual life generated by the new birth (requiring resurrection power–Ephesians 1:19-20) as well as the future resurrection when "this corruptible must put on incorruption, and this mortal must put on immortality" (1 Corinthians 15:53). "God hath given to us eternal life, and this life is in his Son. He that hath the Son hath life" (1 John 5:11-12).

This union with Christ that has secured our newness of life and immortality demands modification in our lives. Since we are new creatures in Christ, our view of life must radically differ from the one we held when we were dead in sin: "Old things are passed away; behold, all things are become new" (2 Corinthians 5:17). In Colossians 3, Paul issues two sweeping imperatives that flow from the fact that we are risen with Christ. First, we are to seek the things that are above where Christ sits at the right hand of God (3:1). Seeking includes more than casual or curious investigation; it requires the concentration of effort necessary to obtain the object of the search. As we live in this world, we are diligently and continually to bring heaven to bear on the issues of life. That we are united to Christ is for us a fact of life that we must factor into life. Second, we are to set our affections on things above (3:2). What the Authorized Version translates as "set your affections" is actually one word and could be translated more literally as "think." We are to be thinking about the things above. You can see that my constant theme and premise is scriptural: what we think about determines what we do. Right thinking always focuses on Christ and our place in Him. That is the essence of Paul's application. Since we have been raised with Christ, think about it. The only question is "Why don't we?"

Union with Christ's Session

By the law of this spiritual and mystical union, believers sit with Christ on His throne. Since we are united to Christ, it is impossible for Christ to be where we are not or for us not to be where He is. As part of His earned exaltation, after His resurrection He ascended into heaven and took His seat of honor at the right hand of His Father. And inexplicably yet absolutely, so did we. I confess that the fact that we are enthroned with Christ as He sits exalted in His session at the right hand of God totally confounds me. It is amazing beyond words. It occurs to me that sometimes we read the Scripture so casually that we do not take the time to let the truths really sink into our minds and hearts. Listen to what the Scripture says, and just think: "Blessed be the God and Father of our Lord Jesus Christ, who hath blessed us **with all spiritual blessings in heavenly places in Christ**" (Ephesians 1:3); "But God, who is rich in mercy . . . hath raised us up together, and **made us sit together in heavenly places in Christ Jesus**" (Ephesians 2:4, 6). If these were predictions of what God would do for us someday, we would have something wonderful to look forward to. But these are not prophecies; they are declarations of what God has already done. So as I sit here struggling over words, I am even now in heaven in throne-union with Jesus Christ. What is more real: where I am here or where I am there?

As confounding as all this may be to reason, what wonder it imports for our faith. The implications of this throne-union to the issues of life are extensive. We ought not to live any part of our life *here* without the consciousness that we are in reality *there*. We need to live in the light of spiritual reality. This throne-union with Christ ought to assure us of our absolute security in the gospel. If we are spiritually present in heaven in Christ now, then there is no possibility that we can ever perish in hell. Union with Christ is an excellent argument for our eternal security. This union ought also to strengthen us through all the struggles and sufferings of this life. Just as certain as suffering is the fact that "we shall also reign with him" (2 Timothy 2:12; see also Romans 8:17 where joint suffering leads to joint glorification). Even when all of life seems to be against us, we have reason for confidence and joy, knowing by faith that appearance and reality are not the same. "Who is he that condemneth? It is Christ that died, yea rather, that is risen again, who is even at the right hand of God, who also maketh intercession for us" (Romans 8:34). Can you see it? Christ died; we died with Him. Christ is risen; we rose with Him. Christ is at the right hand of God; we are sitting with Him. Therefore, no one or nothing can condemn us or separate us "from the love of God, which is in Christ Jesus" (Romans 8:39). May God help us to think more and more about this mystical union and communion that we have with Christ. It will do us good.

UNITED TO CHRIST VITALLY

Believers are also united to Christ vitally. By vital, I simply mean that which is necessary for the existence and continuation of life. Apart from Christ, spiritual life does not exist, but in Christ there is abundant life. Everything necessary to generate and sustain life flows freely from the Savior. Spiritual life and survival, therefore, depend on union with Christ. Paul recognized the vital union between himself and Christ when he testified, "I am crucified with Christ: nevertheless I live; yet not I, but Christ liveth in me" (Galatians 2:20). What was true for Paul is true for every individual believer. The more we are conscious of the animating power within us, the more we can draw from Christ's infinite energy to enable us to live in the flesh by faith in the Son of God who loved us and gave Himself for us (Galatians 2:20). At this point I want to explore three Scriptural analogies of this vital union to increase our understanding of this oneness with Christ. Our success as Christians living in this present evil age will be in direct proportion to the degree to which we see Christ and recognize our place in Him.

The Food and Life Analogy

I suppose that some people live to eat; everyone, though, has to eat to live. I cannot explain how eating works. How the body reacts with food to extract all of the necessary vitamins, minerals, and whatever else is beyond my knowledge. I just enjoy the food and let my body do what it does naturally. Although it is not completely true that we are what we eat, what we eat does become a part of us. From food we get the energy that is essential to life. The Lord Jesus used this daily necessity to teach a fundamental lesson about a far more essential feeding: spiritual eating. After He had miraculously fed the huge crowds with natural food, He identified Himself as the Bread of Life (John 6:48). He then issued this "dietary" ultimatum.

> Except ye eat the flesh of the Son of man, and drink his blood, ye have no life in you. Whoso eateth my flesh, and drinketh my blood, hath eternal life; and I will raise him up at the last day. For my flesh is meat indeed, and my blood is drink indeed. He that eateth my flesh, and drinketh my blood, dwelleth in me, and I in him. As the living Father hath sent me, and I live by the Father: so he that eateth me, even he shall live by me. (John 6:53-57)

To interpret this instruction literally would be linguistically absurd and theologically aberrant. The Lord is obviously making a comparison between eating physically and eating spiritually. Eating Christ is a spiritual act of faith, not a physical act of chewing and swallowing. The point of correspondence is not in the mechanics of the eating process, but in the consequence. Eating is a fitting figure of appropriating to oneself what is necessary for life. As we believe Christ and His gospel we receive life and enter into a mutual bond with Christ: "He that eateth my flesh, and drinketh my blood, dwelleth **in me**, and I **in him**."

In the physical realm we understand the necessity of eating regularly and healthily to sustain life. Without food, our bodies will shrivel and waste away. Without food, we will become faint, having no energy to function. Unless we are physically sick or emotionally unstable, eating is natural, and mealtimes are enjoyable experiences. The same is true spiritually. Partaking of Christ by faith ought to be the normal and happy experience of every believer. We must have a regular, daily diet of eating the Bread of Life and drinking the Living Water if we are going to grow in grace and in the knowledge of God. What is great about eating and drinking Christ is that it is always the right thing to do and it is impossible to eat too much. As I have grown a bit older, I have been instructed to watch what I eat. I can't have this or that because I have to maintain a certain ratio in my cholesterol count. Even as I am writing this, I am drinking a cup of decaffeinated coffee-. I never in my life thought things would come to this! But Christ is always a feast. The more we feast on Him, the more spiritual strength we are going to gain. By faith we must procure to ourselves all that Christ is and all that Christ has for His people. He is our life.

The Head and Body Analogy

Christ is the Head of His people not only in a covenant sense, but in a vital sense as well. Paul expressed his desire for the spiritual growth of the Ephesian believers using this analogy.

> But speaking the truth in love, [we] may grow up into him in all things, which is the head, even Christ: From whom the whole body fitly joined together and compacted by that which every joint supplieth, according to the effectual working in the measure of every part, maketh increase of the body unto the edifying of itself in love. (Ephesians 4:15-16)

Similarly, he identified Christ as "the head over all things to the church, which is his body" (Ephesians 1:22-23). In Colossians he also forthrightly declared that Christ "is the head of the body, the church" (1:18).

The vital connection between head and body is obvious. The head is the command center for all the operations of life. From the head flow all the impulses and instructions for the body to function. A headless body is lifeless. It is only in union with its head that a body can live. What a vivid analogy to illustrate the inseparable connection between Christ and His people! As the body, His people do not and cannot exist without Him. But united to Him, they have everything necessary for spiritual life and function. In addition, they enjoy the security based in the fact that God sees the body only through the head and deals with the body only in terms of the head.

But there is another side to this analogy that should increase our sense of security and our sense of duty. If it is true that a headless body is lifeless, it is equally true that a bodiless head cannot exist. Now follow carefully what I am going to say; I do not want to be misunderstood. Believers cannot exist apart from Christ, and

Christ does not exist apart from His body, the church. I am not saying that the eternal Son of God, the Second Person of the holy Trinity does not exist apart from the church. As God, He is absolutely independent, the eternal and immutable Self-Existent Deity. I am intentionally referring to the Savior as Christ, the title designating Him as the anointed One–eternally chosen to be the one and only Mediator between God and men, the ideal Prophet, Priest, and King. The gracious reason that God ordained His only begotten Son to be that Mediator was that He might become the Son of Man, that He might become Jesus who came to save His people from their sins (Matthew 1:21). Christ, the Messiah, came to save a people, and save a people is exactly what He did. As certainly as there is a Christ, there is a people who belong to Christ–His body, the church. Every believer, therefore, testifies to the existence of the Savior. This is why I say that union with Christ should stimulate our desire to reflect Him. Just as there is a sense in which God sees the body only through the head, there is a sense in which the world sees the head only through the body. It is vital, therefore, that we as members of His body become more and more conformed to His image, the purpose of our predestination to this glorious position (Romans 8:29). Because we are in Christ, God always thinks well of us. Because we are in Christ, may sinners come to think well of Him.

The Vine and Branches Analogy

Perhaps the most thorough analogy describing the believer's vital union with Christ comes from the teaching of Jesus Himself. In John 15, the Lord identifies Himself as the vine and true believers as the branches. The primary point of the analogy is the life connection between the vine and branches. The vine is the stem and root, which supplies the life and fruitfulness of branches. The branches are the natural outgrowth of the vine and have no independent existence. Let me summarize Christ's teaching under three heads.

Union with Christ Explained

Jesus emphasizes two principal aspects of this vital union. First, union involves communion. The verb "to abide" occurs nine times in verses 4-9. This word means to remain, to continue, or to take up residence, and it expresses an intimacy of relationship. This union entails mutual abiding as Christ remains in us and we in Him (15:4-5). The vine shares its life juices with the branches that draw what they need of life from that constant circulation. So the believer shares in and draws from the life of Christ what is necessary for spiritual, eternal, and abundant life.

Second, union implies dependence. The branch cannot function or survive apart from the vine (15:4, 6). Jesus said, "Without me ye can do nothing" (15:5). Note particularly how personal Christ makes this: "without me." Christ is everything to and for His people. Observe as well the absoluteness of Christ's statement: "ye can do nothing." He does not say that we can do things better with Him; He forthrightly says we can't do anything. Why do we then so often endeavor to attempt things without Him? Although we know our flesh is weak, in our spiritual stupidity we often feel obligated to give ourselves a chance before resting upon Christ. Trying to approach sanctification or service without consciously relying on faith in Christ is folly and doomed effort. We can do all things through Christ who strengthens us (Philippians 4:13), and we can do nothing without Him. That's an important lesson to learn.

Union with Christ Evidenced

To be united to Christ shows itself in life: Spiritual life does not look like or act like spiritual death. Jesus highlights two essential proofs of abiding in Him.

First, union with Christ is evidenced by the production of fruit. In verses 6-11, the Lord refers to fruit six times. This fruit is not the result of human effort or achievement; it is the result of abiding in Christ. Note carefully that fruit does not procure union; instead, it reveals the fact of union (15:2, 6, 8). Bearing fruit is not optional; it is an essential mark of union with Christ. Even though Christ is not here specifying the identity or properties of the fruit, we do know that the law of fruit necessitates that kind produces kind. If the life of Christ flows through us, it must be likeness to Christ that emanates from us. As fruit brings glory to the vine, so must we radiate glory to Christ.

It is the fruit that attracts attention to the vine. Some interpreters mistakenly limit the fruit-bearing to efforts in evangelism. Although they are contextually wrong in identifying the fruit as new converts, there is an important sense in which the fruit that we bear–the evidences of spiritual life in Christ–ought to attract men to Christ. It is best to see the fruit as the evidence of a transformed life produced by the Spirit of God. According to Scripture, the kind of fruit required is defined in terms of love, joy, peace, longsuffering, gentleness, goodness, faith, meekness, and temperance (Galatians 5:22-23). The amount of fruit may vary between branches, but the existence of fruit on them does not. As the branch draws from the life juices of the vine, it will yield more fruit. In like manner as by faith we draw from the resources that Christ supplies, the evidences of grace will increase in our lives.

Second, union with Christ is evidenced by the Father's care. In Christ's analogy, God the Father is the husbandman, i.e., the proprietor and gardener (15:1). The branches are not wild growth; rather, they are the objects of special cultivation, care, and concern. The owner of the vineyard does everything that is necessary for the production of fruit (see Isaiah 5:1-2). Good gardening requires great skill, particularly in the pruning of vines and fruit trees. Cutting too much will kill; pruning too little does not further proper growth. Christ reveals that God knows precisely what is necessary for each individual branch to produce fruit. At the beginning of this passage He says, "Every branch in me that beareth not fruit he taketh away" (15:2). On the surface this sounds like a contradictory statement. If the branch is in Christ, how can the branch be taken away? Let me here interject one of the key principles of interpretation: a verse cannot mean what it cannot mean. Christ is unmistakably referring to a branch in Him–a genuine believer. The crux of meaning lies in the verb translated "taketh away," the primary meaning of which is "to raise" or "to lift up." This explains the image: Some branches He lifts up. He carefully raises the branch that has fallen to expose it more advantageously to the light of grace that it might grow. What a beautiful statement this is!

In the second part of this verse, the Savior continues, "Every branch that beareth fruit, he purgeth it, that it may bring forth more fruit" (15:2). God will prune by cutting away what chokes out or competes for the production of fruit. More fruit is His objective. Again it is clear that fruit in the life of the Christian is not the result of natural energies; it is the result of divine operation. The branches can never take credit for fruit, and Christians can never take credit for godliness. Fruitfulness is thriving in grace.

Union with Christ Enjoyed

The benefits that flow from union with Christ are indescribably wonderful. Four blessings stand out in Christ's analogy. Each of these could potentially lead to long discussions, but I am merely going to identify them for your further consideration. First, union with Christ means escape from destruction (15:6). Eternal destiny is linked to where we are in relationship to Christ. The man out of Christ is like a branch that is withered (void of life and vitality) and burned. To be outside of Christ is death now and forever, but to be in Christ is life both now and forever.

Second, union with Christ guarantees the answers to prayer (15:7). The language of this verse is significant. The text marks as a privilege both praying as well as being answered in our prayers. If we abide in Him, we **will ask** and it **will become** reality for us. Prayer is the exercise of our union and communion with Christ. The more conscious we are of that union and our consequent dependence on Him, the more we will pray.

Third, union with Christ assures us that we are the objects of God's love (15:9-10). It is the only way that we can ever personally know and experience the love of God. Christ is the supreme object of the Father's love and those in Christ share in that never-ending, never-changing love.

Fourth, union with Christ produces joy. Christ concludes His analogy with the statement, "These things have I spoken unto you, that my joy might remain in you, and that your joy might be full" (15:11). This is the ultimate issue. The consolation, peace, and satisfaction resulting from our meditation on union with Christ will overwhelm us with spiritual joy and contentment. And in union with Christ, even this joy is mutual. It is easy enough to understand why we should rejoice in Christ, but that He acknowledges His own joy in us is astounding (see similarly in Isaiah 62:4-5–"the Lord delighteth in thee....So shall thy God rejoice over thee"). God, Christ, and we have every reason to be satisfied. Why has the remarkable thrill of this union become so ignored by so many who have every right to enjoy it?

United to Christ Intimately

There is no more intimate relationship on earth than that between husband and wife. Adam, in his yet sinless state, expressed his understanding of the inseparable connection between himself and the partner God had made especially for him: "This is now bone of my bones, and flesh of my flesh" (Genesis 2:23). In his inspired commentary on and application of Adam's statement, Moses made it clear that the marriage bond superseded every other human connection. "Therefore shall a man leave his father and his mother, and shall cleave unto his wife: and they shall be one flesh" (Genesis 2:24). In arguing for the sexual purity of believers, Paul used the theology of Moses to explain the relationship of the believer to Christ: "But he that is joined unto the Lord is one spirit" (1 Corinthians 6:17). He later said to the same group of believers that they had been espoused to one husband, Christ (2 Corinthians 11:2). In Ephesians 5–perhaps the most explicit passage expounding the gospel according to marriage–the apostle goes right back to Adam's confession when he describes the believer's union with Christ: "For we are members of his body, of his flesh, and of his bones" (5:30).

It is not surprising that Scripture so frequently uses marriage as the choice symbol of the intimate and eternal relationship that exists between Christ and His bride, the church. The parallels are many and the theology illustrated is magnificent. In marriage God ordained that two become one flesh; in the spiritual union the believer becomes one with Christ. In marriage two people traditionally share a name; in the spiritual union Christians are called by His name. In marriage two people share one life: in the spiritual union Christians, being one with Christ, are beneficiaries of the grace of His life. In marriage two people have in this life a common destiny: What God has joined together, man cannot put asunder. Likewise, nothing can separate the Christian from the love of Christ. In marriage two people live in constant company and fellowship; so in the spiritual union believers abide in Christ and He abides in them. In marriage two people share a mutual attraction and affection. Each sees something in the other that generates and feeds love. The Song of Solomon portrays a marriage that was a mutual admiration society consisting of two members. Such love points to a love that is even nobler. For Christ loved us first with a love that was not mutual. He loved us, but we saw no beauty in Him that we should desire Him, even though He is the altogether lovely One. But His gracious spirit wooed us and drew us irresistibly to Him, and now we love Him because He first loved us. And here is the real mystery. He loved us not because we were lovely, but in spite of our ugliness and sin. His love for us is single, exclusive, and undivided. It is amazing that Jesus would love even me. But it is an overwhelming thought that in union with Him, Jesus loves especially me. As any bride is special to her husband, so are we believers special to Christ.

Let me suggest one final thought about the wonder of our marriage union with Christ. As a husband, I cherish the union with my wife and have often reflected on what our marriage means as a picture of the marriage between Christ and His church. I pray that in some way our marriage has been a living gospel sermon. Yet as the father of two married sons, I have come to a new understanding and appreciation of the marriage bond. When my first son married, I experienced emotions that I did not know I was capable of. It is difficult to put into words the joy and satisfaction I felt toward my son's bride. Perhaps the strangest and newest thing for me was the total absolute acceptance and family love I have for his wife. Because of her oneness with my son, she is one with my family. So it is for my younger son and his bride. This whole business of having married sons has helped me understand a little of how our Heavenly Father views us as the bride of Christ. The Father is pleased with us because we are united to His Son. United to Christ, the Father loves us as He loves His Son and accepts us completely and unreservedly. In His great intercessory prayer for His people, the Lord Jesus said to His Father, "[Thou] hast loved them, as thou hast loved me" (John 17:23). Amazing!

What a sense of security to know we are loved, to know we are special to God. When we are conscious of the love that binds us inseparably to the Savior, our response should be to reciprocate with mutual love to Him. Christ should be our life–our reason for living. Pleasing Him should be our chief desire.

UNITED TO CHRIST ETERNALLY

There is one final aspect of our union with Christ that I want us to see. It is an indissoluble union, meaning that union with Christ is eternal. The old hymn puts it well.

His forever, only His–
Who the Lord and me shall part?
Ah, with what a rest of bliss
Christ can fill the loving heart!
Heav'n and earth may fade and flee,
Firstborn light in gloom decline;
But while God and I shall be,
I am His, and He is mine.

The Scripture reveals that the believer's mystical union is not just everlasting (no temporal ending), but it is in fact eternal (no temporal beginning, either). There is obviously a temporal beginning of our union when by faith we consciously enter into a saving relationship with Jesus Christ and are baptized by the Holy Spirit into His body. Yet in the mind of God, what transpires in time manifests His eternal purpose. The eternal nature of the believer's spiritual union with Christ puts in boldface the subtitle for this chapter: The security of the gospel.

United Before Time

Ephesians 1 is one of those high watermarks in the Scripture. In this chapter the imprisoned Paul set forth a breathtaking view of God's eternal strategy and purpose in Christ. Paul himself was obviously overwhelmed with the view, because once he started describing it he had a hard time stopping. Verses 3-14 form one complex sentence heaping one glorious truth on top of another. At the end of verse 7 and the beginning of verse 8, he defines it all in terms of "the riches of his grace which he has lavished upon us" (my translation). All of this divinely lavished grace is known in Christ. At least ten times in this run-on sentence Paul uses the construction "in" Christ. God the Father is the source of grace and Christ is the mediator of it. Paul makes it explicitly clear that it is only in union with Christ that men can experience saving grace. Among the many benefits and spiritual blessings that God reveals in Christ is the fact of the believer's eternal election in Him. God has "chosen us **in** him before the foundation of the world" (1:4).

It is sad that the doctrine of election has become such a subject of controversy among Christians, when the Scripture treats it exclusively as a source of blessing. The Bible never makes election a matter of speculation or introspection, but it does present it as a chief reason for praise and confidence in grace. Sinners are never told to ascertain their election before being converted; they are told to come to Christ. But saints, having been converted, are to consider the fact of their election as grounds for their security and peace. I love the way the Savior links these two noncompetitive truths: "All that the Father giveth me shall come to me; and him that cometh to me I will in no wise cast out" (John 6:37). The Father's giving the sinner to Christ guarantees the sinner's coming to Christ. The sinner's coming to Christ is the evidence of the Father's giving the sinner to Christ. God's purpose never fails. As mysterious as the doctrine of election may be, it is clear enough that election does not exist apart from Jesus Christ. All we have to do is get to Christ. And getting to Christ ought to engender confidence when we realize that our getting to Christ is not just a momentary crisis decision on our part: It is time witnessing to eternity. To be in Christ is security.

United After Time

The union that God conceived before time and that we experience now by faith will continue forever. A "time" is coming when time as we know it will cease to exist. The end of time, however, will not mark the end of the believer's union with Christ. Rather, it will magnify it by finally making it not a matter of faith but a matter of sight. In that everlasting day, believers will see His face (Revelation 22:4). "What a day that will be, when my Jesus I shall see!"

Paul draws attention to that moment when our faith will become sight in his great exposition of the Second Coming of Christ. In 1 Thessalonians 4 and 5, the apostle sets down five indisputable facts about the return of the Lord Jesus. (1) Christ's coming will be on schedule (5:1). Although it is not for us to know the day and the hour of His coming (Matthew 24:36), His coming the second time without sin unto salvation (Hebrews 9:28) will be in the fullness of time. (2) Christ's coming will be in person (4:16). It was the Incarnate Christ who ascended into glory; it will be the same Incarnate Christ who in glory returns from glory. (3) Christ's coming will be brilliantly obvious (4:16). His first coming in humiliation was without fanfare–only a few scattered shepherds heard the announcement of His birth. His Second Coming in exaltation will take place with much fanfare–a shout, the voice of the archangel, and the trump of God. (4) Christ's coming will be magnetic (4:14-17). Those in Christ, physically dead or alive, will irresistibly rise and join the Savior. (5) Christ's coming will be a happy event (4:17). This is the primary point of application for us in this discussion. There will be immediate happiness as we meet Christ for the first time face to face in the air. It is hard to imagine what that experience will be like. And Scripture guarantees us unceasing happiness as we shall "ever be with the Lord" (4:17). From that moment on, we will forever know by our glorified sight what we now know only through our so-often weak faith. I cannot possibly add to Paul's inspired application: "Wherefore comfort one another with these words" (4:18).

The truth of union with Christ offers much food for thought; it is an essential component of right thinking about the gospel. It secures for us every blessing of the gospel of grace. Let it be our prayer that God will increasingly enable us to understand and to utilize all that we have in Christ. May God help us to see ourselves as He sees us. May God help us to see Christ.

CHAPTER 6

JUSTIFICATION: THE LEGALITY OF THE GOSPEL

Without laws society cannot function. Laws are essential for maintaining an order and preserving a peace in which a people can happily live. Obedience to the law is a high virtue. Not all citizens, however, are law-abiding. Even in a society where law rules, crimes against law flourish. If law is to have any authority and substance, breaking the law must incur penalty. In our society, a judicial structure exists to enforce law, apprehend suspected offenders, prove the guilt of the accused, and either execute the prescribed penalties or exonerate the accused. There is something quite fascinating about the whole procedure: It is the stuff of news, novels, and television. Not too long ago, America witnessed what was touted as the trial of the century. The nation was riveted to television screens watching the events unfold–from pursuit to apprehension to investigation to trial to verdict. Whether justice was served remains a question, but nonetheless this captivating drama followed a legal process.

In American jurisprudence, the accused is innocent until proven guilty. In a court of law, he has the right to face his accusers and defend himself against any evidence of guilt. The prosecutor uses the evidence to try to build an irrefutable case for guilt, whereas the defense lawyer attempts to explain away the evidence, perhaps not sufficiently to prove innocence, but at least enough to cast some reasonable doubt. Just a reasonable doubt of guilt is grounds for exoneration. How often has justice not been served because one lawyer was more convincing than the other, or because the judge and jury were persuaded by something other than the facts of the case? I suppose that society is filled with guilty people who were legally acquitted because of some legal technicality, a really good lawyer, or a mistake in judgment. But notwithstanding actual guilt, the guilty party is legally exempt from any prosecution. The court declares him innocent and there can be no double jeopardy. I suppose, as well, that the jails may have a few who are in fact innocent of the crime for which they were sentenced. Yet, in spite of a miscarriage of justice, the decision of the court stands and the innocent serves his sentence. The law rules.

So what does this have to do with our understanding and enjoyment of the gospel? The point is that there is a relationship between law and gospel that entails the very heart, essence, and foundation of salvation by grace. I will go so far as to say that we cannot fully comprehend what God's salvation is apart from understanding its relationship to God's law. The element or component of salvation that specifically addresses and redresses the law of God is **justification**. The doctrine of justification pertains to *the legality of the gospel*.

God's law rules, and all who break His law are under the sentence of the just penalty. Whereas in an American courtroom the accused is innocent until proven guilty, before God's court the accused stands guilty until proven innocent. Because human courts are fallible and potentially biased, they sometimes render unjust decisions. God, however, is an infallible and impartial judge. "All things are naked and opened unto the eyes of him with whom we have to do" (Hebrews 4:13), and "we are sure that the judgment of God is according to truth" (Romans 3:2). "There is no respect of persons with God" (Romans 2:11), and "God shall bring every work into judgment, with every secret thing, whether it be good, or whether it be evil" (Ecclesiastes 12:14). There are no miscarriages of justice in God's courtroom. The accused has no excuse or alibi, and no extenuating circumstances are sufficient to prove his innocence. To stand guilty before God is to be guilty beyond even a shadow of doubt. And the truth of the matter is that every man has committed crimes against God's law and has a record that confirms his guilt before God.

Job's question, therefore, has a haunting ring: "How should man be just with God?" (Job 9:2). If man were left to stand alone before the divine Judge in his own defense, he would have no hope, because the Lord "will not at all acquit the wicked" (Nahum 1:3). But thankfully there is hope, because in saving sinners God does not leave man to himself. This brings us again to the gospel–more good news. How a legally guilty sinner can become a legally innocent saint is the issue of the doctrine of justification. Whereas in a human court the acquittal of the truly guilty party would be a miscarriage of justice, in God's court it evidences God's satisfied justice and sovereign grace. God is both just and the justifier (Romans 3:26). To understand how God turns sinners into saints by justification is the very core of the gospel message. Justification concerns the sinner's legal standing–his position–before the law of God. Like every other element of the gospel, justification must be understood in terms of Christ: The justified sinner is exempt from the penalty of the broken law because of Jesus Christ.

Tragically, there are sinners who do not know how to become saints, and there are believers who do not know how to enjoy the benefits of being saints. The message of justification is a saving message for sinners and a liberating message for saints. Justification–the legality of the gospel–is one of the golden links in the unbreakable chain of salvation.

THE MEANING OF JUSTIFICATION

I know of no more succinct definition of justification than the one in the *Westminster Shorter Catechism*. It would be well worth your effort to memorize it and meditate on it often. "Justification is an act of God's free grace, wherein he pardoneth all our sins, and accepteth us as righteous in his sight, only for the righteousness of Christ imputed to us, and received by faith alone" (question 33). The *Baptist Confession of Faith* also offers a fine explanation.

> Those whom God effectually calleth, he also freely justifieth, not by infusing righteousness into them, but by pardoning their sins, and by accounting and accepting their persons as righteous; not

> for anything wrought in them, or done by them, but for Christ's sake alone; not by imputing faith itself, the act of believing, or any other evangelical obedience to them, as their righteousness; but by imputing Christ's active obedience unto the whole law, and passive obedience in his death for their whole and sole righteousness by faith, which faith they have not of themselves; it is the gift of God. (Chapter 11, section 1)

In all theology, precision of definition is important. Before I develop in detail the salient elements of justification, I must define some of the key words that are vital to the definition of this doctrine–all of which are biblical terms.

Righteousness

Both the Hebrew and Greek words translated "righteousness" or "just" have the basic meaning of being straight or conforming to some standard of measurement or judgment. The particular standard of measurement is not inherent in the word and must be inferred from the context. Recognizing that the standard for righteousness varies and is not always theological will prevent some interpretation mistakes. So when Ecclesiastes advises compromise between being overly righteous and overly wicked (7:16-17), it must be addressing some non-theological and non-moral standard, or else the Bible would be contradicting itself in recommending only a moderate holiness. What the exact standard of judgment is here may be open to interpretation, but it cannot be the law of God. We must always examine the context carefully to determine what the ruling guide is.

Particularly in the Old Testament, the word has a wide range of function, referring in varied contexts to God, man, and things. It may apply, for instance, to things in the physical sphere. Balances of righteousness refer to accurate scales; the scales conform to the established standard of weight and measurement (Deuteronomy 25:15; Proverbs 11:1). The word sometimes applies to behavior in a moral or ethical sphere. Jacob's honoring the sheep contract between himself and Laban was an act of righteousness, the right and ethical thing to do; he played by the rules (Genesis 30:33). The word occurs as well in a judicial or forensic sphere to designate those who are legally innocent. Moses instructed judges that when adjudicating a controversy between men, they were to "justify the righteous and condemn the wicked" (Deuteronomy 25:1). Significantly, righteousness is a perfection of God: The Lord is righteous and He loves righteousness (Psalm 11:7). He is His own standard. That God is righteous means simply that God is always God. Who He is and what He does are always in perfect harmony with His infinite, eternal, and unchangeable being and character. That God loves righteousness suggests His standard for evaluating others and what He requires.

Though the word is not strictly a theological concept, it has far-reaching and serious theological implications. When used in a theological context, the absolute standard is always the law of God, particularly the moral law, which reflects the perfections of the righteous God Himself and reveals His absolute demands. Righteousness requires meeting all the requirements of that law; unrighteousness results from failing to meet all the requirements. Because the righteous Lord loves righteousness, righteousness merits the reward of life and unrighteousness merits the penalty of death.

How does all this relate specifically to our justification? When we are justified, God accepts us as though we have obeyed the law completely and are therefore exempt from any penalty. Legally, we are innocent before His unyielding code of morality. As we will see, our status is not the result of blind miscalculation on His part or His ignoring the evidence of guilt. It is, rather, an acceptance based on the righteousness of Christ (i.e., His perfect and total obedience).

To Justify

To justify is the verbal counterpart of the noun "righteousness" and the adjective "righteous"; it is formed from the same root. This key term expresses how those who by their actions are unrighteous can be accepted by God as though they were righteous. To justify means "to declare or pronounce to be righteous." It is a legal expression referring to the adjudication of the Judge that proclaims the defendant to be innocent of the charges against him and not liable to the punishment that guilt would have incurred. The man whom the court decrees innocent is free to go, because the decision of the court is binding and irreversible. This is exactly what God does when He justifies sinners: He declares them to be righteous (completely conformed to His law), thereby freeing them from any penalty.

I need to issue a crucial caution. It is absolutely imperative that we restrict the act of justification to the legal sphere. In other words, justification does not impart or infuse any righteousness into us. It does not create any moral change within us; it is something God does outside of us and not inside of us. Justification concerns how God regards us and deals with us in terms of His law. It is His decision. The importance of this distinction will become clear as we develop the doctrine and see its relationship to other elements of salvation that in fact do impart and infuse righteousness into us.

To Impute

The verb "to impute" is closely related to the verb "to justify." It underscores the objective nature of justification. This is why we define justification as imputed rather than imparted righteousness. The Old Testament word for this concept means "to consider, think about, or reckon" (see Genesis 15:6–and God "**counted** it to him for righteousness"). The New Testament word carries similar implications: to reason, to take something into account, to have an opinion concerning something, to keep mental record, or to charge something to an account. In the theology of justification, the concept of imputation will have a twofold focus. On the one hand, we will see God's imputing our guilt to Christ, and on the other hand, we will see God's imputing Christ's righteousness to us. In other words, God regarded Christ as guilty and dealt with Him accordingly, and He regards us as righteous and deals with us accordingly. This will have important implications for our understanding and application of the doctrine.

Keep these crucial definitions in focus as we consider the specific aspects of justification. The bottom line is that we cannot understand justification apart from the righteousness of God; we cannot understand God's righteousness apart from His perfect law. The gospel *does not replace* God's law; it *fulfills* it for every believer. "Christ is the end of the law for righteousness to every one that believeth" (Romans 10:4). This is why I say that justification addresses the legality of the gospel.

The Need for Justification

We have already learned that justification concerns God's moral law. According to the Lord Jesus, this entire moral law of God is summarized by the two all-encompassing commands to love God totally and to love one's neighbor as self (Matthew 22:37-39, quoting Deuteronomy 6:5 and Leviticus 19:19). Jesus said, "On these two commandments hang all the law and the prophets" (Matthew 22:40). The Decalogue–the Ten Commandments listed in Exodus 20 and Deuteronomy 5–forms the broad outline for these two sweeping statements. Although these commandments are inseparably connected (breaching one breaches all–James 2:10), the first four precepts frame the requirement to love God completely and the last six prescribe what it is to love one's neighbor. Every other command in Scripture is a specific application of one of the ten and, in turn, one of the two. Just thinking about the broad scope of God's law and all the specifics of its application can prove overwhelming. That righteousness demands total obedience both to the letter and to the spirit of the law is equally daunting. It is difficult to keep track of all the laws, let alone obey them all. This suggests two bases on which God's gracious justification is necessary for salvation: God is righteous and man is not.

God's Inflexibility Concerning His Law

The first reason justification is necessary is that God's righteousness causes Him to be inflexible concerning His law.

Remember that God's righteousness means that God is always God and that all the perfections of God are unchangeably and inviolably the same. Justice is one of His infinite, eternal, and immutable perfections. His justice guarantees His impartial fairness and infallible judgments: He never acquits the guilty or punishes the innocent. His justice equally demands that His law be kept perfectly: He must be true to Himself and to His law. God cannot be other than He is. For God to set aside His law or to lessen the criteria for righteousness would be for God to differ from Himself and thus to cease to be God. Such an aberration is absurd and impossible.

On that account, justice demands righteousness–complete conformity to the absolute standard of God's unchanging and inflexible law. In theory there are two ways for man to meet the law's demands. One way, however, is doomed to failure; the other ensures success. I am going to use a couple of words that may be unfamiliar, but stay with me: I will define what I mean. The concept of righteousness can be either stative or fientive. *Stative* refers to a condition of existence; *fientive* refers to activity. In other words, righteousness refers either to what someone is or to what someone does. Stative righteousness can be earned only by a fientive righteousness that does not deviate even slightly from the law.

God's justice grants life to the righteous and calls for the death of the unrighteous. Listen to what Moses and Paul said in describing the righteousness of the law: "The man which doeth those things shall live by them" (Romans 10:5, quoting Leviticus 18:5–see also Galatians 3:12). Man can try to do this on his own, but he will be doomed to fail. As certainly as keeping the law would earn life, failing to keep the law earns death (Romans 6:23). "Cursed is every one that continueth not in all things which are written in the book of the law to do them" (Galatians 3:10, quoting Deuteronomy 27:26).

When my sons were growing up, I often told them that what grade they earned in school was not so important as their doing their best. As long as they did their best, I would be satisfied. God's standard, contrarily, is high and inflexible: God does not require nor is He satisfied with man's best; He requires perfection as the only acceptable "grade." Against the standard of God's law a man is either righteous or unrighteous; there is no such thing as being almost righteous. The chances of our achieving that perfection are exactly nil. The tragedy is that so many try, hoping against hope that somehow God will lower the standard. The only real way to be righteous before God is for God to justify the sinner, declaring him to be legally righteous notwithstanding his personal unrighteousness. That necessitates grace. The good news is that God graciously does exactly this to ensure the requisite legal righteousness.

The bottom line is that a free justification apart from human effort or merit is necessary because God is righteous. If God does not do it, it cannot be done.

Man's Inability to Keep the Law

If the Bible is clear on anything, it is that salvation is all of grace and damnation is all of merit. Judgment is always earned: The wages of sin is death. Therefore, the second reason justification is necessary is that man is incapable of obeying God's law. Every attempt at righteousness by man falls woefully short of the absolute standard, and it is viewed by the righteousness-loving God as filthy rags (see Romans 3:23 and Isaiah 64:6). It is little wonder that Paul concludes, "No man is justified by the law in the sight of God" (Galatians 3:11; see also Romans 3:20). To miss the mark of God's standard is to stand condemned by the law and liable to its just penalty.

Throughout Scripture, when God announces His righteous judgment against the sinner, He always proves His case by giving ample evidence of the sinner's guilt. We would expect no less in any fair trial. Although even a minor infraction of the law would render a man guilty before God, the fact of the matter is that no man ever comes close to keeping the law and thereby earning righteousness. The Bible leaves no doubt about the universality and extent of man's inability: "There is none righteous, no, not one" (Romans 3:10) because "there is none that doeth good, no, not one" (Romans 3:12; see Psalms 14:1-3 and 53:1-3). Just read through the evidence against man in Romans 3:11-18 and you will have to concur that God is absolutely just in His condemnation of sinners. Not only is unrighteousness the condition of all men; it is the condition of all of man. Everything from the inner dispositions of the will to the outward acts of impiety betrays man's total corruption and failure to achieve righteousness. Consequently, there can be no self-defense, for "every mouth [is] stopped," and there can be no other verdict, for "all the world [is] guilty" (Romans 3:19).

The Resolution

Since we need righteousness to escape the penalty of the broken law, and since we are incapable of attaining righteousness, it follows that we must receive righteousness from outside ourselves if we are to be saved. The very fact of our sin necessitates a free and gracious justification. This is exactly the logic of Paul in Romans 3:23-26.

> For all have sinned, and come short of the glory of God; Being justified freely by his grace through the redemption that is in Christ Jesus: Whom God hath set forth to be a propitiation through faith in his blood, to declare his righteousness for the remission of sins that are past, through the forbearance of God; To declare, I say, at this time his righteousness: that he might be just, and the justifier of him which believeth in Jesus.

Before I explain the logic, permit me a personal digression to express my thanks to God for saving my soul. This text will forever have special significance to me because this is the Word that the Holy Spirit used to bring me to see my need of Christ when I was just a child of about seven years old. I hope I never forget that humble and gracious lady, my Sunday school teacher, who pointed me from my sin to my Savior. I admit that I did not then understand all the implications of the imputed righteousness of Jesus Christ, but I did understand that I was a sinner who needed Jesus. I knew that Jesus died and that He died for me, and that was enough. Thank God, it is still enough. Since my conversion, I have learned more about Jesus and what He did for me, and I understand it with more sophisticated and theological precision. Yet the simple fact of the gospel will always be thrilling. This is why I said at the beginning that salvation in Christ is simple enough for a child to understand, yet profound enough that the most mature believer will always have more to learn–if not in facts, certainly in experience.

Now, back to the text. As I suggested, Paul's logic sums up our need for justification by resolving the tension between God's inflexible righteousness and our inability to conform to His absolute standard. I want to discuss this as simply as I can, but my explanation is going to involve some grammatical observations stemming from the Greek text. Just stay with me. Although my concern right now is the link between verses 23 and 24, I should note that Romans 3:23-26 is actually one long sentence. The longer the sentence, the more complicated things can get. I have told my Greek students over and over that when they get stuck, they should always identify the main verb(s) of the sentence and begin their reasoning from there. Everything else in the sentence in one way or another will be subordinate to and will flow from that core.

Let's focus our attention on verse 23 where the only finite verbs occur. Here is one of those grammatical terms. "Finite" verbs are those which are limited by person, tense, mood, and number; simply, they are verbs that require a subject. Once you identify a finite verb, you have found the main verb of any given clause. The core statement is "All sinned and are continuously coming short of the glory of God" (my translation). The rest of the passage flows logically from this all-inclusive statement that underscores man's unrighteousness and his innate inability to attain God's standard. Verse 24 begins with a participle (being justified), one of the chief means in Greek to express subordination between verbal ideas. I would suggest that in this context, the participle indicates the necessary consequence of the main verbs. Let me state the logic explicitly: Because of man's total failure to meet the requirements for righteousness, a free and gracious justification is necessary. Since all have sinned and cannot stop sinning, God justifies freely or else there would be no hope for any sinner. But God does provide hope through His grace and redemption in Christ Jesus. The rest of the sentence explains how this justification works and what it does. Its focus on the person and work of Christ leads directly to the next point of our discussion.

THE GROUNDS OF JUSTIFICATION

Sinners need a free and gracious justification. God's righteousness demands it; Christ's righteousness makes it possible. Grace, notwithstanding its sovereignty, does not operate capriciously. Divine grace does not overrule divine righteousness. Divine righteousness requires the perfect satisfaction of the law or else the just penalty for its breach. Grace and justice would appear to be mutually exclusive. How God can be just and at the same time the justifier is perplexing. Jesus Christ is the answer to this seeming conundrum. "For what the law could not do, in that it was weak through the flesh, God sending his own Son in the likeness of sinful flesh, and for sin, condemned sin in the flesh: That the righteousness of the law might be fulfilled in us" (Romans 8:3-4). Here again is the beauty of the gospel that always brings us back to the Lord Jesus.

The purpose of the Incarnation was that the Son of God might shed His blood and die on the cross to save His people. Saying that He came to die is one thing; understanding why He came to die is the essence of the gospel. As I have been emphasizing, understanding the gospel requires understanding the law of God. The tension between the gospel and law may exist in theological discussion, but not in the Scripture. The gospel of free salvation in and through the Lord Jesus Christ does not replace the law of God; it is the fulfillment and satisfaction of the law of God. I have said that before, but I repeat it simply because I have encountered so many people who erroneously think the gospel is just a new, alternative way of salvation that supplanted the old way of the law. Remember that there can be no salvation unless the righteousness of God is absolutely satisfied: The righteous Lord loves righteousness. The law work of Jesus Christ is the one and only answer to the desperate plight man faces because of sin.

I don't want to labor the point, but I must keep this vital truth in the foreground: God's law demands a total obedience. From the greatest commandment to love God completely to whatever may be the least commandment, God demands absolute righteousness. The law is inflexible, and the least breach of the law carries severe penalty. Because of his sin–that is, his failure to conform to the standard required by the holy law of God-–every man has earned death, the fair wage of sin (Romans 6:23). The justice of God demands the full payment of that earned wage, and, therefore, sinners are doomed to the full payment of not only physical but also spiritual and eternal death.

Jesus Christ, God's Son and our Savior, is the solution to that problem. What man cannot do in earning life under the weight of God's holy law, Jesus Christ did. This is to me the great beauty of the gospel: What man cannot do for himself, God in His grace through His eternal Son has done. Christ came to free man from the law's bondage. He freed us not by changing the rules but by obeying the rules in our place and suffering the consequences of our disobedience. Two things were necessary for God to be just in saving sinners: the demands of the law had to be completely obeyed, and the penalty of the broken law had to be completely paid. Jesus Christ did both, and both are foundational to the gospel.

The Life of Jesus Christ

Throughout His earthly life, the Lord Jesus obeyed the law of God, earning both life and the right to die in place of His people. Theologians refer to this righteous living of Christ as His *active obedience*. It is important to realize that this active obedience of Christ, or His life, was just as vicarious as His death. Not only can a Christian say, "Jesus died for me," but he can also say, "Jesus lived for me." In fact, had the Lord Jesus not lived the life that He did, His death could not have counted as a substitutionary death at all.

Christ Earned Righteousness

The New Testament places significant emphasis on Christ's obedience as an essential part of His mission. Galatians 4:4 plainly says, "When the fulness of the time was come, God sent forth his Son, made of a woman, made under the law." "Made of a woman" implies the virgin birth and asserts the real humanity of the Savior. If I may put this colloquially "made under the law" means that Christ did not receive any special break or special treatment in regard to the law. He was not exempt from the rules; He was born under the same rigid, inflexible, unchangeable law that every other man is born under. In fact, according to words attributed to Christ Himself, He came to fulfill that law, which reflects God's perfect will: "Lo, I come (in the volume of the book it is written of me,) to do thy will, O God" (Hebrews 10:7, quoting Psalm 40:7-8). But whereas that law condemns us and calls for our death, it vindicates Christ as having been absolutely righteous. First Timothy 3:16 says that the God who was manifest in the flesh was justified by the Spirit; that is, He was vindicated or proven to be righteous. In absolutely every way, Jesus Christ conformed to the absolute standard of righteousness, God's Law. We earn death; Christ earned life.

I must clarify that I am not referring to the inherent and eternal righteousness that Christ has by virtue of His deity. It is wonderfully true that as God He is righteous. But the righteousness that "counts" for our salvation is that which He earned every day and every moment for the thirty-some years He lived on earth. Paul, in that great Christological text in Philippians 2, declares that an essential element in the Lord's self-humiliation was that He became obedient all the way to death. As strange as it may sound, the Lord Jesus had to learn obedience. Although He was impeccably perfect, He had to achieve perfection. Hebrews 5:8-9 says, "Though he were a Son, yet learned he obedience by the things which he suffered; And being made perfect, he became the author of eternal salvation unto all them that obey him." Literally verse 9 says, "He became one who was perfected." Ethically and morally,

Christ matured to evident perfection (cf. Hebrews 2:10). Never a wrong deed, never a wrong thought–He kept the law in its perfect spirit to the minutest detail of its letter. Only of Jesus Christ could it be said that he was "holy, harmless, undefiled, separate from sinners" (Hebrews 7:26; see also 1 Peter 1:19).

Christ Earned Righteousness Vicariously

The entire obedient life of Jesus Christ was vicarious. This simply means that He lived a substitutionary life for His people. Every moment of His perfect life–every holy thought, His baptism, His temptation, His every act of kindness, everything to His cross–was for the benefit of believers and in their place. Christ lived the righteous life that God required of man.

Although the Gospel narratives and General Epistles give evidence of Christ's sinless life, it is Paul who explains the theology of it. Romans 5 is a crucial text that explains how God could regard Christ's righteous life as substitutionary. Here the apostle expounds the relationship between Adam and Christ. Paul explains that **legally** God deals with humanity in terms of two men–either Adam or Jesus. Through the sinful disobedience of Adam, the entire human race is justly guilty before God and under the necessary sentence of death (5:12, 17-19). Through the righteous obedience of Christ, the entire "believing part" of the human race is justly righteous before God and freed from the necessary penalty of death: "So by the obedience of one shall many be made righteous" (5:19; see also 15, 17, 18). As God justly imputed Adam's sin to the human race–which was in Adam and which consequently, was involved in his sin–so He justly regards Christ's obedience as applying to those who believe in Christ. Adam's disobedience was not confined to himself; Christ's obedience was not confined to Himself.

This is precisely how God maintains His absolute justice while at the same time pardoning the sins of everyone who trusts in Christ and Christ alone. When God saves a sinner, He considers the demands of the law to be completely, righteously satisfied because of the righteousness earned by the perfect, active obedience of Jesus. Theologians like to debate the mechanics and logic of this legal imputation, often confusing the matter and making it more complicated than God wants it to be for us. Let me make it as simple as I possibly can. Here are the basic facts. (1) God demands perfect obedience to His law. (2) Man cannot obey perfectly; so he earns death, the penalty for breaking the law. (3) The man Christ Jesus obeyed the law perfectly; so He earned life, the reward for keeping the law. (4) God graciously lets the perfect obedience of Christ count for all and any who trust Christ, thereby freeing them from the penalty of death. This is why Paul says that Christ is the end of the law for righteousness to those who believe (Romans 10:4). For believers, Christ has fulfilled the law. Unbelievers are still on their own in Adam, and they continue, therefore, under condemnation. Being in Christ is man's only hope.

The Death of Jesus Christ

God cannot let bygones be bygones when it comes to sin. For man's salvation to be possible, every claim of the law had to be addressed. There could be no outstanding debts. Whereas the life of Christ took care of the positive demands of the law, His death paid the penalty of the broken law. Theologians refer to His dying for His people as His *passive obedience*. This does not appear to be a precisely accurate expression, because Christ was not a passive victim in His death. No man could take His life; He voluntarily, deliberately, lovingly, and joyfully submitted Himself to the shame and suffering of the cross (John 10:17-18; Hebrews 12:2). In fact, perhaps we should see His death as the last, triumphant demonstration of His active obedience in completely fulfilling the will of God. The coiners of this expression, however, did not intend to imply that Christ was inactive in His death; rather, they used the term "passive" according to its Latin derivation that meant "capable of suffering." This is better, although it could wrongly suggest that there was no suffering during His life of active obedience. Nevertheless, as long as we define the term properly and understand that passive obedience refers to His obedient death on the cross (Philippians 2:8) without implying that Christ was just a victim of uncontrollable circumstances or that He experienced no suffering before His passion, we can use the term legitimately.

Although infirmities, miseries, and sufferings filled the whole life of Christ, they reached their indescribable climax at the cross and in the events immediately leading to the cross. When we consider the atonement of Christ, we are approaching the deepest and highest theological truths in the Bible. Theologians have argued about the purpose of the death of Christ, the extent of its application, even the shape of the cross. It is not my purpose here to consider all the theories of the atonement, but to set down two key aspects of Christ's death that are essential and fundamental to justification.

An Actual Death

Christ's perfect obedience earned two things: for His people, life, and for Himself, the right to die in payment for their sins. His death could pay the penalty for our sins because it did not have to pay the penalty of His–He had no sin. Part of His total obedience was His becoming "obedient unto death, even the death of the cross" (Philippians 2:8). By that death, He paid the penalty of sin, received the just wages of sin, and thereby blotted "out the handwriting of ordinances that was against us, which was contrary to us, and took it out of the way, nailing it to his cross" (Colossians 2:14). On that cross, He took the curse of sin and suffered the full penalty of the broken law: "Cursed is every one that hangeth on a tree"(Galatians 3:13). This is why the Bible so unequivocally stresses that the death of Christ was real.

The first component in Paul's classic definition of the gospel is "that Christ died for our sins according to the scriptures" (1 Corinthians 15:3). The form of the verb "died" lays stress on the simple fact that it was a real, actual death that occurred in history. The death of Christ is not just a theological doctrine; it is a historic fact. On an actual day in history, Jesus of Nazareth shed His blood and died on a Roman cross. To say that a man died is hardly unusual, for "it is appointed unto men once to die" (Hebrews 9:27). This, however, is not just any death that Paul is talking about. He refers to the death of the only Man who had ever lived or will ever live who did not deserve to die. Yet He died a death that was not only real, but also sacrificial and eternally planned. It is not without significance that the Gospel narratives devote so much attention to the crucifixion of the Lord Jesus. Although Christ lived over thirty years and accomplished so much that John said the world would not be able to contain the books if everything about His life were written (John 21:25), all four Gospels focus on the events of the last week of His life. The Gospels may be temporally lopsided, but they are theologically balanced. This is one reason we call them the Gospels and not the biographies of Jesus Christ. Each of the Gospels narrates the real sufferings that Christ endured at the hands of wicked men. The gospel of salvation in Christ remains only religious theory unless founded on the real historic fact of the death of the Son of God.

A Vicarious Death

The death of Christ was a substitutionary sacrifice. Christ died instead of us; He died in place of us. That He fulfilled our obligation to die in payment of our sins is the very heart of the gospel; it is also why His death had to be real. If Christ did not really die, our debt to the law and justice remains ours. The line in the old hymn says it well: "It is enough that Jesus died and that He died for me." For us to pay the penalty of our own sins would take forever because we have offended the infinitely holy God. Salvation would never eventuate if sinners were left to themselves either to obey the law or to make full payment for breaking it. Salvation for sinners requires a Savior outside themselves. Salvation for sinners requires that the penalty of sin be paid by one whose death could have infinite value. Jesus Christ is the only One qualified to be such a Savior. Because He was completely pure and holy with no unpaid debt to the law, He was able to suffer and die for others. Both the Old and the New Testaments declare over and over that Jesus died not for Himself but for sinners. I could offer many texts as evidence, but consider these few. Christ "was delivered for our offences" (Romans 4:25). "In due time Christ died for the ungodly" (Romans 5:6). "While we were yet sinners, Christ died for us" (Romans 5:8). "Christ hath redeemed us from the curse of the law, being made a curse for us" (Galatians 3:13). "Who his own self bare our sins in his own body on the tree" (1 Peter 2:24). "For Christ also hath once suffered for sins, the just for the unjust" (1 Peter 3:18). "Christ died for our sins according to the scriptures" (1 Corinthians 15:3). "For he hath made him to be sin for us, who knew no sin" (2 Corinthians 5:21).

This last verse requires explanation. Paul is not saying that Christ became a sinner. There are two orthodox interpretations of the statement. Some interpret it to mean that Christ was made a sin offering for us. This is certainly true and would establish a clear link between Christ's sacrifice and the Old Testament, which uses the word "sin" to designate the sin offering. Others interpret the statement as using the language of imputation. Christ was considered guilty of sin and liable for its penalty. On the cross God dealt with Christ as though He were legally a sinner, though in actual fact He was always the pure and spotless Lamb. For what it's worth, I favor the second interpretation. I believe this imputation aspect of Christ's passive obedience parallels the imputation aspect of His active obedience. The doctrine of justification involves a double imputation: Our guilt imputed to Christ and His righteousness imputed to us. Legally, God deals with believers in terms of Christ's righteousness. Legally, God dealt with Christ in terms of our sins. By God's legal transaction, the life that Christ earned becomes ours and the death that we earned became His. The life and death of Jesus Christ have provided the just grounds for our justification (Romans 3:25).

THE RESULT OF JUSTIFICATION

Because Christ's life and death satisfied the principle of divine justice, divine justice is satisfied for those persons for whom Christ lived and died, those who believe in Him. According to the *Shorter Catechism*, two great consequences result from God's gracious declaration of justification: sins are forgiven and sinners are accepted before God as being righteousness. Therefore, as far as the law is concerned, God sees believers the same way He sees Christ: legally perfect and innocent. There can be no condemnation for those who are in Christ Jesus (Romans 8:1). The law has nothing against believers.

Pardon from Guilt

Pardon from the guilt of sin and immunity from the penalty of sin go hand in hand. On the grounds of the work of Jesus Christ, God forgives our sin, removing every impediment to spiritual life and every liability to punishment. When God justifies sinners, He does not impute their trespasses to them (2 Corinthians 5:19). In other words, He does not consider, take into account, or factor in their sins when dealing with them. So closely connected is pardon with justification that Paul equates the imputation of righteousness with the non-imputation of sin. Listen to how he interprets David's statement:

> Even as David also describeth the blessedness of the man, unto whom God imputeth righteousness without works, saying, Blessed are they whose iniquities are forgiven, and whose sins are covered. Blessed is the man to whom the Lord will not impute sin. (Romans 4:6-8)

This is a quote from Psalm 32:1-2. The New Testament never changes the meaning of the Old Testament, so let's look directly at what David said in order to understand precisely the import of what Paul is saying. The Psalm makes three significant statements about the nature of God's gracious pardon.

Forgiveness

First, "transgression is forgiven" (Psalm 32:1). The word "transgression" refers specifically to rebellion against the authority of God–crimes against His law. Paul maintains the idea of legal transgression by translating the word as "lawlessness" ("iniquities" in the AV). Both words picture sin as a violation of the righteousness of God's law and suggest the consequent culpability and legal guilt of the transgressor. In the Psalm, the word "forgiven" means literally "to lift up" or "to take away." Similarly, the New Testament counterpart means "to dismiss" or "send away." What a beautiful truth this is and how well the children's chorus expresses this profound theology: "Gone, gone, gone, gone, yes, my sins are gone."

Covering

Second, "sin is covered" (32:1). Both the Old and the New Testament picture sin as a missing of the mark, a failure to meet God's perfect standard. This failure to conform to the law is the unrighteousness that incurs guilt in the sight of God. But God graciously covers the sin: He hides it from His sight. This word means "to conceal" and serves as a synonym for another Old Testament word meaning "to cover," which in turn is the theologically technical word designating the atonement. Although David here does not use the theological word, he nonetheless avers the same truth. This concealing of sin implies and demands the atonement.

Again, let me urge you to avoid the notion that God's covering and concealing sin refers to His sweeping it under a rug only to bring it out again to deal with it more thoroughly in the future. The point of David's testimony is that blessedness belongs to the man whose sin God does not see. I guarantee you that God can see through a rug. But God cannot see through the blood of atonement. When sin is covered with the blood, there is absolute pardon. One of the nice things about Hebrew poetry is that one line generally helps to interpret the other. The "cover" of the second line of verse 1 parallels the "take away" in the first line, meaning that this cannot refer to a temporary concealment. Sin cannot be taken away and left at the same time. The same parallel occurs in Psalm 85:2–"Thou hast forgiven the iniquity of thy people, thou hast covered all their sin." Similarly, Nehemiah 4:5 treats God's not covering iniquity as His not blotting out sin. The linguistic evidence warrants the theological conclusion. God's covering sin is tantamount to God's removing sin. God does see what is not there (see Isaiah 44:22; Psalm 103:10-12).

Non-imputation

Third, God does not impute iniquity (32:2). The word "impute," remember, is one of our key terms in the vocabulary of justification. It means simply "to think about" or "to take into account." Although the word "iniquity" depicts sin as twisted and perverted behavior, it is also the standard word in the Old Testament to designate the consequent legal guilt before God and His law that any and every sin occasions. The sense of guilt is particularly relevant in this context. Let's put this together. The essence of pardon is that in justifying the guilty sinner, God does not take into account or regard his guilt against him. For God not to regard our guilt means that He sees us as legally innocent. If there is no guilt, there can be no condemnation and no penalty. That's what justice is all about.

Keep in mind several points when thinking about this divine pardon. First, the pardon of justification concerns our legal standing before the bar of God's justice. God issues a legal pardon that remits the guilt of all our sins against His law–whether past, present, or future. This legal justification is a singular act. The claims of the law as the sole possible condition for life will never and can never be raised against us again. Christ has satisfied those claims for us. We are forever free from the penalty of the broken law. We cannot again be legally judged or condemned, because the guilt demanding our punishment was imputed to Christ. There can be no double jeopardy. There is absolutely "no condemnation to them which are in Christ Jesus" (Romans 8:1).

Second, the pardon of justification concerns our legal guilt and liability to penalty, not our sense of fault or the consciousness of guilt which we experience when we sin. Maintaining the distinction between our legal position and daily experience is crucial both to understanding and to enjoying the benefits of the gospel. Our present and future sins will certainly rob us of the joy of fellowship with God and should make us miserable in our souls, but they cannot change our legal standing before the law. When we sin, we must seek the Lord for forgiveness to restore the fellowship and remove the misery, but not even our failures can change God's verdict. This is both the ground for assurance and the motive to holiness. But be careful here. To interpret this unchangeable sentence as giving a license to sin is an aberration of the truth that betrays no understanding and very likely no experience of its reality.

Positioned in Christ

The second great consequence of God's gracious justification is that believers are accepted as righteous in God's sight, but only for the righteousness of Christ imputed to us. As essential as pardon from sin and guilt is, forgiveness alone is not enough to establish for us a perfect standing before God. Forgiveness removes our guilt, but it does not address the continuing and eternal demands of the law for perfect righteousness. If God were to pardon our sins and then leave us on our own to make a fresh start at maintaining righteousness, we would be immediately right back where we were. But God does not leave us thus naked; He clothes us with the garments of salvation, even the robe of righteousness (Isaiah 61:10). He positively imputes righteousness to us (Romans 4:6).

A vivid, divinely given illustration of this occurs in Zechariah 3. The passage begins with a judicial scene in which Joshua, the high priest, is standing before the Angel of the Lord and is being accused by Satan. As the high priest he is serving as man's representative, an accurate picture of how every man on his own stands before God. He stands silently, dressed in detestably filthy garments with no self-defense before the Judge. This scene graphically pictures how man appears before God in all the filthy rags of his own righteousness. Seemingly out of the blue God rebukes Satan and rescues Joshua as a brand plucked from the burning. Joshua is accepted before the Lord and allowed to stand in His presence. The text highlights two essential elements of that acceptance. (1) The Lord graciously pardoned sin. This is pictured by the removal of the filthy garments and explained directly: "I have caused thine iniquity to pass from thee" (3:4). The guilt and, therefore, the liability for punishment and penalty was removed. (2) The Lord provided righteousness. Not only were the filthy garments removed, but they were replaced with costly and glorious clothes which represent that robe of righteousness, the garment of salvation, that renders the wearer presentable before the Lord. In justification, God both pardons sin and imputes the righteousness of Christ.

The righteousness God imputes is not theoretical; it is the actual righteousness that Jesus Christ earned in His perfect humanity by His active obedience. Listen to how Paul put it: "By the righteousness of one the free gift came upon all men unto justification of life. . . . So by the obedience of one shall many be made righteous" (Romans 5:18-19; see also 5:15-17). By His life our precious Lord Jesus wove for us that garment of salvation, that robe of righteousness, that God considers to be ours. Here's where the imputation factors in again. Just as God regarded Christ as a sinner by charging Him with our guilt, so God regards us as righteous by attributing to us His righteousness. Imputed righteousness does not make us in *person* righteous any more than imputed guilt made Christ in *person* a sinner. Instead, it concerns how God regards us and how God deals with us.

This is the mind-boggling and heart-thrilling truth: As justified sinners, God sees us and deals with us only through the righteousness of Christ. Before the bar of God's justice, we are just as righteous and holy as Jesus Christ Himself. That would be a blasphemous statement if we were comparing our righteousness to His. But we are not comparing degrees of righteousness: We are sharing in His. As the old hymn says, "No merit of my own His anger to suppress. My only hope is found in Jesus' righteousness." I'm about to break out in song. Zinzendorf had it right when he wrote, "Jesus, thy blood and righteousness my beauty are, my glorious dress." Wesley had it right when he wrote, "No condemnation now I dread; Jesus, and all in Him is mine! Alive in Him, my living Head, and clothed in righteousness divine." M'Cheyne certainly had it right when he wrote, "When I stand before the throne, dressed in beauty not my own . . . then, Lord, shall I fully know–not till then–how much I owe." There is some great theology in hymns. Pay attention to what you sing.

If it can sink into our souls that by virtue of our justification God regards us as legally righteous as Jesus Christ, it will liberate us. This means that nothing we do can add to or distract from that acceptance. Nothing we do can get God to love us any more than He already does. How tragically often Christians labor and struggle doing this or that with the intent of working off some sense of guilt or meriting some increased favor with God. Too many Christians live with a constant, shameful sense of inadequacy and under the burden of anxiety that they aren't quite measuring up to God's expectations, rather than appropriating and confidently enjoying what they are in Jesus Christ. To know that God loves us as He loves His Son and that God accepts us as He accepts His Son ought to put the real joy in serving Jesus.

THE MEANS OF JUSTIFICATION

Justification, this act of God's free grace based on the merits of Jesus Christ, is received by faith alone. When a sinner accepts Christ by faith, he is granted at that moment a pardon by God, thereby gaining acceptance before God. As the hymn declares, "The vilest offender who truly believes, that moment from Jesus a pardon receives." The Scripture constantly links justification to faith. Consider this sample data. "And he [Abraham] believed in the Lord; and he counted it to him for righteousness" (Genesis 15:6; quoted in Romans 4:3). "Therefore we conclude that a man is justified by faith without the deeds of the law" (Romans 3:28). "But to him that worketh not, but believeth on him that justifieth the ungodly, his faith is counted for righteousness" (Romans 4:5). "The just shall live by his faith" (Habakkuk 2:4; quoted in Romans 1:17, Galatians 3:11 and Hebrews 10:38). "Wherefore the law was our schoolmaster to bring us unto Christ, that we might be justified by faith" (Galatians 3:24). "And be found in him, not having mine own righteousness, which is of the law, but that which is through the faith of Christ, the righteousness which is of God by faith" (Philippians 3:9). I think you start to get the idea.

Galatians 2:16 highlights the focus that I want us to keep in considering justifying faith. "Knowing that a man is not justified by the works of the law, but by the faith of Jesus Christ, even we have believed in Jesus Christ, that we might be justified by the faith of Christ, and not by the works of the law: for by the works of the law shall no flesh be justified" (see also Ephesians 2:8-9). This text makes two things clear: (1) Saving faith and self-effort are mutually exclusive; (2) Saving faith finds its sole object in Jesus Christ.

This evangelical or saving faith justifies because it **rests** on Christ alone as He is offered in the gospel and **receives** as a free gift all that He offers. The saving value of this faith is in its object and not its exercise. I'm sure that over the years I have told my students hundreds of times, "The value of faith is determined by the object of faith. Saving faith is saving faith because its object is Christ." The exercise of faith will never be perfect, but the object of saving faith is. This is why we can take seriously what Peter says in writing "to them that have obtained like precious faith with us through the righteousness of God and our Saviour Jesus Christ" (2 Peter 1:1). The Greek word translated "like precious" literally means "of equal worth." That statement always puzzled me when I compared the fervency and boldness of Peter's faith with what I knew to be the weakness of mine. How could my faith be of equal worth to that of the great apostle? But that is a false comparison. What makes our faith of equal worth with Peter's is not the exercise of it, but the object of it–Jesus Christ.

It would not be particularly good news if God required from us a perfect faith any more than it would be good news if we had to perform perfectly the works of the law. Neither is possible for us. That demand would diminish faith to frustrating and futile effort as we tried to make sure that we believed enough, believed sincerely, or believed really. I don't know any genuine believer who, when looking inside of himself to evaluate the degree of his faith, will ever be satisfied with what he finds. Our prayer must always be, "Lord, I believe; help thou mine unbelief" (Mark 9:24).

God does, however, require perfection, and both He and we find that perfection in Christ. When Paul says that "faith is reckoned for righteousness" (Romans 4:5), he is not saying that faith is reckoned "as" righteousness. Faith is not "in place of" God's absolute standard of perfection, but it is with a view to righteousness. Faith is the means of obtaining the perfect righteousness that God requires, found only in the Lord Jesus Christ. Consequently, because all saving faith is of equal worth, every justified sinner has exactly the same standing and acceptance before God. Every believer is equally justified. What assurance and boldness this ought to give us! Down with the notion that some Christians will enter heaven by the skin of their teeth. Nobody just slips into heaven's glory: Every believer in Christ can anticipate a full and welcome entrance because he enters on the perfect merit and righteousness of the Savior. "I stand upon His merit. I know no other stand, not e'en where glory dwelleth, in Immanuel's land." Saving faith sets aside all effort, lays hold of Christ, and trusts God to keep His word that He is "the justifier of him which believeth in Jesus" (Romans 3:26).

> Justifying faith is a saving grace, wrought in the heart of a sinner by the Spirit and word of God, whereby he, being convinced of his sin and misery, and of the disability in himself and all other creatures to recover him out of his lost condition, not only assenteth to the truth of the promise of the gospel, but receiveth and resteth upon Christ and his righteousness, therein held forth, for pardon of sin, and for the accepting and accounting of his person righteous in the sight of God for salvation. (*Westminster Larger Catechism*, question 72)

Justification is a mighty doctrine that we ought to devote conscious, careful, and constant thought to. If we can learn to think rightly about this component of the gospel, it will enable us to live rightly. In fact, right thinking about justification is foundational to right thinking about every other link in the gospel chain. Living in the reality that God has pardoned our sins, freed us from the penalty of condemnation, and consequently accepted us as He accepts His own dear Son will liberate us from the oppression of guilt that hinders full enjoyment in the daily experience of our salvation. Justification is the basis for our assurance, peace of conscience, joy in the Holy Spirit, and pure motive to serve and to please God. Let's sing again: "Complete in Thee! No work of mine may take dear Lord, the place of Thine . . . Yea, justified! O blessed thought!"

CHAPTER 7

Reconciliation: The Peace of the Gospel

"Your iniquities have separated between you and your God, and your sins have hid his face from you" (Isaiah 59:2). With prophetic precision, Isaiah summed up man's horrible condition before God. The *Westminster Larger Catechism* delineates that horrible condition when it asks, "What misery did the fall bring upon mankind?" The answer compresses the teaching of Scripture: "The fall brought upon mankind the loss of communion with God, his displeasure and curse; so as we are by nature children of wrath, bond slaves to Satan, and justly liable to all punishments in this world, and that which is to come" (question 27). Although man was created upright (Ecclesiastes 7:29) with a positive bias toward holiness and in a state of perfect fellowship with God, he willfully sinned against that bias, grievously offended his God, and tragically lost both the desire and any possibility of fellowship with the Lord. Separation from God was the first symptom of spiritual death. When fallen Adam and Eve heard the Lord coming in the garden, they immediately hid themselves from His presence (Genesis 3:8). Hiding from God was the first act of the fallen will, and Adam's entire fallen race has willfully followed him behind those trees. Indeed, sin has lost man so deep in those woods that finding the way out is impossible. The terrible truth is that sinful man does not naturally want to find the way out. Adam and Eve were not playing a game of hide-and-seek; in their sin they would have been happy had the Lord not found them.

This brings us to the beauty of grace. Although Adam and Eve offended God, God came to them and showed the way back to His presence and fellowship. In the first declaration of the gospel, the Lord announced the coming of the Seed (the Christ), who would reverse the curse by crushing the head of the serpent (Genesis 3:15) and thereby remove the enmity that separated men from God. It is by the gospel of Jesus Christ that the Lord has graciously, yet justly, removed the impediments to peace and fellowship between Himself and sinners. The Scripture calls this aspect of salvation *reconciliation*. This component in the salvation chain is closely linked to justification. In fact, Romans 5:1 declares, "Therefore being justified by faith, we have peace with God through our Lord Jesus Christ." Two key thoughts combine in this declaration. First, Paul reasons from cause to effect: because we have been justified, we have peace. Second, he identifies Christ as the agent through whom this peace is mediated. In justification God acquits the guilty sinner and imputes to him Christ's righteousness. This frees the sinner from the curse and liability of the law and grants the sinner a perfect legal acceptance on the ground of the infinite merit of Jesus Christ. *In reconciliation, God restores the justified sinner to a place of peace, fellowship, and communion by means of the atoning work of Jesus Christ.*

How different this is from typical human relationships. If there is friction or alienation between two people, we expect the offending person to make amends and do whatever is necessary to win back the favor of the one he has offended. When my boys were growing up, one would occasionally slug the other for no apparent reason. It was always my parenting policy to make the slugger apologize to the sluggee. That was not only evidence of father's knowing best, but also good, common sense. In the gospel, however, the opposite is true. The offended God took the initiative and did everything necessary to reclaim the offender.

The Bible suggests three lines of thought for our consideration of reconciliation: its necessity, its character, and its results. As we learn more of this great spiritual blessing purchased by Christ, may our response echo Isaiah's when he thought on the same truth: "O Lord, I will praise thee: though thou wast angry with me, thine anger is turned away, and thou comfortedst me. Behold, God is my salvation; I will trust, and not be afraid: for the Lord Jehovah is my strength and my song; he also is become my salvation" (Isaiah 12:1-2). Peace with God is certainly something to sing about.

The Necessity of Reconciliation

In order to understand the grace and the full beauty and benefit of this gospel truth, it is important for us to consider why it is necessary for God to reconcile sinners. It is good for believers to remember that although God was angry with them, now He is not. Reflecting on that change of relationship will generate praise and thanksgiving in our hearts just as it did in Isaiah's. It is essential for unbelievers to know that so long as they are rejecters of Jesus Christ, they are God's enemies and are subject to His wrath. The sinner's usually casual view of sin coupled with his invariably perverted view of God tends to engender a false sense of well-being. Unfortunately, the bumper-sticker gospel that encourages all and any to smile because God loves them has become the popular theology of our day and parallels the preaching of the old false prophets who preached peace when there was no peace (Jeremiah 8:11). Although it does not promote a feel-good mentality, it is better to hear the word of the Lord: "There is no peace, saith my God, to the wicked" (Isaiah 57:21). Scripture gives two essential reasons that reconciliation between God and men is necessary.

Because Men are Enemies of God

The first reason reconciliation is necessary is that men are enemies of God. Although many texts of Scripture mark sinners as children of wrath and enemies of God, two key passages link man's natural enmity against God with God's gracious reconciliation of sinners. In Romans 5:10 Paul says, "When we enemies, we were reconciled to God by the death of his Son." Similarly, Colossians 1:21-22 says, "And you, that were sometime alienated and enemies in your mind by wicked works, yet now hath he reconciled in the body of his flesh through death." The full force of the words "enemy" and "alienated" cannot be ignored. The word "enemy" connotes an intense and active hatred; the word "alienated" suggests a state of estrangement. Sinners, therefore, are not only foreigners and strangers to God and grace, but they are downright hostile in their attitudes and behavior toward God. The battle lines are drawn; man is at war with God.

Those battle lines were drawn the moment Satan and the angels following him sinned against God and fell from their estate. From that moment, the battle of the ages between God and Satan, light and darkness, and good and evil has raged furiously (see Revelation 12 for an overview of that battle). It was Satan's strategy as the "god of this world" (2 Corinthians 4:4) to enlist newly created man, who was at perfect peace with God, in his rebellion against God. In his temptation of Eve, the serpent successfully blinded her mind, and she, being deceived (1 Timothy 2:14), shifted her allegiance to Satan's side against God. Adam, however, was not deceived when, contrary to his holy bias, he deliberately crossed the line in his transgression (1 Timothy 2:14). As the first man and head of the entire race of humanity, Adam, by consciously exercising his free will, took his position against his Creator and in the process took his entire posterity with him. "By one man sin entered into the world, and death by sin; and so death passed upon all men, for that all have sinned" (Romans 5:12). Consequently, every man is guilty of that original sin. This is that estrangement that Paul refers to in Colossians. By birth and by instinct, every man is in a state of alienation and hostility toward God. We are naturally the children of wrath (Ephesians 2:3). As Adam was cast out of paradise, so in Adam we are born out of paradise, foreigners to God's kingdom.

We cannot, however, put the whole blame on Adam; we are all individually as guilty as he was. Not only are we all the children of wrath by nature, but by behavior we are the children of disobedience (Ephesians 2:2). Nature always determines behavior: We do what we do because we are what we are. Since men are born enemies of God, they demonstrate that animosity with actual transgressions against God and His law. Paul describes the sinner as walking according to the course of this world, following both the prince of the power of the air (Satan) and the desires of his own flesh (Ephesians 2:2-3). According to James, such association with this world is enmity with God: "Whosoever therefore will be a friend of the world is the enemy of God" (James 4:4). We have all sinned (Romans 3:23), and every sin we commit is an affront against the infinitely holy God.

Because God is the Enemy of Sinners

The second reason reconciliation is necessary is that God is the enemy of sinners. Although this statement seems to run contrary to the popular theology that declares "God hates sin, but loves the sinner," it is nonetheless a biblical truth that recognizes the justice of God and ultimately magnifies the grace of God revealed in the gospel. There is a wonderful sense in which that popular theology is biblically accurate, yet it ignores essential truths. As we must see, in an equally biblical and terrible sense God "hates" sinners. It is a mistaken and unscriptural view of God that sees Him as a God of love who overlooks and tolerates sin. The separation between God and sinful men is mutual and very personal.

The biblical evidence is clear. Notice the focus on the sinner personally. Psalm 11:5 says, "The Lord trieth the righteous: but the wicked and him that loveth violence his soul hateth." The expression "his soul" when referring to God is an intensive way of designating His Person. In other words, the Psalmist says of the Lord, "**He Himself** hates the wicked." In another Psalm, David in a prayer addressing the Lord affirms, "Thou hatest all workers of iniquity" (Psalm 5:5). Understanding these statements correctly requires a proper definition of the word "hate." Whereas we tend to think of hatred as an intense emotion expressing strong aversion, dislike, or abhorrence, the Hebrew word used in these passages is primarily a volitional term of choice: to hate is to reject. Conversely, the Hebrew word for "love" is more than an intensely emotional one expressing strong like or affection; it also is a volitional word of choice: to love is to choose. Consequently, God's hating sinners does not mean that He intensely dislikes them but that He rejects them. In His justice, He must refuse them His holy presence. So, for instance, when the prophet declares, "Yet I loved Jacob, And I hated Esau" (Malachi 1:2-3), he is not speaking of God's affection for one and aversion to the other. Rather, he declares that God chose the one and rejected the other. That God hates sinners means, therefore, that He rejects them from His presence and fellowship and places them under divine wrath and condemnation because of their sin.

However, the point is that this rejection is personal. God in His just wrath will sentence sinners, not sin, to hell, the place of eternal punishment (Revelation 21:8). The same text that declares God's love for the world also warns that unbelievers (not their unbelief) are under the sentence of condemnation (John 3:18). Remember how Isaiah personalized his song of praise: God, who had been angry with him, was not angry anymore (Isaiah 12:1). The prophet rightly knew that God's anger was not directed toward his sin as some abstraction but that it was directed to him personally. The Bible is clear: The holy God cannot, does not, and will not peacefully or passively deal with sinners.

If it were not true that a righteous God rejects sinners and sentences them to damnation, there would be no need of a gospel at all. But there is a need for a gospel. And the wonder of all wonders is that there is a gospel. This is why I say the statement that God is the enemy of sinners ultimately magnifies the grace of God revealed in the gospel. By sovereign grace, the need for reconciliation gave rise to the reality of reconciliation. In spite of the sinner's alienation from and animosity to God and notwithstanding His just and necessary wrath against the sinner, God so loved and gave His only begotten Son. Here is the amazing grace, beauty, and mystery of the gospel: "But God clearly and visibly proved His own innate love in regard to us in that Christ died in our behalf in spite of the fact that we were still sinners" (Romans 5:8; my translation).

THE CHARACTER OF RECONCILIATION

How the tension between God's wrath against sinners and God's love for sinners is resolved and how the chasm between God and sinners is bridged brings us to the heart of the doctrine of reconciliation. In human conflicts–whether personal or national–cessation of hostilities usually follows long and heated sessions of negotiation and compromise between the warring factions. Each side reluctantly gives a little so that each can take away something of what the parties were fighting over. History books are replete with references to various "peace talks" that ostensibly determined the terms for peace for many wars. History records too frequently that a great many of those peace agreements failed because one or the other faction could not live with the terms. Peace talks and peace accords may be able to address the attendant circumstances of conflict and disagreement between parties, but they are powerless to change the inbred hatred and long-lived suspicions that have the potential of exploding again in open warfare. Man-achieved peace is always tenuous at best. In wonderful contrast, the reconciliation provided by the gospel is permanent. The gospel has addressed and resolved the core issues of hostility and has achieved an unbreakable peace between the offended God and offending sinners. Two essential features of this element of the gospel guarantee its success: It is a divine work, and its terms are nonnegotiable.

Reconciliation is Divine Activity

From start to finish, reconciliation is the work of God. Before looking at the biblical evidence that underscores this important truth, I need to define the key word for this study. The Greek verb usually translated "to reconcile" means simply "to change." In literature outside the New Testament, the word applied to changing anything from currency (a banking term) to political or personal relationships. When referring to persons (either groups or individuals), it signified replacing a relationship of hostility with one of peace–enemies became friends. The corresponding noun, "reconciliation," refers to the ensuing state or condition of restoration to favor. In other words, those who have been reconciled (received into favor) enjoy the benefits of that reception into favor. In the New Testament, the significance of this word heightens when applied to the change of relationship between God and man. Theologically, the word refers to God's receiving someone into favor who was once in disfavor and reestablishing a friendship and fellowship. Even the most cursory survey of the biblical data on this doctrine reveals two outstanding truths that assure a successful peace.

God is the Source

First, God *is the initiator of reconciliation*. Although the hostility between God and sinners is mutual, God has taken the initiative in providing for peace and thereby restoring fellowship. Just as God made the first move to find Adam and reveal to him the way back to fellowship, so He has sought out Adam's race to lay the groundwork for restoration. If anything is clear from the biblical revelation about this doctrine, it is that reconciliation is the unique work of God. Whenever the verb "to reconcile" occurs in this theological context, God is always the subject or agent of the activity. Paul says, "God was in Christ, reconciling the world unto himself" (2 Corinthians 5:19). Again he says, "It pleased the Father...to reconcile all things unto himself. . . . And you, that were sometime alienated and enemies in your mind by wicked works, yet now hath he reconciled" (Colossians 1:19-21). This is far more than simply a grammatical observation; it is the only hope for helpless sinners. If sinners–if we–were left alone to devise a peace plan to appease God's just anger, we would be forever the objects of His wrath. Sinners left alone have neither the desire nor the ability to sue for real peace with God. All human effort to apologize and try to do better (man's typical plan) falls infinitely short of dealing with the issues that separate us from God. Anything that we would imagine could make amends would be an affront and an insult to His perfect holiness.

Unless God Himself chose to reconcile sinners, reconciliation would be impossible. Here is grace. The offended God in His good pleasure effected the reconciliation of sinners to Himself. The reason for this gracious reconciliation resides within the mind of God: He thought it to be good (Colossians 1:19). We must understand that God was under no obligation to open again the gates of paradise for sinners to return to fellowship with Him. Remember that when Satan and his angels rebelled against God, God justly condemned them and made no overtures of peace to restore them. But in His good pleasure, God has devised "means, that his banished be not expelled from him" (2 Samuel 14:14). Interestingly, in Colossians 1 when Paul attributes the work of reconciliation to the good pleasure of God, he uses a special compound of the verb "to reconcile" that intensifies the action: God *completely* reconciled. In His grace, God took care of everything and anything that had to be done to make peace. This is good ground, therefore, for our confidence and enjoyment. We ought to be sure that if God has taken the initiative and has set the terms of peace, He will be well satisfied with His own terms.

Not even sovereign grace, however, can move God to overlook or ignore the issue that caused the separation and hostility. A holy and just God will not excuse sin; He cannot allow bygones to be bygones without ceasing to be God. In his song in praise of God's majesty, Nahum underscored that inflexible justice of God: "God is jealous, and the Lord revengeth; the Lord revengeth, and is furious; the Lord will take vengeance on his adversaries, and he reserveth wrath for his enemies" (Nahum 1:2). What a dilemma this is: How can God be holy and at the same time receive sinners? How God does this brings us to the second great truth that assures the peace. As is true for every other element of the gospel, to understand reconciliation we must come again directly to the Lord Jesus Christ. "And all things are of God, who hath reconciled us to himself by Jesus Christ" (2 Corinthians 5:18).

Christ's Death is the Means

Second, *Christ's atoning death is the means of reconciliation.* To be at war with God is fatal. Sinners are under the sentence of death, and death there must be. Whereas God's love graciously provides a way to peace, God's justice demands the death of His own Son as the only way to achieve that peace. I have intentionally used the word "demand" to accentuate the absolute necessity of Christ's atonement. The cross was not just one of many options available to God in decreeing His plan to reclaim sinners. The New Testament asseverates that if man could attain righteousness by keeping the law (and, by implication, through any other means), then "Christ is dead in vain" (Galatians 2:21). To claim that God chose this way to save sinners only because it would be an effective way of convincing sinners that He really loved them is an absolute perversion of the person of God and His perfections–especially His love and His holy justice. The death of Jesus Christ is the greatest evidence of God's altruistic love for sinners and at the same time of His rightful wrath against them. That God gave His Son to be "the propitiation for our sins" (1 John 2:2) declares how seriously God takes sin and silences those who claim that Christ's death was not necessary.

Let the Bible speak for itself. Over and over again the Scripture links reconciliation to the atoning death of Christ. Here are some the key texts.

> And, having made peace through the blood of his cross, by him to reconcile all things unto himself; by him, I say, whether they be things in earth, or things in heaven. And you, that were sometime alienated and enemies in your mind by wicked works, yet now hath he reconciled in the body of his flesh through death. (Colossians 1:20-22)

> But God commendeth his love toward us, in that, while we were yet sinners, Christ died for us. Much more then, being now justified by his blood, we shall be saved from wrath through him. For if, when we were enemies, we were reconciled to God by the death of his Son, much more, being reconciled, we shall be saved by his life. (Romans 5:8-10)

> But he was wounded for our transgressions, he was bruised for our iniquities: the chastisement of our peace was upon him; and with his stripes we are healed. (Isaiah 53:5)

Note that although Isaiah does not use New Testament language or terminology, his theology equals Paul's (because it is all God's theology). In this great song describing the atoning work of the Suffering Servant, Isaiah explained that the chastisement or punishment that the Servant endured was for the purpose of achieving our peace. That is the work of reconciliation.

Christ's death was the successful means of achieving reconciliation because it propitiated God's wrath. According to the apostle Paul, God set Christ forth "to be a propitiation through faith in his blood" (Romans 3:25). Similarly, the apostle John, addressing the heart of the matter, identified Jesus Christ the righteous as "the propitiation for our sins: and not for our's only, but also for the sins of the whole world" (1 John 2:2). It is best to see the preposition translated "for" as expressing cause: Because of sin, Christ is the propitiation. If there were no sin in the world, there would be no need for the work of Christ. But there is sin; and Christ is, therefore, the necessary propitiation. That is the heart of the matter. I know that propitiation is one of those big, intimidating theological terms, but it is far better to learn what it means than to shy away from it and miss the blessing it conveys. It is a great word that explains how Christ's death is the effective means of reconciliation, of making peace with God. It simply means to appease, to satisfy, or to bring into a state of calm and quiet. Now factor that definition into what Christ accomplished by His atoning sacrifice. When the Lord Jesus sacrificially shed His precious blood on the cross of Calvary, He appeased God's wrath, satisfied divine justice, and silenced every legal claim that condemned guilty sinners. By His shed blood and sacrificial death, Jesus Christ swept away every impediment and every barrier to fellowship and peace with God. When the Holy Father sees the precious shed blood of His holy Son, all is well. What more can justice possibly demand?

The best illustration of this that I can think of is one God Himself gave to us. Before the Incarnation and actual accomplishment of the work of atonement, God often explained great theological truths by using visible object lessons. He did not just drop a load of theological terms from heaven, expecting man to figure things out on his own. These divinely defined object lessons (symbols and types) which revealed Christ in the Old Testament dispensation are still valuable in illustrating Christ and His work. In my book *Beginning at Moses: A Guide to Finding Christ in the Old Testament* (Ambassador-Emerald International, 1999), I explain the principles to use when interpreting these "picture-prophecies" and provide a synopsis of many of the most important of the divinely inspired analogies (chapters 8 and 9). One of those Old Testament types in particular illustrates what I want us to see about the propitiatory aspect of Christ's atonement.

Remember the events on the Day of Atonement (Leviticus 16). This was the one day of the year when the high priest entered into the Holy of Holies, the most restricted room in the Tabernacle. This remarkable day declared and illustrated three essential gospel truths: (1) the need for a mediator, (2) the need for a sacrifice, and (3) a sure salvation. The second of these truths highlights the need for propitiation. Although several sacrifices were offered on the Day of Atonement, one event, in two parts, constituted the principal message: the ritual involving the goat for the sin offering and the scapegoat. The two goats together paint a beautiful picture of the full atonement accomplished by Christ. But for the moment, our attention is on the first goat. This goat was slain, thereby declaring the necessity of death and bloodshed. With the blood of that goat, the high priest entered behind the veil into the Holy of Holies and sprinkled the blood directly onto the mercy seat, that atoning lid that covered the Ark of the Covenant.

Seeing the significance of this depends on our understanding the import of the Ark of the Covenant. The Ark was simply a box that symbolized the presence of the Lord. Although it functioned primarily as an object lesson, the restrictions guiding its construction, content, location, and transportation were rigid and inflexible. God was declaring that there is something wonderfully fearful about His presence; man cannot trifle with the Most Holy God. I see five important lessons concerning the Ark that are relevant to our discussion. (1) Its being overlaid with gold declares the sovereign majesty of God. (2) Its being overshadowed by the cherubim declares the holiness of God. (3) Its containing a pot of manna and Aaron's rod testifies to God's gracious provision for His people. (4) Its containing the tablets of the law, the Decalogue, speaks of God's righteousness and His inflexible demand for righteousness. (5) Its being covered with the mercy seat, the atoning lid, proclaims the gospel of hope. Without the lid, the law cried for righteousness and demanded condemnation for unrighteousness. If the box were left open, man had no hope. But the closed box declared the sinner's salvation. The mercy seat was God's visible pledge that He will be satisfied with the atonement and will by virtue of that atonement dwell in fellowship with men. When the blood of the goat was sprinkled on the atoning lid, the impediments to fellowship with God were removed. The blood was a propitiation or satisfaction of God's just wrath against the sinner. The blood was placed over the demands of the law and all was well.

As clear a picture of the gospel that the Ark was, it was only a picture. All that the ancient box pictured, Jesus Christ is. This is what Paul declares to us. When he said that God set forth Christ to be a propitiation (Romans 3:25), he used the same word for propitiation that the Septuagint, the Greek version of the Old Testament, used to translate the Hebrew word for "mercy seat." I submit that Paul was aware of that usage and made an intentional link between Christ and the Ark. What the sprinkling of the blood on the mercy seat pictured–the stilling of the law's demand and the appeasing of God's righteous wrath–was accomplished for real when Christ entered heaven with His own blood (Hebrews 9:8-28). So in seeing what the high priest did on the Day of Atonement, we can begin to understand something of what Christ did by His death. By putting the lid on the wrath of

God, He opened up the way whereby we can be at peace with God. The wrath of God cannot break out from under the precious and powerful blood of our Savior.

Reconciliation is Nonnegotiable

The second essential truth about the character of reconciliation is that its terms are nonnegotiable. The terms of peace with God are divinely fixed, having been determined and achieved without any input or contribution from man. Reconciliation is objective; that is, it is something external to our thoughts and feelings. In other words, this saving reconciliation was something accomplished *for* us, not *in* us. The love of God manifested in reconciliation is not focused on the moment a man believes as evidence of his changed attitude about God; rather, it is focused on the objective, historic event of the cross where Christ died. Reconciliation is not primarily concerned with man's attitude about God but with God's attitude about man. It is only because of the Godward result of the cross (propitiation) that the many manward benefits of the cross can be applied.

Listen to the Bible again. "While we were yet sinners, Christ died for us" (Romans 5:8). "When we were enemies, we were reconciled to God by the death of his Son" (Romans 5:10). Christ attained our reconciliation without our ever taking a step toward God or extending to Him any white flag of surrender. This is why Paul concludes this explanation of reconciliation by saying, "We also joy in God through our Lord Jesus Christ, by whom we have now received the atonement" (Romans 5:11). The word "atonement" is actually our word "reconciliation." It is something that we receive, not achieve. There is nothing we can add. The finished work of Jesus Christ broke down every barrier between God and sinners and achieved a peace at infinite cost. To gain access to this condition of restoration to favor with God, sinners must receive by faith what God has already done in Christ. That is good news indeed. There is no need to worry whether we have done enough to satisfy and appease God. All we have to do to enjoy peace and to experience divine love is get to the cross. God is always satisfied with His Son and with those who come to Him in and through His Son. We come to peace with God on His terms–no negotiation.

THE RESULTS OF RECONCILIATION

What is true about the gospel in general is true for reconciliation in particular–it works. There are two significant results of God's reconciling sinners to Himself: peace without and peace within. The peace without refers to the cessation of hostility between God and us. The peace within refers to the actual experience of the changed relationship. The peace without is the basis for the peace within. The subjective experience flows from the objective reality. This is the link that we see over and over again in the gospel. Experience in the gospel emanates from the truth of the gospel. Therefore, the more we understand the truth, the more we can experience the realities. Right thinking about the gospel produces right living in the gospel.

Peace Without

God's reconciling sinners to Himself through the atoning death of the Lord Jesus Christ means simply that the war is over. Where once there was enmity, animosity, and hostility, there now is peace. Enemies are now friends. This is not wishful thinking; it is the sure Word of God. Colossians 1:20 forthrightly declares that Christ made peace through the blood of His cross. We have already considered something of what the blood did in accomplishing that peace, so I will not go over that again. I simply want to emphasize at this point, praying that the truth of it sinks into our souls, that Christ was absolutely successful in acquiring that peace. There is no such thing as a "maybe" gospel. It is an absolutely irrevocable fact that divine wrath is no longer a threat to those in Christ. This truth needs to be part of our thinking. The degree to which we enjoy peace will be in proportion to how much this truth grips us. If sinners are not at peace with God or saints are not feeling at peace with God, it is not because peace with God is unavailable. The reality of a restored relationship with God in and through Christ allows the inward peace of mind, contentment, and assurance of soul that all is well with God.

Peace Within

Just as certainly as there was a Godward effect of the cross, so will there be a manward effect. Indeed, it is because of the successful Godward result that there can be the successful manward application of grace. Knowing that God is satisfied with the gospel is an important step in our coming to the full enjoyment of our salvation. It certainly removes a load of pressure to know in our hearts that we can truly be at peace with God without our having to figure out something that can appease God's wrath against us.

Appropriating the peace of reconciliation requires a subjective, inward change within man. Just as the hostility between God and man was mutual, so will be the peace. Our enjoyment of reconciliation requires our accepting the nonnegotiable terms of peace. Either we have peace with God on His terms or we cannot have peace. Although reconciliation is the work of God in Christ, Paul the preacher issues the imperative to sinners, "Be ye reconciled to God" (1 Corinthians 5:20). This puts the claims of Christ before sinners and demands their response. This passive imperative conveys a tolerative (the grammatical term for allowing something to happen) or permissive notion: "allow yourselves to be reconciled." Being reconciled does not require anything on our part except to receive the benefits of the purchased peace. Obeying the command to be reconciled is tantamount to receiving reconciliation (Romans 5:11). To be reconciled is to raise the white flag of faith. Surrendering in faith is the only way that we can sue for peace with God. Surrendering in faith means that we rest on, rely on, appropriate, and claim personally what Christ has done. By faith in Christ, sinners embrace, experience, and enjoy God's provision of reconciliation. To reject the provision of Christ is to remain an enemy of God.

Just as sinners were enemies of God by both nature and behavior, so reconciled sinners, having changed sides in the spiritual conflict and war, evidence the new relationship with God by their character and behavior. According to the apostle Paul, the objective of God's reconciling us was to present us "holy and unblameable and unreproveable in his sight" (Colossians 1:22). Similarly, "if any man be in Christ, he is a new creature: old things are passed away; behold, all things are become new. And all things are of God, who hath reconciled us to himself by Jesus Christ, and hath given to us the ministry of reconciliation" (2 Corinthians 5:17-18). So great is the change that those who were once enemies with God are now ambassadors for Christ (2 Corinthians 5:20). As ambassadors not only do we represent our King, but we have been assigned the commission to recruit others into His kingdom of peace: God has committed to us (literally, placed in us) the word of reconciliation (2 Corinthians 5:19). As the old hymn exults, "What a wonderful change in my life has been wrought since Jesus came into my heart."

The doctrine of reconciliation is a message of hope for saints and one of warning for sinners. Since God has done everything necessary to provide for peace, believers should never despair that something else must be done to gain or keep that peace and fellowship. Since God has done everything, unbelievers must beware of the folly of their own attempts to make things right with God. Self-effort and the works of the flesh only make matters worse. Bonar's hymn expresses this beautifully with biblical precision:

Not what I feel or do, can give me peace with God;
Not all my prayers, or sighs, or tears, can ease my awful load.
Thy work alone, my Saviour, can ease this weight of sin;
Thy blood alone, O Lamb of God, can give me peace within.

There is only one way to peace with God. To come by that way is peace indeed. May God help us to understand more and enjoy more of this great benefit of the gospel. To be complete in Christ means that we have complete peace with God. That is no small blessing.

CHAPTER 8

ADOPTION: THE PRIVILEGES IN THE GOSPEL

Family is special. The bonds created by family are unlike those of any other relationship. Notions of love, loyalty, sympathy, intimacy, sharing, caring, mutual responsibility, and privilege flood the mind when we think of family. The sense of belonging that family provides is one of the great blessings of life. To be alone without family support, nurture, and fellowship–either by divine providence or personal preference–is a sad condition indeed. Unfortunately, at times families may grow apart through distance or disagreements, but no number of miles or hurt feelings can reverse the fact of family. The benefits of family may not always be enjoyed or appreciated, but family is family. The family structure is defined by God and is one of His gracious gifts to mankind for our good.

In helping us to understand the truth of the gospel, God often uses familiar aspects of life to illustrate or define His gracious salvation. Throughout Scripture, He characterizes the relationship between Himself and His people in terms of family. Sometimes He uses the relationship between husband and wife, sometimes that between father and son. That these human relationships may from time to time disintegrate and disappoint does not detract from the intent and force of the spiritual counterparts. To be a part of the family of God is never to know disappointment, because this family is fixed and preserved by unfailing, unwavering, divine love. To be members of the family of God puts us in a position of indescribable privilege and belonging.

These human family units, however, commence differently. Marriage, for instance, begins with a choice. Who makes the choice may differ from culture to culture, but a choice is made. I chose my wife, and she consented to be chosen. It was her choice to say yes or no to what I regarded as an irresistible proposal. Once the marriage choice has been made, the relationship is maintained both by love and by law. In a parent-child relationship, children are born into the family. Once the baby is born, the biological and natural relationship between parent and child is irreversible; the relationship is fixed by blood. There are times, however, when law can create a family that takes precedence even over natural bonds. By adoption, a couple can bring a child into their family structure who was not born naturally to them. Although no blood connection exists, the law guarantees for the child all the rights and privileges of belonging to that family.

Interestingly, the Lord describes salvation with each of these family analogies. Whereas marriage represents the intimate union believers have with Christ (see Chapter 5) and being born again depicts the mystery of regeneration (see Chapter 4), adoption addresses specifically all the guaranteed rights and claims that believers legally possess as members of God's family. The *Westminster Shorter Catechism* succinctly sums up the doctrine of adoption: "Adoption is an act of God's free grace, whereby we are received into the number, and have a right to all the privileges of the sons of God" (question 34). Knowing what this status involves is essential to our fully enjoying it. If we can think rightly about belonging to the family of God, we will more and more benefit from the pledged blessings. As I have already stated many times, right thinking about the gospel always produces right living in the gospel. In this chapter I want to expound the Scripture's teaching on adoption and thereby highlight the consequent privileges which belong to every child of God.

DEFINITION OF ADOPTION

Although the attendant blessings and privileges of adoption are frequent themes in the Bible, the actual word "adoption" occurs only five times and only in Paul's epistles. As a compound of the word "son" and the word "to place," the Greek word translated "adoption" is rather transparent: It means *placement as a son*. The usage of the word confirms this obvious meaning. Notwithstanding the rarity of the word in Scripture, adoption was a common concept in the New Testament world, a fact Paul utilized as he explained key elements of the gospel. Adoption was a term applied to the legal transaction by which one unrelated by blood became a member of a new family. Sometimes adoption insured that a childless couple would have provision in old age; sometimes government authorities would use adoption to choose their successor to power. Although the motives for adoption in the worldly sector were seldom altruistic, once adopted, the legal son was in every respect under the law a full-fledged member of the family with the same rights as a natural-born son, including addition to the will of the father. Interestingly, these legal transactions were often performed as public events before witnesses in order to safeguard the adopted son's status in the family should any dispute ever arise.

This background closely parallels Paul's spiritual application of the concept. Unlike some of the pragmatic, egoistic adoptions of the Greeks and Romans, God's adopting sinners secures no gain for Him. God's placing believers as His sons in His family, while testifying to His grace and goodness, is for the sole benefit of the believer. The New Testament emphasizes the privileges of sonship. So in this sense, Paul elevates the concept of adoption to a level unparalleled in the secular sphere. To be adopted by the God of heaven and thus to be appointed to the status of God's children is incredibly amazing. The Father has placed us into His family, has made us joint-heirs with His Son, Jesus Christ, and has given to us the Holy Spirit as a witness to validate all the legal rights and claims belonging to the sons of God.

Development of the Doctrine

To arrive at a full comprehension and enjoyment of what it means to be the sons of God, we must learn and understand the propositional truths revealed in the contexts of adoption. To that end, I want to examine four theologically defining passages: Ephesians 1:5; Galatians 4:5; Romans 8:15; and Romans 8:23. I should note that Paul uses the term "adoption" again when he lists the many advantages that belonged to Israel: "Who are Israelites; to whom pertaineth the adoption, and the glory, and the covenants, and the giving of the law, and the service of God, and the promises" (Romans 9:4). This text is theologically significant in that it shows that adoption is not uniquely a New Testament truth. However, since it does not add to the definition of the doctrine, I will not deal with it in this discussion. In the four defining passages, however, four wonderful truths boldface the privileges of the gospel that we enjoy as the adopted sons of God.

Believers are Sons by Choice

Ephesians 1 is one of those Grand Canyon and Mt. Everest texts in the Bible. It is impossible to fathom its depth or scale its height. It heaps up spiritual blessing on top of blessing until it takes away our breath; it is absolutely awe-inspiring. I confess that as I come to this passage I am out of my league: all I can do is try to describe what is here and pray that its realities will overwhelm us all. One of the potential problems with these magnificent texts is that they are so great that they almost defy credence. Consequently, theologians and commentators tend to explain away the sublime to confine it within the borders of human understanding. If you have ever visited the Grand Canyon, you know that is exactly what the park authorities have done there. Rather than giving the credit and glory to God for the dazzling parnoramic beauty of His handiwork, they have constructed their own evolutionary models to explain how it all happened. I do not want to be guilty of explaining away Ephesians 1 either by filling in its depths or by whittling down its heights to mundane levels. We must never limit truth to understanding. Matters of faith are never unreasonable, but they are often beyond reason.

So, let us be overwhelmed with what the Bible says. Paul begins with praise to God who has "blessed us with all spiritual blessings in heavenly places in Christ" (1:3). He then proceeds with the statement that teaches us something about adoption.

> According as he hath chosen us in him before the foundation of the world, that we should be holy and without blame before him in love: Having predestinated us unto the **adoption** of children by Jesus Christ to himself, according to the good pleasure of his will, To the praise of the glory of his grace, wherein he hath made us accepted in the beloved. (1:4-6)

The Fact of the Choice

This text forthrightly declares that God has chosen and predestinated us to adoption. To choose simply means to make a selection. To predestinate means to separate by setting borders around something or someone. With these two words the apostle identifies God the Father as the chooser of His children. When we put this in the context of adoption, it should not be hard to understand. In the natural family, parents take what they get. Years ago, the Lord graciously gave my wife and me two boys. More recently, He has given us a granddaughter and two grandsons. I love them all beyond words and would not trade them for anything. But when they were born, that was it. We had no choice whether to receive them as family or not: by birth they were Barretts. It is completely different when a couple decides to adopt. Without coercion, they have the right to choose to adopt whom they desire. Once they have made their choice and have received the child into their homes, they are often the objects of admiration. Their choice of child testified to their unselfish love and desire for family. I have never known of adoptive parents being charged with coldness or unfairness because they did not adopt the entire orphanage.

Let's plug this into spiritual adoption. Rather than making God's gracious choice of sinners a matter of controversy because we can't figure out how God's choice and man's choice fit together, or because we think it unfair that God's choice of sinners was not universally inclusive, let us simply rest in the wonderful truth of it. Let us just stick to and not stray from what the Bible says. In contrast to theologians, the Scripture never speaks of God's electing sinners as a matter of controversy and never sets God's choice in opposition to man's will. On the contrary, divine election is presented as the cause and foundation of every spiritual blessing. Even if we cannot comprehend it completely (and nobody can), let us accept the truth of it. Let its reality generate within our hearts assurance, joy, and humble gratitude. It is a vital part of the good news of the gospel without which we have no hope. According to Paul, God's choosing us to be His adopted children is just one portion of "the riches of His grace which He has lavished upon us" (1:8, my translation). By nature we are the children of wrath; by grace we are the sons of God. What a blessing that is!

The Time of the Choice

The text explicitly identifies the time of God's choice to be "before the foundation of the world" (1:4). This is one of the expressions that the Scripture uses to designate what we can comprehend only in terms of eternity past–that "time" before time. To proffer a definition of eternity and to explain its existence are beyond both the scope of this discussion and my intelligence. At best I can say that eternity is that reality that had no beginning and will have no end. Eternity is virtually the antithesis of time. Time consists of successions of moments during which everything in time is subject to change. In eternity, however, there is no time to pass; and therefore, what is eternal is not subject to change. There is a sense in which the eternal God is always now; He is always the same. Although time began and continues and will sometime end, eternity has always been "is" and will forever be "is." This is getting thick, so let me just get to the blessing part of it as it relates to our adoption.

Our sonship rests on a love that never began as well as a love that will never end. In eternity before the beginning of time and obviously before the beginning of us, God chose to make us His children. The gospel was not God's afterthought or even His forethought; it was His eternal thought. In eternity the whole scheme of the gospel was mature in the mind of the unchanging

God. What God does in our time to call us to Himself and to place us personally in His family is the fulfillment of His eternal purpose. Our adoption is therefore certain because there can be no change in His eternal purpose. What God has purposed in eternity is guaranteed for time; there is no possibility of failure. Let's not trouble ourselves speculating about the mechanics of God's eternal choice of us; let us be glad for the fact of it. Faith rests on the unwavering foundation of God's eternal purpose and engenders confidence and thanksgiving for divine grace. Because He chose us before the foundation of the world, our sonship is sure. Grace is eternally certain, and those upon whom that grace has been lavished are eternally secure. That is certainly a gospel blessing to revel in and to think about.

The Basis of the Choice

The text bases our adoption on "the good pleasure of his will," which testifies "to the praise of the glory of his grace" (1:5-6). The reason for this gracious adoption is found within God and not us. Therefore, we don't have to worry about whether we have what it takes to get God to choose us–whatever we might think that to be. The phrase "the good pleasure of his will" refers to the deliberate and beneficent resolution of the eternally independent will. God's adopting us is not something He needed to do; it is something that He desired to do. There are many things that I desire to do that remain undone because I do not have the wherewithal to achieve my desire. But such is not the case with God. His pleasure is His will, and that always translates to reality. The Psalmist expressed this clearly when he mused, "But our God is in the heavens: he hath done whatsoever he hath pleased" (Psalm 115:3). Therefore, our selection to membership in the family of God, having been eternally purposed according to His benevolent and generous resolve, proves itself in time when we by faith trust in Christ. That God's gracious will is the basis of our adoption ought to produce within us a confident assurance that our sonship guarantees every divinely intended privilege. We are sons of God, after all, "not of blood, nor of the will of the flesh, nor of the will of man, but of God"(John 1:13). What grace conceives, grace achieves.

It is important to note that the good pleasure of God's will is not a cold, arbitrary, heartless exercise whereby God played a game of "eeny, meeny, miney, mo" as He capriciously scanned humanity. Although it is true that the reason for God's choice rests in God and not in us (for which we should rejoice), two key factors give witness to the fact that the divine choice was anything but cold and heartless.

First, God's choice was motivated by love. The verse division between Ephesians 1:4 and 1:5 indicates that the prepositional phrase "in love" governs the statement "that we should be holy and without blame before him." Although this makes legitimate sense, I would suggest that the phrase more appropriately governs the following statement: "*in love* having predestinated us unto the adoption of children." Remember that the chapter and verse divisions that help us locate and identify texts so easily were not included in the text as written by the inspired authors, so it is okay to change the divisions when necessary. This shift of "in love" from verse 4 to verse 5 puts election in the proper perspective. God's choice according to the good pleasure of His will operated within the sphere of and by means of divine love. This love describes the essence of God: "For God is love" (1 John 4:8). It is an active love that moved God to choose us and to send Christ in realization of that loving choice: "In this was manifested the love of God toward us, because that God sent his only begotten Son into the world, that we might live through him. Herein is love, not that we loved God, but that he loved us, and sent his Son to be the propitiation for our sins" (1 John 4:9-10).

Why God would or should love us is beyond comprehension. Thankfully, it is not because of something lovable in us. If God would love only those about whom He found something attractive or appealing, then none would ever be loved. He loves us simply, yet profoundly, because He loves us (see Deuteronomy 7:7-8). There is little wonder that Paul concludes his exposition on adoption by attributing it all to grace: "To the praise of the glory of his grace" (Ephesians 1:6). What a word is "grace"! All theologians agree that grace refers to that display of God's goodness and mercy to those who do not deserve it–indeed, to those who deserve divine wrath. Although all seem to agree on what grace means, some seem to be apprehensive about its implications. To try to figure out why God demonstrates grace contradicts the very definition and concept of grace. Grace is not the reward for some potential virtue or latent merit; grace is grace. Let grace be grace, and let us humbly delight in its reality. This amazing and wondrous grace is our only hope. Listen again to the Scripture:

> The kindness and love of God our Saviour toward man appeared, **Not by works** of righteousness which we have done, but **according to his mercy** he saved us, by the washing of regeneration, and renewing of the Holy Ghost; which he shed on us abundantly through Jesus Christ our Saviour; That being justified **by his grace**, we should be made heirs according to the hope of eternal life. (Titus 3:4-7)

Although Paul does not specifically use the word "adoption" in this text, he nonetheless refers to the theological concept when he says, "We should be heirs." Being an heir of God is one of the privileges of adoption, and it is all of grace.

Second, God's choice inheres in Christ. This truth also gives witness to the real heart of God in His choosing us to be His children. To try to understand anything of God's electing grace apart from Jesus Christ is folly, and it inevitably gives rise to some misunderstanding or abuse of the glorious doctrine. Note how in Ephesians 1:3-6 the apostle identifies Christ as the locus of all spiritual blessing (v. 3–in Christ), election (v. 4–in him), and acceptance (v. 6–in the beloved). The adoption of children is specifically defined as being accomplished through the agency or mediation of Jesus Christ (v. 4). The Lord Jesus as the Second Person of the Holy Trinity is the eternal object of His Father's love. Christ testified to this eternal love in His great intercessory prayer: "Thou lovedest me before the foundation of the world" and thou "hast loved them, as thou hast loved me" (John 17:24, 23). To be the objects of God's love, displayed in His predestinating us unto the adoption of children, is to be loved in the same way as and with the same infinite dimension with which the Father loves His only begotten Son. God does not treat His adopted children as second-class members of the family; He loves them as He loves Christ. This defies explanation but demands belief.

It is only in Christ that sinners will enjoy and experience any of the blessings of grace and salvation, including election to sonship. Paul makes this explicitly clear in verse 6. After attributing the sum of God's saving work in adoption "to the praise of the glory of his grace," he concludes that it is in that grace that God "hath made us accepted in the beloved." The word translated "made accepted" means "to endue with grace." Let me offer this more expressive translation: "By which [grace], He endued us with grace in the One who continuously has been and still is loved." Receiving grace and the consequent knowing of grace are only in the person of Christ. This makes the issue and evidence of election simple enough. All we have to do is get to Christ. Getting to Christ is only way we can know we are the adopted sons of God. Once we know our sonship, we can know that we are loved with everlasting love. Once we know that everlasting love, then we can share in Paul's testimony: "For I am persuaded, that neither death, nor life, nor angels, nor principalities, nor powers, nor things present, nor things to come, Nor height, nor depth, nor any other creature, shall be able to separate us from the love of God, which is in Christ Jesus our Lord" (Romans 8:38-39).

The Purpose of the Choice

Although the ultimate aim of our adoption is to testify to the praise of God's glorious grace, there is a corollary purpose for us as well. God's intention for us is "that we should be holy and without blame before him" (Ephesians 1:4). The word "holy" designates separation, both from sin and to God. It is the purpose of grace to set us apart from the evil of the world and to place us in a position of fellowship with God. The phrase "without blame" is a sacrificial term that describes the victim for sacrifice that was to be without spot or blemish. The victim was open to inspection to insure the required perfection. Although these words could describe our legal position and privilege before God by virtue of our acceptance in Christ, I think that in this context they instead define the proper behavior for members of God's family. What demonstrates the glory of grace more than hell-deserving sinners' not only being made fit for the family of God but also living in a way that reflects well on the family name? Interestingly, both of these words that mark the purposed character and behavior of believers elsewhere in the New Testament apply directly to Christ. As the adopted sons of God, we are to imitate the only begotten Son. Therefore, for us to be holy and without blame is simply to be like Christ. Being like Christ fulfills the purpose of our predestination (see Romans 8:29). To profess membership in God's family and yet to live like the children of disobedience and wrath that we once were is a gross contradiction of grace. It is both our privilege and our duty to be like the Lord Jesus. As we live like Christ, we will give credibility to our sonship and witness to the praise of lavished grace.

Before I move to the next wonderful truth associated with adoption, I need to digress for a moment and issue a couple of caveats. I have been around long enough to know that this wondrous truth is often abused or explained away, so, I feel this digression is warranted. It is too bad that we can take a truth that God has revealed to bless us and turn it into a cause for worry or an excuse for sin. First, note that election is the ground for assurance and comfort for believers, not a playground for speculation by either saints or sinners. The Bible never tells lost sinners to figure out whether they are part of the elect before they can believe. The Bible commands sinners to believe and then to rejoice, confidently knowing that before they chose to believe, God had graciously chosen them. In Ephesians 1 Paul directs his discussion of God's gracious election to believers to enable them to know their manifold blessings as saints (see the apostle's prayer in 1:16-23). Second, note that the Bible never limits evangelism to the elect. It is a perversion of truth to refuse a free proffering of the gospel to one and all. The Bible commands all men to repent and believe the gospel. To refuse to offer the gospel to sinners indiscriminately or to think that praying for sinners is unnecessary reflects aberrant theology and unbiblical application. Never use theology to justify disobedience. On the contrary, God's gracious election of sinners in Christ ought to motivate and propel hearty and fervent evangelism. Put it all in terms of Christ and all objections and abuses vanish. Right thinking about the gospel always produces right living in the gospel.

Believers are Sons by Purchase

Adoption is expensive. I have known couples who have spent many thousands of dollars to secure their adopted children. Substantial legal, medical, and adoption agency costs to finalize and guarantee the adoption can mount up formidably. The willingness to pay such a high price testifies to the sincere and earnest desire of the parents to do whatever necessary to procure the right to make the child their own.

Our adoption into the family of God was likewise purchased with great expense. The redemption cost for our spiritual adoption, however, is beyond monetary calculation and exceeds human resources. The Scripture makes it clear that no man, regardless of his wealth, is capable of redeeming another, because "the redemption of [the] soul is precious [that is, extremely valuable]" (Psalm 49:6-8). Consequently, we have been purchased not "with corruptible things, as silver and gold . . . But with the precious blood of Christ" (1 Peter 1:18-19). God's willingness to pay the necessary and terrible price for us testifies to His immense love and relentless resolve to make us His children.

In Galatians 4, the apostle Paul itemizes the great cost of our adoption, making it clear that we are sons of God by purchase. Two great tolls had to be paid: The one required Christ's life of humiliation; the other required His atoning death.

> But when the fulness of the time was come, God sent forth his Son, made of a woman, made under the law, to redeem them that were under the law, that we might receive **the adoption of sons**.

> And because ye are sons, God hath sent forth the Spirit of his Son into your hearts, crying Abba, Father. Wherefore thou are no more a servant, but a son, then an heir of God through Christ. (4:4-7)

If we can merely begin to comprehend something of what it cost God and His Son to redeem us, it will generate within us a sense of gratitude and confidence. Gratitude as we think about the divine love that spared no expense in purchasing for us all the privileges of sonship. Confidence as we think about the full payment that leaves no outstanding debt that could jeopardize our sonship. Gratitude and confidence because Jesus paid it all.

Although this rich text encompasses several essential elements of the gospel generally and adoption specifically, I want to restrict my comments here to the cost of our adoption. I want us to see why a payment was necessary, what that payment required, and what that payment purchased. Further, the several aspects of the work of Christ that Paul here relates to adoption, the Scriptures elsewhere relate to other components of salvation. I want you to see that in one way or another, every benefit of salvation flows from the person and work of Jesus Christ. Never cease thinking of Christ and never fail to factor Him into both your understanding and your enjoyment of the gospel.

The Necessity of the Purchase

Galatians 4:5 consists of two clauses that indicate the purpose or reason for God's sending forth His Son (v. 4). The first clause, "to redeem them that were under the law," is prerequisite to the second clause, "that we might receive the adoption of sons." It is the first clause that shows us why a payment was necessary. The phrase "under the law" describes the horrific condition of those who by grace were destined to become sons by adoption. According to Galatians 3:13, being under the law is being under its curse. In that same context, Paul explains why those under the law are under the curse: "Cursed is every one that continueth not in all things which are written in the book of the law to do them" (Galatians 3:10; quoted from Deuteronomy 27:26). It is the law of God that delineates the divine requirements for righteousness and holiness without which no man can see God (see Hebrews 12:14). Because God demands absolute conformity (righteousness) or obedience to His law (see Chapter 6), man remains hopelessly unrighteous since he is innately incapable of perfect obedience. To be under the obligation of perfect obedience without the ability to obey puts man in a slavery from which he cannot liberate himself. Christ Himself made this clear when He said, "Whosoever committeth sin is the servant of sin" (John 8:34). Every self-effort of man only tightens the chains that bind him in his sin. Left alone under the law, man is nothing but a slave under the sentence of death. Escape from that bondage is impossible.

Here again is the beauty of the gospel: What man cannot do for himself God does. God sent Christ to redeem. "Redeem" is a great word in gospel vocabulary. The specific word that Paul uses in Galatians 3:13 and 4:5 is a compound of a verb that means "to buy in the marketplace." Outside the New Testament, this particular root frequently occurred in the context of purchasing or ransoming slaves. It suggested an image that would have been immediately understood by those to whom Paul wrote, and I believe that Paul was using the image in this context to accentuate God's liberating us from the bondage of sin, the curse of the law. To this basic word, Paul adds the preposition "out of" to boldface two ideas: the translocation of whatever was purchased in the marketplace, and the full payment that exhausted every cost. In other words, those whom Christ redeemed are no longer slaves to the bondage of the curse, and they need never dread the reappearance of an unpaid debt to enslave them in the former bondage. Those freed by Christ are freed indeed (John 8:36). Because Jesus paid it all, sin no longer dominates the redeemed; they are "not under law, but under grace" (Romans 6:14; see also 6:7, 17-18). So why was a purchase necessary? The answer is simple. Before we could be placed in the privileged position of sonship, we had to be freed from the slavery of sin.

The Cost of the Purchase

Any consideration of the price of our redemption brings us face to face with Christ. Salvation is free to us, but it cost Christ His life and His death. I will not go into much detail here, because we have considered these remarkable truths in some depth in the chapter on justification. The overlap, however, should not be surprising since adoption is inseparably linked to justification, both referring to legal components of the gospel. As part of its definition, the *Westminster Larger Catechism* explains that adoption is that act of God's grace "whereby all those that are justified are received into the number of his children" (question 74). Adoption flows from justification and is necessarily based on the same foundation.

The first foundation payment for our adoption is the life of Christ. Galatians 4:4 is one of the great texts on the Incarnation of Jesus Christ, heralding both the fact and the function of the Incarnation. That He was "made of a woman" suggests His virgin birth and demands His full-fledged humanity. This is the fact of the Incarnation: The eternal Son of God became man–"God was manifest in the flesh" (1 Timothy 3:16). That He was made "under the law" suggests the function of the Incarnation. Christ lived under the same obligations of the law as every other man. Not only was He under the same law, but the Lord Jesus was under the same potential curse of the law if He did not obey it completely. The warning of Deuteronomy 27:26 and Galatians 3:10 is universally true: "Cursed is every one that continueth not in all things which are written in the book of the law to do them." But whereas the law condemns every other man as guilty, the law proved Christ to be "holy, harmless, undefiled, separate from sinners" (Hebrews 7:26). In regard to the law, Christ was in a class all by Himself. By His impeccable obedience, He earned a perfect righteousness that satisfied the requirements of the law (see Romans 5), and God graciously imputes it to us in our justification. Our trespass was a debt that had to be paid if we were ever to become the children of God.

The second foundation payment for our adoption is the death of Christ. Although the immediate context of Galatians 4:4-5 does not directly refer to His atoning death, it implies and demands it when it uses the word translated "to redeem." The cost of redemption was the precious blood that Christ shed on the cross. In the preceding chapter Paul puts it together: "Christ hath redeemed us from the curse of the law, being made a curse for us: for it is written, Cursed is every one that hangeth on a tree" (Galatians 3:13). We broke the law, but He became the curse. We deserved to die, but He died for us. Although Christ earned life by His obedience, God imputed the guilt of our disobedience to Him, and He paid the penalty of the broken law. That debt had to be paid. By His life and by His death all the demands of the law were satisfied, and all the impediments to sonship were removed. So how much did our adoption cost? Again, the answer is simple: It cost Christ everything–His life and His death.

The Result of the Purchase

Remember the two clauses in verse 4 that indicate the purpose or reason for God's sending forth His Son. I don't want to get grammatically or logically technical here, but there is a relevant point that I want us to discern. I have identified the two statements in verse 4 as expressing the purpose of Christ's coming, but the heading of this discussion is "the result of the purchase." There is a logical link between the *purpose* of an action and the *result* of an action that has theological importance for us. Both notions express the intention of an action: Logically, *purpose* designates the intended consequence to be accomplished whereas *result* expresses the intended purpose that has been accomplished. I have often attempted to do certain things with sincere intention to achieve a particular end, only to fail miserably. My purpose does not guarantee results. Now, here is my point: God's purpose always guarantees the result; His intentions always become reality. Whereas the first clause of this verse, "to redeem them that were under the law," explains why Christ had to pay such a tremendous price for us, the second clause, "that we might receive the adoption of sons," sums up what He purchased at such terrific cost. He got what He paid for: He got us. What Christ purchased by His active and passive obedience was our freedom from the curse and our placement into the family of God. That is what He came to do and that is exactly what He did.

Our freedom from the curse consists of not only a legal freedom by which we are exempt from any further execution of justice, but also an actual freedom in which we can experience all the benefits of being the sons of God. Verses 6 and 7 enumerate some of those glorious benefits: the indwelling Spirit, access to the Father, and being a legal heir of God through Christ. These benefits parallel closely those detailed in Romans 8, so I will discuss them all together in the next section. Let me wrap up this part by reaffirming that our sonship, having been purchased by Christ, is complete and certain. The more we consciously link our sonship to the person and work of Jesus Christ, the more we can be confident that all the privileges of sonship are really ours.

Believers are Sons in Experience

Although adoption is primarily a legal concept that insures the standing of a person as a member of a family, it also grants family privileges to the adopted. For a couple to go to all the expense of adopting a child and then to leave the child in the orphanage would make little sense. The child might be theirs on paper, but unless the child entered the home to enjoy the family experience, what was on paper would have little immediate value. It would be a tragedy for an adopted child to live still as an orphan.

The spiritual parallel to our adoption into the family of God is patently clear. In our adoption, not only does God guarantee for us the legal rights fixing our standing in His family, but He also brings us "home" to experience all the benefits of sonship. We are not just the sons of God "on paper"; we are the sons of God in our daily experience. The tragedy is that so many believers continue to live in the orphanage without taking advantage of all that belongs to them.

In Romans 8, another of those Grand Canyon texts, Paul outlines the daily benefits that ought to be the experience of every child of God. We need to live in the reality of what we are: the sons of God.

> For as many as are led by the Spirit of God, they are the sons of God. For ye have not received the spirit of bondage again to fear; but ye have received the Spirit of adoption, whereby we cry, Abba, Father. The Spirit itself beareth witness with our spirit, that we are the children of God: And if children, then heirs; heirs of God, and joint-heirs with Christ. (8:14-17)

There are three great truths in this passage that should encourage us to take advantage of the position we have as the children of God.

God is Our Father

The first privilege and evidence of our adopted sonship is that we have access to God as our Father. To recognize God as our Father is to acknowledge His special love and concern for us and to express our trust in His wisdom to do for us what is best. God's fatherly love, concern, counsel, provision, and discipline are family blessings not just in theory but in experience for every believer of the gospel. Paul sums up the greatness of this privilege with the simple yet amazingly profound statement that by virtue of our adoption, "we cry, Abba, Father" (Romans 8:15). Approaching and addressing the Holy God of heaven as our Father becomes the right and should be the spontaneous and earnest expression of every child of God. That Paul uses the term "Abba" with reference to our access to the Heavenly Father underscores the far-reaching import of this gospel right and privilege. Unfortunately, much has been said about this word that tends to minimize and even trivialize its sacred significance. Thus, I want to take time to explain the word and expound briefly the passages where it occurs.

Abba is a transliteration of the Aramaic word for "the father" and it occurs only three times in the New Testament. However, these three appearances speak volumes. Before considering the three texts, I must define the word. The *ab* part of the word is the standard Semitic term meaning "father"; the *ba* part of the word reflects the Aramaic way of making a word definite. In other words, *Abba* does not just mean "father"; it means **the father**. Notwithstanding the phonetic simplicity of the word, it is not to be equated with the equally phonetically simple expressions "dada" or "daddy" that English-speaking children so easily utter as their first appellation for their earthly fathers. *Abba* is not a nickname; it is not a childish term of sentimentality or endearment. Rather, it is an honorific title that expresses the utmost reverence and respect due to any father–and infinitely more so when referring to the Heavenly Father. The Lord Himself asks, "If then I be a father [Hebrew *ab*], where is mine honour?" (Malachi 1:6). Although every child of God has the privilege of approaching God as his Father and so addressing Him, none has the right to address the Lord as "Dad" or "Daddy." It may be cute and endearing when a child refers to his father in those terms, but it would be the height of irreverence to use such language in addressing God. The fact that the term *Abba* is easy to say is irrelevant to its honorific significance.

Although not a trivial term of endearment, *Abba* does express the intimacy of the father-child relationship. Its three occurrences in the New Testament highlight this truth.

Mark 14:36 is the first passage, and it sets the tone for our understanding the other two texts. Mark is giving his account of the agony suffered by Christ in the garden of Gethsemane on the eve of His crucifixion. In the throes of that indescribable spiritual battle, the Lord Jesus prayed, "Abba, Father, all things are possible unto thee; take away this cup from me: nevertheless not what I will, but what thou wilt." In that moment of crisis, the eternal Son of God knew the closeness of His Father and expressed His implicit trust in His Father. If we can grasp nothing else about this word, may we grasp this: As the adopted children of God we have the right to address God in the same terms as Jesus Christ Himself. That is no small privilege.

Indeed, it seems almost presumptuous that we would address God in such an intimate way; we would not dare to speak in these terms on our own. This is where the next text helps. Galatians 4 reveals a divine prodding that incites and enables us to cry, "Abba, Father." Having addressed the fact of our purchased adoption (verse 5), Paul identifies the immediate consequence: "And because ye are sons, God hath sent forth the Spirit of his Son into your hearts, crying, Abba, Father" (verse 6). The Greek text makes it explicitly clear that it is the Spirit who cries, "Abba, Father," and not our hearts. The Holy Spirit of God graciously ministers to us by proclaiming and by implanting within our hearts the assurance of sonship. He convinces and instructs us not only that it is permissible to address the Lord in this Christlike manner, but also that we should. It is our right as the sons of God.

The third text, Romans 8:15, brings doctrine to practice and theory to reality. Here Paul directly says that by adoption we are crying, "Abba, Father." We manifest in our own expression Christ's manner of addressing His Father; what the Spirit has implanted and instructed within us translates itself into our own experience. The tense of the verb "cry" suggests that this access to the Father is always open: We can constantly cry, "Abba." What a glorious truth this sets before us. Fatherly wisdom may withhold any number of things from children, but a good father will never withhold his presence. Indeed, any father delights when his children confidently know that he is always available for them and sensitive to their needs. Any father is gratified when his children take full advantage of his wisdom and welcome his presence. So it is infinitely true with God our Father. He is constantly available to us and keenly sympathetic to our needs. Let us learn to follow the example of our Savior and the prodding of the Spirit in taking full advantage of our relationship to God as our Father.

Let me finish this section by explaining why I think the New Testament preserved the Aramaic word in these three texts and what the vital lesson is for us. Although the New Testament was written in Greek, Aramaic was the native language of Palestine in New Testament times. It was the everyday language of both Jesus and Paul. It is not surprising that when Christ was in Gethsemane pouring out His heart before His Father, He would have spoken in His native tongue. Indeed, most likely the entire prayer would have been in Aramaic. Mark, under the supernatural influence and inspiration of the Holy Spirit, recorded the prayer in Greek, yet preserved exactly what Christ prayed. I believe that he retained *Abba* to underscore the intimacy and fervency of the prayer. Writing initially to a Roman audience who would not have known Aramaic, he then immediately translated it into the Greek equivalent, *ho pater*. Similarly, Paul, when contemplating the privilege of adoption, became so overwhelmed that he lapsed into his native tongue in referring to God as *Abba*. He then immediately translated it ho pater for the primarily Gentile audiences. What *Abba* means in Aramaic, *ho pater* means in Greek. The English word "Father" is the equivalent of both.

The point is this. God knows Aramaic and Greek and English and every other language. We don't have to learn some liturgical language or formula for our approach to our Heavenly Father. There is no official language for prayer. Whoever we are, wherever we are from, and whatever language we speak, we can address the Lord in our own tongue. He will understand. After all, He is our Father, and we are His sons.

Christ is Our Elder Brother

The second privilege and evidence of our adopted sonship is that Christ is our elder Brother. If God is our Father and we are His sons, then we are His heirs through Christ (Galatians 4:7). In Romans, Paul takes the logic even further: "And if children, then heirs; heirs of God, and joint-heirs with Christ" (8:17). The word "heir" is a compound form comprising the word for "lot or portion" and the word for "law." An heir legally has a share in the family fortune. That claim is mind-boggling when the family happens to be the family of God: The inheritance that belongs to the children of God is beyond reckoning. We have received an inheritance according to God's eternal will (Ephesians 1:11), and God has given us by His Spirit the guarantee of "our inheritance until the redemption of the purchased possession" (Ephesians 1:14; see also 2 Corinthians 1:22). Part of the ministry of the Spirit is to help us understand "the things that are freely given to us of God" (1 Corinthians 2:12). As heirs of God, we now experience all the blessings the Father bestows: His power, presence, protection, provision, love, and more are our great possessions–our lot in life. And listen to this: The best is yet to be!

As amazing as this is, Paul adds that we are joint-heirs with Christ. This reminds us again that there is no element or blessing of the gospel that can be understood independently of Jesus Christ. In the theology of adoption, Jesus Christ is our elder Brother. Paul suggested this relationship when he wrote that one of the objectives of our predestination is that Christ may be the firstborn among many brethren (Romans 8:29). Similarly, the apostle declared that Christ was not ashamed to call those whom He had saved brothers (Hebrews 2:11). What an elder brother the Lord Jesus is– unlike any other. Remember how selfish and unsympathetic the elder brother was in the parable of the prodigal son (Luke 15:25-32). My own younger sister could probably testify to some of my selfishness and sadistic delight when she received any amply merited discipline from our parents. I'm over that now, but the point is that I was not always an ideal older brother. The Lord Jesus, however, freely and lovingly shares all that belongs to Him.

The word "joint-heir" simply adds a prefix meaning "with" to the word "heir." What we inherit, we inherit in association with Christ Himself. What Christ inherits, we inherit. Merely to begin listing all that the Father has given His Son would be staggering. Just listen to this one promise from the eternal Father to the eternal Son: "Thou art my Son; this day have I begotten thee. Ask of me, and I shall give thee the heathen for thine inheritance, and the uttermost parts of the earth for thy possession" (Psalm 2:7-8; for my exposition of this text see *Beginning at Moses*, pp. 301-303). Whatever is included in that magnificent promise we will share with Christ. All His riches become our riches. Astounding! He shared our poverty that we might share His wealth. "For ye know the grace of our Lord Jesus Christ, that, though he was rich, yet for your sakes he became poor, that ye through his poverty might be rich" (2 Corinthians 8:9). Let me pose a searching question: Why do we so often live as spiritual paupers when all the riches of Christ are ours? To think right about the gospel will at the very least enrich our lives. If we are Christ's, all things are ours (1 Corinthians 3:21, 23).

The Holy Spirit is Our Witness

The third privilege and evidence of our adopted sonship is that the Holy Spirit is our internal witness that God's Fatherhood and Christ's Brotherhood are personally true. It is marvelous enough to know that the doctrine of adoption is objectively or factually true; it is even more special to know that it is subjectively or experientially true. Just as Roman laws required witnesses to verify and validate the proceedings and consequent claims of adoption, so the Lord has given the Holy Spirit to testify to the validity and authenticity of every believer's individual status among the children of God. In the argument of Romans 8:14-17, Paul identifies two specific operations of the Holy Spirit intended to confirm our membership in the family of God.

First, the Holy Spirit leads: "For as many as are led by the Spirit of God, they are the sons of God" (8:14). Being led by the Spirit is positive proof of sonship. This Spiritual leadership is an emancipating power that frees us from the bondage of fear, distrust, and sin and that brings us to the liberty of confidence, faith, and holiness (see the reference to the "glorious liberty of the children of God" in Romans 8:21). It is a leadership that guides us away from the deeds of the flesh to follow the way of righteousness (Romans 8:12-13). In simple terms, the Holy Spirit leads us to more and more conformity to Christ; He changes us from glory to glory (2 Corinthians 3:17-18). In Galatians 5, Paul associates the leading of the Spirit (verse 18) with the fruit of the Spirit (verse 22). A Spirit-changed life that follows the leading of the Spirit in manifesting love, joy, peace, longsuffering, gentleness, goodness, faith, meekness, and temperance is an excellent witness to sonship. It is appropriate to apply Peter's conclusion to

Paul's statement: "For if these things be in you, and abound, they make you that ye shall neither be barren nor unfruitful in the knowledge of our Lord Jesus Christ" (2 Peter 1:8). There is no condemnation to those who walk after the Spirit (Romans 8:1).

Second, the Holy Spirit testifies: "The Spirit itself beareth witness with our spirit, that we are the children of God" (8:17). I must confess that this is easier to experience than to explain. This is not a witness of private vision, audible voice, or enthusiastic fancy. The Holy Spirit gives power to the Word of God and produces receptiveness in the heart in order to bring the two into perfect harmony. He subjectively confirms the objective truths of the gospel by graciously convincing us of all the things freely given to us by God (1 Corinthians 2:12). Assurance of sonship does not come from wishful thinking; it comes by the sweet ministry of the indwelling Spirit. That constant, unceasing, abiding presence of the Holy Spirit within every child of God is incontrovertible proof of a genuine relationship to Jesus Christ (Romans 8:9-11). To have the witness of the Spirit now is to have the guaranty of every right of our sonship.

Paul highlights this certainty when he says of believers, "Ye were sealed with that holy Spirit of promise, Which is the earnest of our inheritance until the redemption of the purchased possession, unto the praise of his glory" (Ephesians 1:13-14). Two words in particular picture the absolute certainty of sonship: "sealed" and "earnest." The "seal" had three essential functions: to identify something as property, to stamp something as genuine, and to render something secure. The Holy Spirit does all three when He seals us as the sons of God. In ancient Greek, the "earnest" was a commercial term designating a partial payment made in advance to secure the rights of purchase–the first installment or down payment confirming the intent of the purchaser to pay in full. In modern Greek, it designates an engagement ring, which is a token confirming the intent of a couple to go through with the marriage. It has been a long time since I was engaged to be married, but I can still remember when I proposed and gave a ring to my prospective bride. When Sander (my term of endearment) took that ring, she knew she had me. And she was right.

The point is clear. If God has given us His Holy Spirit to seal us, He will not renege on His promise to give us every other part of our inheritance purchased in full by His Son. Although Paul was not using the image of an engagement ring, he was employing the commercial image of the first installment that guaranteed payment in full. The Holy Spirit is the down payment of our full salvation. Nevertheless, I think the engagement ring analogy works well. As we experience the fellowship and influence of the indwelling Spirit, let us look at His presence as the ring on a future bride that testifies to commitment and generates joy and anticipation of the future. The Holy Spirit is a witness to the certain future for the children of God.

Believers are Sons Forever

The final occurrence of the word "adoption" assures that sonship is forever. After describing the tension and suspense of all creation as it waits for the final revelation of glory and manifestation of the sons of God (Romans 8:19-22), Paul points to the future prospect of the children of God–their glorification. Christ's redemption is complete: Not one part of redeemed man will ever ultimately perish. Christ saves us–body and soul. Here is the text.

> And not only they [the creation], but ourselves also, which have the firstfruits of the Spirit, even we ourselves groan within ourselves, waiting for the adoption, to wit, the redemption of our body. (Romans 8:23)

That Paul defines adoption as the redemption of the body brings us to the realization of the final and ultimate inheritance of the children of God–the sure end of every regenerated, justified, sanctified, and adopted soul. This is the full purchase secured by the down payment we now possess. What a glorious hope! Our bodies that now experience corruption will be raised in incorruption. Our bodies that now are plagued with dishonor and weakness will one day be transformed in glory and power. This natural, physical body will become a glorified, spiritual body like that of Christ (1 Corinthians 15:42-44). I don't know any other text that sums up this blessed hope better than 1 John 3:1-2.

> Behold, what manner of love the Father hath bestowed upon us, that we should be called the sons of God. . . . Beloved, now are we the sons of God, and it doth not yet appear what we shall be: but we know that, when he shall appear, we shall be like him; for we shall see him as he is.

What can I possibly add to that? We are the sons of God now, but the best is yet to be.

These four Scripture texts containing the word "adoption" and the propositions they suggest give us much to think about. However, many of the attendant truths associated with adoption occur in passages that do not actually use the word. As you meditate on these great gospel truths and study them even more in the Scripture for yourself, you may find the statements of the *Westminster Larger Catechism* and the *Baptist Confession* to be of some help in directing your thoughts. Each offers a useful and comprehensive definition and synopsis of the doctrine.

> Adoption is an act of the free grace of God, in and for his only Son Jesus Christ, whereby all those that are justified are received into the number of his children, have his name put upon them, the Spirit of his Son given to them, are under his fatherly care and dispensations, admitted to all the liberties and privileges of the sons of God, made heirs of all the promises, and fellow-heirs with Christ in glory. (*Westminster Larger Catechism*, question 74)

> All those that are justified, God vouchsafed, in and for the sake of his only Son Jesus Christ, to make partakers of the grace of adoption, by which they are taken into the number, and enjoy the liberties and privileges of the children of God, have his name put upon them, receive the spirit of adoption, have access to the throne of grace with boldness, are enabled to cry 'Abba, Father,' are pitied, protected, provided for, and chastened by him as by a Father, yet never cast off, but sealed to the day of redemption, and inherit the promises as heirs of everlasting salvation. (*Baptist Confession of Faith*, Chapter 12)

May God help us to understand and may we be sensitive to our resident Witness as He applies the facts to life. If anything is clear from our study of adoption, it is that what God has begun in us,

He will finish (Philippians 1:6). The choice that God made in eternity ends with the chosen in eternity. What a perfect ending to a purposed beginning!

CHAPTER 9

SANCTIFICATION: THE EFFECT OF THE GOSPEL

Grace never leaves a man where it finds him. Grace always transforms the sinner into a saint–a holy man. "For we are his workmanship, created in Christ Jesus unto good works, which God hath before ordained that we should walk in them" (Ephesians 2:10). God's will is for His people to be holy. The objective of His electing grace is to bring us into conformity to the image of Jesus Christ (Romans 8:29), and every true Christian has a desire for that Christlike holiness. Yet, notwithstanding God's will and the Christian's desire, the experience of holiness does not come easy. We seem to be in constant struggle against the external enticements to sin that so effectively appeal to the internal impulses of our own carnal desires. Every victory that we win over sin seems only to increase the intensity of the next battle. Every defeat weighs heavily on our conscience as we wonder if God will forgive us again. The question presses us: How can we achieve victory over sin and live the Christian life successfully? Is such victory even possible?

Sadly and wrongly, many Christians give up, resigning themselves to what appears to be the fact of the matter–they can't quit sinning. Consequently, Christianity has become for some people nothing more than a theoretical set of beliefs that have little bearing on life; for others it is a rigid set of standards that relentlessly rule life. Neither of these alternatives produces much joy in the Lord, and neither leads to a victorious life. Whatever initial enthusiasm existed at conversion dwindles, and disillusionment sets in; faith loses its attraction. Further testifying to the problem are the plethora of how-to books offering supposedly new formulas for successful Christian living and the proliferation of para-church seminars offering practical, character-building principles or psychological tricks for increasing personal resolve. Many well-meaning but ultimately deleterious efforts have capitalized on the dissatisfaction of Christians who have somehow failed to understand what the Bible teaches about the Christian life. The tendency has been to substitute virtuous character traits for genuine holiness. Too much stress as been placed on being like some person or even like some animal mentioned in the Bible. It is little wonder that Christianity degenerates to the drudgery of doing this or not doing that when Christians ignore the God-given key to holy and happy Christian living. I submit that successful Christian living and victory over sin are possible if we stick to the path God has laid down for us in His Word. I hope by this time you know where I'm headed. The key to happy holiness is the gospel of Jesus Christ.

The doctrine that concerns our daily duty of holiness is *sanctification*. Sanctification is God's will for every believer. First Thessalonians 4:3 is explicitly clear: "For this is the will of God, even your sanctification." Doing the will of God is our duty, but, as always, duty must flow from doctrine. The more we understand the doctrine of the gospel, the more we can do our duty. Remember our analogy of the gospel's being like a chain with many inseparable links. Successful sanctification is going to depend on how we see sanctification coupled together with the other links. Too often I have seen Christians frustrated in their efforts at holiness because they have uncoupled and isolated sanctification from all the other gospel components. Attempting to live a Christian life apart from the bedrock of Christian theology is presumptuous folly, but it is not a new mistake. Paul saw this same proclivity for will power rather than gospel power among the Galatians: "Are ye so foolish? having begun in the Spirit, are ye now made perfect by the flesh?" (Galatians 3:3). His right answer to their mistake was to direct their eyes again to Christ who had been "evidently set forth" before them (Galatians 3:1). Seeing Christ and our place in Him is going to be the solution for us as well. We are *complete in Him*.

In this chapter, I want to expound the doctrine of sanctification and show its connection to our complete salvation. Very simply, we are going to see that sanctification is the application of the gospel in our daily lives. Perhaps our axiom–"Right thinking about the gospel produces right living in the gospel"–applies more directly to this element of salvation than to any other. Whereas other links in the gospel chain focus on our position, privileges, and prospects in Christ, sanctification concerns where and how we live right now. I like to think of sanctification as the believer's becoming in experience what grace has purposed him to be. Sanctification is living in the reality of gospel grace. Since in our justification God regards us as holy and righteous, we should live as though we are. Although holiness is not the prerequisite for salvation, it is the evidence of it. This is why I say that sanctification is the essential and certain *effect of the gospel*.

THE PRINCIPLE OF SANCTIFICATION

The *Westminster Shorter Catechism* provides a succinct definition of biblical sanctification: "Sanctification is the work of God's free grace, whereby we are renewed in the whole man after the image of God, and are enabled more and more to die unto sin, and live unto righteousness" (question 35). This definition suggests two key truths: (1) Sanctification is something God graciously does in us; (2) Sanctification is something we obediently do in response to and in evidence of what God does. In other words, we cooperate with God. If we remain passively inactive in the face of sin, waiting for God to do it all, we will be overrun. If we are active in the face of sin without conscious reference to what God has done, we will be overrun. Leviticus 20:7-8 effectively unites these two essential elements. The Lord first commanded His people, "Sanctify yourselves therefore, and be ye holy." Then He affirmed, "I am the Lord which sanctify you."

Before considering the salient elements of the theological definition and how they all work, I want to address some basic issues that will help us in properly understanding and applying the doctrine of sanctification.

Key Word

Accurate definition of the key theological vocabulary is always the first step in understanding any theological proposition. Therefore, we must understand the significance of the biblical terms translated "to sanctify" or "sanctification." The words for sanctification in both the Old and the New Testaments have the same essential idea: holiness. In both Hebrew and Greek, the fundamental concept of holiness is separation. The concept of sanctification, therefore, refers to the act or process of setting something apart, thereby making it holy–separate and distinct from something else.

Be aware that particularly in the Old Testament, the word does not always occur in a salvation or gospel context. For instance, the fourth commandment says, "Keep the sabbath day to sanctify it" (Deuteronomy 5:12). This simply means that the Sabbath is to be set apart and treated differently from all the other days of the week. In another instance, the Lord identified the Medes as the particular people that He had sanctified or set apart for the specific purpose of defeating the Babylonians (Isaiah 13:3). They certainly were not a godly people. However, when the word does occur in the context of salvation or the gospel, it refers to separation from sin unto God. A sanctified life is a distinct and separated life–consecrated to God and pure from sin.

I want to make you aware of another dimension of this word in Scripture. The New Testament uses the word group (different forms of the same root) "to sanctify" to refer to three inseparable, yet individually identifiable, aspects of salvation. The failure to recognize the multiple use of the word has led to some significant errors in the theology of sanctification; so we want to be careful in our interpretation.

First, it refers to *positional* sanctification. This is most likely the sense intended by Paul when he identified the believers in Corinth "as sanctified in Christ Jesus, called to be saints" (1

Corinthians 1:2; see also 6:11). The whole point of the epistle is that in practice, the Corinthians were not acting like saints (literally, holy or sanctified ones), although in reality and fact they were saints. This positional sanctification essentially equates with justification and designates the acceptance the believer has before God in Jesus Christ. At conversion, every believer is set apart unto God and guaranteed a full salvation. Positional sanctification is entirely the gracious act of God.

Second, it refers to *perfected* sanctification–every believer's ultimate glorification. This meaning looks to that time when we will experience total separation from sin's power and sin's presence. This is the ultimate end of Christ's sanctifying His bride: "That he might present it to himself a glorious church, not having spot, or wrinkle, or any such thing; but that it should be holy and without blemish" (Ephesians 5:27). In death, to be absent from the body is to be present with the Lord and, therefore, to be removed from sin's presence (2 Corinthians 5:8). At death, every saint takes his place in the heavenly Jerusalem with "the spirits of just men made perfect" (Hebrews 12:23) The word "perfect" in Hebrews 12:23 is a different word, meaning "to be brought to maturity." But to be separated from sin by death is not the end. Perfected sanctification will at the end include our bodies as well as our souls. This final act and eternal condition of sanctification is again the sole agency of God. With a power that is uniquely divine, God will "change our vile body, that it may be fashioned like unto his glorious body" (Philippians 3:21).

Third, it refers to *progressive* sanctification. This concerns the course of life between the moment of our positional sanctification that separates us from sin's penalty, and our perfected sanctification that separates us from sin's presence. Progressive sanctification is the experience of separation from sin's power in our daily lives. As the catechism says, we are "enabled more and more to die unto sin, and live unto righteousness." Remember the statement in Hebrews 12:23. The fact that it is in heaven that the just men have been brought to maturity indicates that none of them had achieved spiritual maturity or perfection before they died. According to Hebrews 12:14, this sanctification is something that we must pursue: "Follow peace with all men, and holiness [sanctification], without which no man shall see the Lord." The verb "follow" suggests a couple of key thoughts. (1) Its literal meaning–"to chase" or "to pursue"–implies an expenditure of effort. (2) Its tense intimates that this fervent pursuit is constant and unceasing. (3) Its mood (imperative) directs the issue to our wills and demands obedience. Whereas positional and perfected sanctification require no effort on our part, progressive sanctification requires trust and obedience. We must trust what God has done in making us holy and obey what He commands to achieve that holiness. In short, we are to live distinct and separated lives, performing our duty in the light of God's provision.

So although the word "sanctification" in the Bible encompasses salvation from start to finish, the *doctrine of sanctification* concerns the application of the gospel during the journey from start to finish. It is the day-by-day effect of the gospel. Knowing that the primary significance of the word "sanctification" is separation (from sin to God) will help us to identify key passages in Scripture pertinent to the doctrine of sanctification, even if the actual word does not occur. Any passage directing us to quit sin or to do right concerns progressive sanctification.

Key Distinction

Although the term "sanctification" sometimes applies to justification and glorification as well as sanctification, it is vital for us to maintain the distinction between these gospel components while at the same time maintaining their inseparable connection. The doctrines are not to be confused, but neither are they to be disjoined. If there is justification, sanctification in this life and ultimate glorification in eternity necessarily and certainly follow. The main confusion concerns the relationship between justification and sanctification.

It is not my intent at this point to review everything that we have already learned about justification or to preview what we are going to learn about sanctification. However, I do want to highlight a couple of thoughts that I think will help as we discuss the doctrine and seek to implement holiness into our behavior.

Position vs. Experience

First, we must maintain a distinction between our legal position and our daily experience. Justification concerns our legal position before the bar of divine justice, where God pardons our guilt and regards us as righteous by imputing Christ's righteousness to us. Sanctification, on the other hand, concerns our everyday experience in which we strive by faith in Christ to be righteous, yet never attain that perfect righteousness in this life. Justification is a legal transaction outside of us, whereas sanctification is moral transformation within us. Legally, believers are as righteous as Jesus Christ; experientially, believers are not. Believers are accepted completely by God and, on the basis of that acceptance, they desire to please God. Position is irrevocably fixed; experience fluctuates.

The failure to grasp this difference stirs up many questions. Students, for instance, have often asked me, "If God has pardoned all our guilt and will never condemn us, why must we continue to confess our sins, seeking forgiveness from God?" I am happy they recognize that sin requires confession and necessitates forgiveness, but I grieve that many labor under the impression that their failures to please God somehow jeopardize their standing before God. I have often used marriage to illustrate the issue. My marriage to Sander is a legally binding relationship. When we got married, we bought a license that had to be filed with the state. I have been married for almost thirty years, and I suppose that if I looked hard enough, I could find the papers to prove it. Notwithstanding that legal relationship and the unforced desire I have to please her, I have over the years done a few odd things that have hurt Sander's feelings and created a bit of friction between us. She cries, and I feel bad. I don't like it. I have learned to admit that it is always my fault, to say I'm sorry, and to ask for her forgiveness so we can enjoy each other once again. So far, she has been most willing to forgive. Now here's my point. My stupid behavior does not in the least alter the fact that I am married to Sander; our marriage is established by law. However, my behavior often mars the experience because I am not a perfect husband.

So it is with our relationship to God. Justification legally and irrevocably fixes the relationship. Sanctification pertains to the unforced desire of those justified to please God. Our failure to please God may rob us of the joy of fellowship, but it does not change our legal standing. The only way to restore the marred relationship is to admit our fault, confess our sorrow at grieving Him, and seek His forgiveness. Thankfully, "If we confess our sins, he is faithful and just to forgive us our sins, and to cleanse us from all unrighteousness" (1 John 1:9). Don't confuse position with experience.

Monergistic vs. Synergistic

Monergism and synergism may be strange-sounding words, but they are easily definable. Monergism simply means "working alone." Synergism means "working together." It is imperative to keep these notions distinct when comparing justification with sanctification. Justification is monergistic–it is the work of God alone. Remember that in justification God graciously pardons a guilty sinner, exempts the pardoned from the penalty of his sin, and regards the sinner to be righteous–all on the basis of the righteousness of Jesus Christ. It is a single, judicial, completed act done outside of the individual without causing any change in character but resulting in an equal standing for all so justified. The sinner makes no contribution; by faith he simply receives and rests on what God has done in and through the Lord Jesus Christ.

Sanctification is synergistic–that is, it is the cooperation of God and the believer working to produce actual holiness. Failing to see the synergism of sanctification results in two potential errors: either passivity in waiting for God to do it all, or frustrating hyper-activity by trying to do it all alone. Sanctification is not a divine "zap" that automatically makes the believer irreversibly holy. There is a common saying, "Let go, let God." That is true enough for justification, but it does not apply to sanctification. Neither is sanctification simply the exercise of will power, although the Christian must exercise his will not to sin. In sanctification God makes the believer a new creature, renews him in the image of God, imparts righteousness, removes the pollution of sin, and defeats its power–all on the basis of the work of Jesus Christ. In sanctification the believer reacts to all that God has done inside of him, gradually changing more and more into the image of Jesus Christ by obeying God's Word and by appropriating through faith all that Christ has done.

Israel's conquest of the Promised Land is perhaps one of the clearest illustrations of this necessary cooperation between God and the believer. Over and over again God told the nation to possess the land because He had driven out every enemy. God achieved and assured victory for His people by virtue of His promises to give them the land and to expel the Canaanites who stood in the way of their possessing the promise. The Israelites, nonetheless, had to cross the Jordan and drive out the enemy for themselves in deadly battle. Listen to what Moses told them on the border of the land (Deuteronomy 9:3; see also 7:2). "Understand therefore this day, that the Lord thy God is he which goeth over before thee; as a consuming fire he shall destroy them, and he shall bring them down before thy face." That was God's part. "So shalt thou drive them out, and destroy them quickly, as the Lord hath said unto thee." That was their part. Both parts were essential for victory.

The Canaanites did not roll over and play dead or pack their bags and leave voluntarily; they fought back. The Canaanites were naturally stronger than the Israelites, and the Israelites stood little chance against them in their own strength (Deuteronomy 7:1). But believing that God had given them the victory, they entered and fought in the light of that certain victory. Unconventional tactics, such as marching around Jericho or praying for the sun and moon to stand still, testified to God's supernatural intervention, but the Israelites conquered Jericho only by obeying God's command and they defeated the coalition of nations only by using their swords in conjunction with God's hailstones. Note this lesson as well: One victory led directly to the next conflict–there was always an Ai to follow Jericho. The battles to possess the land were unrelenting, and the possession of new territory was gradual.

Similarly, Christ has achieved our victory over sin. But sin does not flee from us just because we have been saved; it does not give up its hold on us without a fight. If we attempt to battle against sin in our own strength, defeat is certain, because sin is stronger than we are. Conversely, if we do not strive to fight against sin, defeat is just as certain. But if we enjoin the conflict claiming all that God has promised and Christ has won, and fighting against sin with all our renewed resolve, we can enjoy the victory. Even when we experience victory, though, we can never let our guard or our faith down because we live in a world filled with the Canaanites of sin and temptation. One victory only leads to the next conflict. Remember how the catechism definition of sanctification suggested this necessary cooperation. "Sanctification is the work of God's free grace, whereby we are renewed in the whole man after the image of God, and are enabled. . . ." That's God's part. "More and more to die unto sin, and live unto righteousness." That's our part.

In Appendix 1, I have isolated some of the key distinctions as well as some essential links between justification and sanctification. I hope that it will give you a clearer picture of how these two vital truths work together and find their focus together in Christ. Also see the Appendix "Who Fought the Battle of Jericho?" for a more thorough comparison between the conquest and salvation.

THE PROBLEM FOR SANCTIFICATION

That every believer struggles against sin and temptation requires no argument. Experience proves it. It is not insignificant that Israel's conquest of Canaan stands as the great type (inspired analogy and picture prophecy) of the Christian's battle for sanctification. Because sanctification is not a single, perfect act making us holy once for all, simply living in this world means that we are surrounded by temptations. Throughout the Bible, we see examples of the most godly of men, the great heroes of the faith, failing and falling. Even Job, who was "perfect and upright" (Job 1:1) and in his day the most holy man on earth (Job 1:8), struggled with bitterness and doubt in the fray of his great battle. He confessed his own awareness of his moral imperfection: "If I justify myself, mine own mouth shall condemn me: if I say, I am perfect, it shall also prove me perverse" (Job 9:20). His perfection consisted in his wholehearted dedication and consecration to fear God and turn from evil, but he recognized it did not actualize in sinlessness. So we have to face it: Every Christian is in a battle for holiness. The problem for sanctification is that we cannot avoid encountering the enemy. In any war, identifying the enemy is essential. The battle for sanctification rages on two fronts.

The External Enemy

The Bible is clear that there are two principal enemies that assault the believer from the outside: the world and Satan.

The World

James 4:4 draws the battle line. "Know ye not that the friendship of the world is enmity with God? whosoever therefore will be a friend of the world is the enemy of God." Therefore, as believers we are not to be "conformed to this world" (Romans 12:2). James and Paul use two different words to designate the world that opposes Christians in their pursuit of holiness. The word "world" in James 4:4 refers not to the planet earth, but to the organizational orders, viewpoints, systems, and philosophies of the inhabitants of this planet that scheme and conspire against the order of God. Paul's word choice defines the world as a temporary, transient place that will soon pass away. This temporary world is a hostile environment for Christians. This world is no friend of grace; it never has been and never will be.

To side with the world is to stand against God. How foolish it is for Christians who are destined to eternal glory to be consumed and taken in by an anti-God and anti-Christ system that is doomed to destruction. Following this path leading along the broad way to hell may be easier than travelling the narrow way, but the eternally different destinations make the narrow way the only way to go. The problem is that for now, the broad way with all of its attractions is still in plain view as believers walk the narrow way; and therefore, the temptation is always present to go the way of the world. There are so many things in the world that can get us. We are surrounded, frequently ambushed, and too often subdued by sin. Therefore, we must be on constant guard. It is encouraging beyond words to know that our blessed Savior has prayed for us as we live in this hostile place: We are in the world, but we are not of the world (John 17:15-16).

I think that the Old Testament laws of cleanness and uncleanness (Leviticus 11-15; Deuteronomy 14) provide a great illustration of this conflict that every believer faces by living in the world. I am well aware that these sections of the Old Testament seem strange, and it is easy to get bogged down or sidetracked just trying to figure out what a "pygarg" or a "chamois" is. Notwithstanding the specific difficulties for us and for the Israelites in discerning what was clean or unclean, there was a very obvious lesson that God was teaching His people and one that we must learn as well: Fellowship with God demands purity. Whatever else may have been the point in all the regulations, it was clear that to be unclean precluded participation in the rituals and ceremonies of worship. Therefore, Israel was to be vigilant in avoiding whatever would produce uncleanness.

Even though I may not be able immediately to identify every pollutant, I get the impression every time I read these laws that there were many, many things constantly surrounding the people that could potentially render them unclean and thus rob them of fellowship with God. That should be the primary point and warning for us. We can't walk in this world without being surrounded by unclean things that can potentially defile us and rob us of our enjoyment in the Lord. Therefore, as we walk we must be vigilant in avoiding whatever would render us unclean. Fortunately, in the Old Testament there was always an appropriate sacrifice to restore to cleanness. And there still is–the blood of Jesus Christ keeps on cleansing us from all sin (1 John 1:7).

Satan

Behind all the worldly attractions and assaults against our progress in holiness is the "god of this world" (2 Corinthians 4:4) who hates God, Christ, and all that belong to Them. We, therefore, must not be ignorant of Satan's devices lest he "should get an advantage of us" (2 Corinthians 2:11). First Peter 5:8 says, "Be sober, be vigilant; because your adversary the devil, as a roaring lion, walketh about, seeking whom he may devour." Similarly, Paul warns about our dangerous spiritual enemies and admonishes us "to put on the whole armour of God" so that we "may be able to stand against the wiles of the devil" (Ephesians 6:11-12). Satan's attack against Job, attempting to put a wedge between him and God by provoking him to sin against God, was not a unique or isolated occasion. A spiritual battle rages between God and Satan, and believers are very often the battlefield (see Revelation 12 for a synopsis of that the spiritual warfare). Satan's efforts to thwart the sanctification of those Christ has delivered from his realm persist, even though he is a defeated enemy and his power over the believer has been subdued by the Lord Jesus Christ. In crushing the serpent's head, Christ both conquered Satan himself and destroyed his works (Genesis 3:15; 1 John 3:8; Hebrews 2:14). We will consider more about the provision for victory that we have in the Lord Jesus, but for now we are simply identifying our enemy. Although defeated and doomed, Satan now is running around like the proverbial chicken with its head cut off. He is frantic, but ultimately he will fall. In the meantime, we must be on guard.

The Internal Enemy

In this battle against sin, we are our own worst enemies. The temptations outside would not be such a threat were it not for the spiritual traitor inside. Every Christian has residing within him that which answers to sin and finds it appealing. The Scripture identifies this traitor as the flesh or the old man. "For the flesh lusteth against the Spirit, and the Spirit against the flesh: and these are contrary the one to the other: so that ye cannot do the things that ye would" (Galatians 5:17). Even Paul confessed, "For I know that in me (that is, in my flesh,) dwelleth no good thing: for to will is present with me; but how to perform that which is good I find not" (Romans 7:18). Every Christian knows by experience the inner struggles with sin and the constant frustrations caused by succumbing to sin. Inside is where the battle rages most fiercely.

It is important not to confuse what the Bible calls "the flesh" or "the old man" with what we theologically refer to as "nature." The term "nature" refers to the intrinsic and essential characteristics of something. The most common analogy I have heard over the years to describe the inner struggle for sanctification has been conflict the between the black dog and the white dog. These two dogs presumably represent the two natures of the Christian. Both dogs are barking and battling for attention and dominance. Whichever dog we choose to feed wins: Thus, all we have to do to be holy is feed the white dog and starve the black dog. This sounds simple enough, but it either exhibits or leads to some fundamental theological errors. It reflects a careless or incorrect understanding of the new nature that the believer has. The believer, just like the unbeliever, has only one nature. The new nature is different from the old, but it is not an additional nature. The black dog–white dog theory implies that alongside the original sin nature, which is totally corrupt and depraved without any desire or ability to please God, is placed another nature that is perfectly holy and pure. This suggests that the Christian can be governed sometimes by the old nature that has no interest in God, and sometimes by the new nature that is perfectly in tune with God. Neither of these options is true or even possible. I have seen too many Christians beating themselves up and driving themselves spiritually crazy trying to control the dogs. If we don't identify the enemy properly, we will have little success in fighting him.

Although this inner struggle is unavoidable, it should not discourage us or paralyze us in the conflict. *Don't begrudge the struggle, for the struggle is itself an evidence of grace.* Sin finds a peaceful existence in the old nature, but it never exists peacefully in the new. David expressed the feeling of every genuine believer when he acknowledged that his sin was ever before him as a constant hostile presence (Psalm 51:3; cf. Psalm 32:3-4). When God renews in us the whole man after His image, He does not eradicate every element of the old man. In regeneration, God gives us a new nature. It is new, but it is not perfect. The *Westminster Confession of Faith* succinctly describes the situation:

> This sanctification is throughout, in the whole man; yet imperfect in this life, there abiding still some remnants of corruption in every part; whence ariseth a continual and irreconcilable war, the flesh lusting against the Spirit, and the Spirit against the flesh. (Chapter XIII, section 2; note as well the *Baptist Confession*, Chapter 13, section 2 for an almost identical statement.)

No analogy is perfect, but I prefer the following one. In renewing the whole man after His image, God plants within the believer the seed of holiness that sprouts, takes root, grows, and bears fruit. The corruption within us tends to choke and slow the progress of growth, but there will be growth. We must be on guard and vigilant in pulling the weeds. The Confessions put it this way:

> In which war, although the remaining corruption, for a time, may much prevail; yet, through the continual supply of strength from the sanctifying Spirit of Christ, the regenerate part doth overcome; and so, the saints grow in grace, perfecting holiness in the fear of God. (*Westminster Confession of Faith*, Chapter XII, section 3)

> In which war, although the remaining corruption for a time may much prevail, yet through the continual supply of strength from the sanctifying Spirit of Christ, the regenerate part doth overcome; and so the saints grow in grace, perfecting holiness in the fear of God, pressing after an heavenly life, in evangelical obedience to all the commands which Christ as head and King in his Word hath prescribed them. (*Baptist Confession of Faith*, Chapter 13, section 3)

There is hope after all. Having identified the enemies, we are ready to get the victory.

THE PROVISION FOR SANCTIFICATION

The fact of the conflict is the occasion for conquest, not retreat. The only way we can conquer sin and win the victory is by living in the reality of what God has provided for us in and through the Lord Jesus Christ. Our battle against sin really should not be a fair fight because God has given us everything we need to live godly lives. Listen to this amazing promise.

> According as his divine power hath given unto us all things that pertain unto life and godliness, through the knowledge of him that hath called us to glory and virtue: Whereby are given unto us exceeding great and precious promises: that by these ye might be partakers of the divine nature, having escaped the corruption that is in the world through lust. (2 Peter 1:3-4)

Remember our adage: Right thinking about the gospel produces right living in the gospel. Practical piety (our duty) is the product of sound theology (our doctrine). In this section, we are going to consider the right thinking. I want you to see how sanctification requires the implementation of the truths of the gospel. Some of the links in the gospel chain that I will be highlighting here, I discuss in greater detail elsewhere in separate chapters. My objective for now is for us to see the importance of letting grace permeate our daily lives. "Victory in Jesus" is more than a song.

A New Source of Life

Every military campaign has a base of operation. For the Christian in his campaign against sin, union with Christ is that base. The significance and implications of union with Christ are manifold. It is a precious link in the gospel chain that is too frequently ignored. I discuss it more thoroughly in Chapter 5; here I want to focus on its ramifications for sanctification. Union with Christ provides spiritual life, incentive, and power to be holy. I can think of no other text in Scripture that so explicitly links sanctification to union with Christ than Romans 6. In Appendix 3 I have reprinted my detailed exposition of Romans 6:1-14 that explains the passage more thoroughly than I can do here. I hope that you will read it and meditate on it. But for now, notice these key points of the passage that outline the logic of sanctification based on the truth of union with Christ: *know, believe, obey*. Each point is essential, and the order of points is unalterable. To leave out a step or reverse the order will lead to bondage and frustration.

Knowledge of Union with Christ

The process of sanctification begins with knowing that we are united to Jesus Christ. Having established the fact of a free justification in Christ (Romans 3-5), Paul begins to reason from the fact of the believer's position in Christ to his duty to live free from sin: "How shall we that are dead to sin, live any longer therein?" (Romans 6:2). He then immediately leads the believer into thinking about his union with the Savior. Three times in the first fourteen verses, Paul mentions something that we are supposed to know fully: our baptism into Christ's death (6:3); our crucifixion with Him (6:6); and Christ's victorious resurrection (6:9).

Knowledge of Baptism

The baptism here is obviously spiritual; no amount of water can effect this vital relationship to the death of Christ. I cannot begin to fathom, let alone explain, the mechanics of this spiritual baptism that places us inseparably into Jesus Christ and links us to His death. It is a mystical, inexplicable, yet real, union. Positioned in Him, we are where He is and accepted by God in Him, the Beloved (see Ephesians 1). Being united to His death means that somehow in the mind and purpose of God, when Christ died, we died. We are, therefore, partakers of all the benefits and blessings that He accomplished by His atoning death. What He purchased, we enjoy (i.e., forgiveness, deliverance, peace, adoption, and on it goes). Significantly, one of the reasons that Christ gave Himself for His church was "That he might present it to himself a glorious church, not having spot, or wrinkle, or any such thing; but that it should be holy and without blemish" (Ephesians 5:27). Our being holy is possible only because we are united to Christ.

The corollary to union with Christ's death is union with His burial. Being buried with Christ "by baptism into death" (6:4) refers to one of the great consequences of our union. In physical burial, a corpse is removed from the land of the living; so in Christ we are separated from the world of sin. Outside of Christ, we were dead *in* sin; inside of Christ, we are dead *to* sin. There is an eternity of difference. And it gets better. If we are buried with Him, we are raised with Him unto "newness of life" (6:4-5). Union with His death guarantees union with His life. Just as Christ's resurrection was the certain consequence of His atoning death, so a sanctified life is the certain consequence of our dying with Him.

Knowledge of Christ's Resurrection

The third thing Paul wants us to know for our sanctification concerns a key implication of Christ's resurrection (6:9). (I know that I am reversing Paul's order of presentation here, but bear with me. I will come back to the second thing in just a moment.) In verses 9 and 10 the apostle stresses the irreversibility of Christ's resurrection. Christ died to sin once and "death hath no more dominion over him" because He lives unto God. Christ will never die again: He lives in the power of an endless life (Hebrews 7:16). Paul's purpose in describing the permanent life of the risen Christ is to show that all who have been united to His death and resurrection likewise share in a life that is permanently free from sin. United to Christ, there is no more spiritual deadness in sin. Our new life source is irreversible. This is a key piece of information.

Knowledge of Our Crucifixion

The second thing Paul wants us to know concerns our crucifixion with Christ and the consequent liberation from sin's dominion (6:6). I have intentionally left this for last because of Paul's use of a different word for "know" from that which occurs in the other two texts. Although the verbs in verse 3 (being ignorant of facts) and verse 9 (knowing facts) are not the same, they both refer principally to intellectual perception. The verb in verse 6, on the other hand, refers principally to experiential knowledge. In this text,

Paul personalizes for every Christian the fact of union with Christ's death. This union is not just theological theory; it is wonderful reality. We must factor into our constant experience the knowledge that when Christ died, we died. We must factor into our experience the purpose of that crucifixion, to put to death the "old man" with its bent to sin. We must factor into our experience the new life we have in Christ with its bent toward holiness that frees us from having to sin. Knowing all of this to be personally true is crucial artillery in the battle against sin.

Appropriation of Union with Christ

On the basis of what we know, we are to believe. Faith is the link between doctrine and duty–between what we know and what we are to do. If saving faith rests on and receives Christ as He is offered to us in the gospel, sanctifying faith specifically appropriates all that we have received and upon which we rest. In general terms, knowledge is purely objective. It is true, whether we believe it or not, that Jesus died and rose again. Faith, on the other hand, is the subjective, personal experience of objective truth. By faith, I know that Jesus died for me. Faith does not make union with Christ a reality, but it does claim a personal union with His death and resurrection that makes living in the reality of what is objectively true a personal experience. Without faith in the finished work of Christ and our place in Him, efforts toward sanctification tend to be guilt-driven and doomed to frustrating failure. Remember that the object of faith always determines the value of faith. To trust in personal resolve and will power is folly; to trust Christ, appling the truth of our union with Him to individual struggles, means victory.

In this Romans text, Paul uses two different words for faith, both of which accentuate the appropriation of absolute facts. In verse 8 he says, "Now if [since] we be dead with Christ, we believe that we shall also live with him." Faith recognizes the essential connection between dying with Christ and living with Him. Paul's logic is sound: Union with His death flows inevitably into union with His life. In verse 11 he says, "Likewise reckon ye also yourselves to be dead indeed unto sin, but alive unto God through Jesus Christ our Lord." I love this word "reckon." It is the same word we talked about in our discussion of justification, whereby God considers Christ's righteousness to be ours. Whereas in justification God is the subject of the verb, in sanctification we are. But what we reckon to ourselves is the same thing God reckons to us–the benefits of Christ's atoning death. Notice carefully the statement of what we know in verses 9 and 10 (Christ's irreversible resurrection, His emancipation from death, and His living unto God) and compare that with what we reckon to ourselves in verse 11 (our death to sin and life unto God). What is true about Christ, we claim for ourselves!

Faith in this provision–I do believe–is the secret to sanctification and victory over sin. If we can learn to put the cross between us and the onslaughts of temptation, we can win the battles because Christ has won the war. Sin will lose its appeal when we see it in the shadow of the cross. How can sin be attractive when we realize that sin is the reason Christ died for us and that we died with Him? Let the cross run interference for us and protect us from the surrounding enemy set on our defeat.

Obedience in the Light of Union with Christ

Trust always issues forth in obedience. That's why we so often sing, "Trust and obey." That is good theology. It is only after Paul focuses knowledge and faith on the fact of union with Christ that he issues the commands, "Let not sin reign. . . . Neither yield ye your members as instruments of unrighteousness unto sin: but yield yourselves unto God" (6:12-13). To begin the appeal for sanctification with the command not to sin would be injurious to spiritual welfare. No genuine Christian needs to be told not to sin. He knows that he should not sin, and grace has changed him so that he doesn't want to sin. Simply commanding holiness without teaching the basis for holiness and how to implement holiness is futile. But once we know the facts and believe the facts to be personally relevant, we have the necessary ammunition to enter the conflict. And enter the conflict we must.

A New Principle of Life

Sanctification operates within a whole new sphere of life. Before conversion, we all were dead in our sins without any spiritual understanding, interests, desires, or abilities (see 1 Corinthians 2:14). Sanctification–living a holy life–was absolutely impossible. In order to become holy in life, we first had to be alive spiritually. God by His grace gave to us the necessary spiritual life: "Even when we were dead in sins, hath quickened us together with Christ" (Ephesians 2:5). To quicken simply means "to make alive." The theological term for God's making us spiritually alive is regeneration (the new birth). I discuss this component of the gospel more thoroughly in Chapter 4. At this point I want you to see how progress in sanctification connects to this vital link in the gospel chain.

Regeneration makes us new creatures with a new outlook on life. We once had an anti-God bent to sin, but now we have hearts that are inclined to God, holiness, and behavior that is pleasing to the Lord. Paul puts it this way: "Therefore if any man be in Christ, he is a new creature: old things are passed away; behold, all things are become new" (2 Corinthians 5:17). Again he says, "For we are his workmanship, created in Christ Jesus unto good works, which God hath before ordained that we should walk in them" (Ephesians 2:10). God implants within us the principle of spiritual life, thereby creating within us a whole new disposition toward holiness that influences our desires and choices. The very desire a Christian has to die more and more to sin and to live more and more to righteousness evidences God's gracious intervention and active interest. The Bible makes clear that "it is God which worketh in you both to will and to do of his good pleasure" (Philippians 2:13).

The relevance of this new principle of life to our sanctification should be apparent. We live holy lives not in order to attain spiritual life; we live in a holy way because of spiritual life. Sanctification flows *from* spiritual life, not *to* it. It is a growing in grace, not a striving to merit grace. We should have the confidence, therefore, that in regenerating us, God changed us from the inside out. Knowing that the very desire to be holy is God-given should encourage us to draw from that provision of life. If we are spiritually alive, there is no reason that we should behave as we did when we were spiritually dead. Sanctification is living in the reality of the new birth. Think about this.

A New Life Companion

I have stressed the importance of seeing sanctification as synergistic–a cooperation between God and the believer. Although God does His part and we are to do our part, God in His amazing goodness has not left us alone even to do our part. We have a Companion with us who never leaves us alone–the blessed Holy Spirit. The indwelling Holy Spirit is the irrefutable evidence that we belong to Christ: "Now if any man have not the Spirit of Christ, he is none of his" (Romans 8:9). The Spirit that raised up the Lord Jesus from the dead and made us spiritually alive (Romans 8:11) is the same Spirit that constantly abides with us. Every believer has dwelling within him that death-defying infinite Power as a constant resource in the daily battles for holiness. Although the presence of the indwelling Spirit provides the believer with many blessings and benefits (assurance, fellowship, guidance, conviction, etc.), the primary ministry of the Spirit in our sanctification is to incite and enable us to holiness. It is "through the Spirit" that we are able to "mortify the deeds of the body" (Romans 8:13). God's promise to Zerubbabel applies to sanctification as much as to any other work for the glory of God: "Not by might, nor by power, but by my spirit, saith the Lord of hosts" (Zechariah 4:6).

I don't know precisely how the Spirit operates in our sanctification except that He directs us to the application of the gospel. We have received "the spirit which is of God; that we might know the things that are freely given to us of God" (1 Corinthians 2:12). It is by the Spirit of the Lord that we are changed into the image of Christ from glory to glory (2 Corinthians 3:18). In the light of this provision, it should be our daily prayer "to be strengthened with might by his Spirit in the inner man"(Ephesians 3:16). God has given us the infallible Guide to lead us to walk contrary to the flesh (Romans 8:4). Indeed, the promise is that if we walk in the Spirit, we "shall not fulfill the lust of the flesh" (Galatians 5:16). Paul's argument is that since "we live in the Spirit," we should "also walk in the Spirit" (Galatians 5:25). The particular word for "walk" in this verse brings the issue down to the basics. We are literally to walk in a straight line or row, step by step following the path set by the Holy Spirit. The way of holiness is certainly not a game, but it does involve "following the Leader." In another well-known text Paul says, "And be not drunk with wine wherein is excess; but be filled with the Spirit" (Ephesians 5:18). The analogy is clear and expressive. To be drunk with wine affects a person's walk, talk, and thought. So to be under the influence of the Spirit will affect the way we walk and talk and think. We must submit ourselves to that Holy influence and follow God's provision, our faithful Companion, relying on His might to lead us to victory. Following the lead of the Holy Spirit and being under His influence will lead us not only away from sin but also toward the positive marks of godliness: "love, joy, peace, longsuffering, gentleness, goodness, faith, Meekness, temperance" (Galatians 5:22-23).

THE PERFORMANCE OF SANCTIFICATION

Right thinking about the gospel produces right living in the gospel. We have been thinking about what we should be thinking about; now we must consider how we are to behave. Although it is God who works in us "both to will and to do of his good pleasure," we are to work out our "own salvation with fear and trembling" (Philippians 2:12-13). By faith in what is true, we behave as though it really is true. Obedience is always the meter of faith.

Do

One of the New Testament words of sanctification is "godliness" (also translated "devout" or "godly" in the Authorized Version). This word is the sum of true piety and practical holiness. Based in the fear of God, godliness involves the proper worship of the Lord and the obedience generated by that worship. A life of godliness elevates God to the place He deserves in our thoughts, our devotion, and our lives. A study of this word in the New Testament reveals some significant truths.

(1) Godliness is focused on Jesus Christ (1 Timothy 3:16; 2 Peter 1:3).

(2) Godliness flows from truth (1 Timothy 6:3; Titus 1:1).

(3) Godliness is motivated by the consciousness of eternity (2 Peter 3:11-18).

(4) Godliness is practiced in both antagonistic and amicable surroundings (2 Timothy 3:12; 2 Peter 1:6-7)

(5) Godliness is marked by a reverential fear (John 9:31)

(6) Godliness begins at home (1 Timothy 5:4).

(7) Godliness matures through effort (1 Timothy 4:7; 6:11).

All of these are relevant to the doctrine of sanctification, but the last point is our concern here.

Exercise

Paul uses two images to describe the effort required in sanctification. In both images, Paul's point is clear. Godliness does not just happen. It requires discipline and duty. First, he compares it to bodily exercise: "Exercise thyself rather unto godliness" (1 Timothy 4:7). Athletes prepare for competition with a single-minded focus on the contest; they are totally consumed with that goal. Athletic skill does not just happen; it is not achieved just by reading how-to books on proper techniques. Over the years I have read innumerable books and articles on the golf swing. I know the theory of the golf swing as well as anyone, but all that reading has done little good. I know what I ought to do, but I have neither the ability nor the time to put it into practice–to make it reality. So it is that knowing the doctrine of godliness and sanctification is not enough. Merely reading the inked words of Scripture does not produce holiness. Every believer must consciously and purposefully work it out.

As an athlete will consistently and repetitively practice the techniques that are fundamental to his sport, so must the Christian focus on the basics of holiness and work on his areas of personal weakness. When I learned a few years ago that I was going to become a grandfather and that it would not be too much longer before I would approach middle age, I started working out at a fitness center. Throughout the room were various machines labeled with different muscle groups, each designed to exercise and strengthen that particular part of the body. Similarly, we need to note our particular areas of spiritual weakness and work to strengthen them. That requires concentrated spiritual effort. (Unfortunately, about the only thing I gained from my gym experience was this analogy.)

Pursue

Second, Paul compares our efforts toward sanctification to military action: "Follow after . . . godliness" (1 Timothy 6:11). The word "follow" involves more than just a casual game of "follow the leader." It means to pursue or chase after something. The word can designate either military or hunting activity, both of which require strategy and strenuous effort. The word suggests an intense resolve to catch and to conquer. Since the next verse says, "Fight the good fight of faith," the military idea is the one most likely in view. Soldiers struggle passionately and vigorously, because their lives frequently depend on their efforts; so must we fight with might and faith in order to win the victory, which is godliness. This chase after godliness will take us through hostile territory and threats of ambush, but we must keep on pursuing, using all of the armor and weaponry in our arsenal.

What to Do

Doing is not sufficient in itself; doing the right thing is vital. Too many Christians, in their good zeal to be holy, take off in a spiritual frenzy without a clear course of action. Remember that God's Word is our rule not only for faith but also for practice. The Bible clearly sets the course for sanctification. It does not specifically detail every minute step, but it does put up clear signs designed to keep us on track. The Bible tells us what to do.

Break with the World

Since the world is one of the enemies of our sanctification, it is logical that we must break with the world if we are going to experience holiness. This is exactly what the Scripture demands in two well-known texts.

1 John 2:15

First John 2:15 commands us to stop loving the world: "Love not the world, neither the things that are in the world." John uses a particular form of prohibition (negative command) that orders the cessation of an action that is taking place. The simple fact that he tells believers to stop loving the world addresses the natural propensity within even the Christian to love the world's systems and philosophies. This word "love" refers more to a conscious and willful choice than to emotional affections. In essence, John is telling us to quit choosing the way of the world with all of its attractions and allurements that are contrary to the way of holiness.

But the fact of the matter is that we cannot live in indifference; we have to love something. This is where the right thinking comes in. The only thing that will oust our love for the world is our love for Christ. We must remember that in the cross of the Lord Jesus, the world is crucified unto us and we unto the world (Galatians 6:14). Christ "gave himself for our sins, that he might deliver us from this present evil world, according to the will of God and our Father" (Galatians 1:4). I suggest both by observation and, sadly, by personal confession that the only reason Christians have difficulty not loving the world is that at any given moment or circumstance they fail to let the cross interfere and stand between them and the world.

Romans 12:2

In Romans 12:2 Paul says something similar. "And be not conformed to this world: but be ye transformed by the renewing of your mind, that ye may prove what is that good, and acceptable, and perfect, will of God." Like John, Paul puts this command in the present tense: stop being conformed . . . constantly be transformed. I think we have already learned that the "world" in this passage focuses on the transience of the age in which we live in contrast to the eternity that awaits us. This word implies what John explicitly declared: "The world passeth away" (1 John 2:17). The prohibition is simple. We are not to get wrapped up with the things of time and circumstance; we are to resist the temptation of living for the present and putting our treasures here where they will certainly corrupt (Matthew 6:20-21). The thinking of this age is diametrically opposed to spiritual and godly pursuits; therefore, we must set aside any likeness to this age.

The positive side is that we are to be constantly transformed. This Greek word is the root from which we get metamorphosis, that word generally used to describe a caterpillar's transition to a butterfly. I don't want to read the English usage back into the Greek, but the idea of a metamorphosis is appropriate. The word depicts a revolutionary change. It requires the outward expression of the inner reality. What God has graciously changed on the inside must show itself on the outside. Rather than masquerading as worldlings, believers are to live like the new creatures they are. This gradual but persistent transformation takes place by the renewing of the mind. Here is the link again between thinking and doing.

There is something unusual and noteworthy about this command to be transformed by the renewal of the mind. The command is in the passive voice, a fact that raises a logical question. I will try not to get too technical about this, but it is a significant point. Imperatives (commands) are directed to the will of the addressee, and the accomplishment of the command depends on his choice to obey. The passive voice means that a different agent is acting upon the subject of the verb. The will of the subject is not a factor. So that's the problem: What's the point of giving a command to one who is not the agent of the action? There have been many times over the years that I have been tempted to walk into one of my classes and say, "Be taught," and then walk out. But the student's being taught depended on my teaching them, so I would always stay. Nevertheless, their being taught also depended on their being teachable; they had to allow themselves to be taught. This is the idea I want us to see. Our being transformed by the renewing of the mind depends on an agent outside ourselves to transform us. That agent is the Holy Spirit. We, in turn, must allow ourselves to be transformed; we must submit and yield to His work. The Holy Spirit has renewed our minds, and we must use the mind that He has given us. Think right! If we use the mind the Spirit has given us, we will always break with the world.

Resist the Devil

Satan, along with the world, is the other great enemy of our sanctification; therefore, we must do battle against him. "Resist the devil, and he will flee from you" (James 4:7). The word "resist" more literally means "take a stand against." Sounds easy enough. However, before we get all bold and take our stand against Satan out in the open on our own, we need to pay attention to where James issues this command and promise of victory. He sandwiches the command to resist the devil between the two imperatives to submit to God and draw near to God (4:7-8). That's the secret. The only way we can successfully take our stand against Satan and find the way of escape from every temptation (1 Corinthians 10:13) is to be surrounded by God and His provision for our protection. Perhaps the most important passage that instructs us about God's battle provisions and how we are to take our stand against Satan and his demonic forces is Ephesians 6:10-17. Here are the key orders.

Preparation for Battle

"Be strong in the Lord, and in the power of his might" (6:10). Preparation for battle is essential. The first order is to acknowledge that we cannot muster the strength and courage for the conflict from within ourselves. No amount of self-effort or psychological pumping up is sufficient to stand against the spiritual enemy that is so far superior to us. We must from the start submit to the Lord's infinite strength that is abundantly effective to win in any conflict against any enemy. Being strong in the Lord is the exercise of faith: it is depending and relying on Him. When we are the most empty of ourselves and the most conscious of our own weakness and timidity, we can be the most full of God's power. Our courage is going to be pumped up in proportion to the confidence we have in the Commander, who has already triumphed over the enemy (Colossians 2:15). He who rushes into spiritual warfare without thinking of Christ, without trusting Him, and without claiming the victory in union with Him is demented and doomed to defeat. Resisting the devil begins with right thinking.

Arming for the Battle

Twice in the battle plan Paul issues the order to arm ourselves with the armor of God (6:11, 13). God is not only the source for inner strength and courage but also the provider of the necessary means to defend ourselves and to assault the enemy. Fighting without this protection is the equivalent of a suicide mission because of the nature of the conflict. Between the two commands to put on the armor, Paul describes the enemy and the kind of warfare confronting us. The enemy is spiritual and the warfare is personal: "For we wrestle not against flesh and blood, but against . . . spiritual wickedness in high places" (6:12). This is the only place in the New Testament where this word "wrestle" occurs. It vividly stresses the personal hand-to-hand combat that we will encounter. Every Christian soldier is going to be on the front lines, and every contest will be a fight to the finish: Either we have downed the opponent, he has downed us. Because this enemy is not flesh and blood and we are, he has the advantage. Something more than human strength and strategy is needed: the armor of God.

This armor of God is designed for victory. After each of the commands to put on the armor, Paul states the purpose for doing so: "That ye may be able to stand against the wiles of the devil" (6:11) and "That ye may be able to withstand in the evil day, and having done all, to stand" (6:13). The Christian armor is not for parade or show; it is for battle and for victory. Satan's methods of warfare (his wiles) may be anything from guerilla tactics to frontal attacks to sleeping gas, but wearing the God-given armor will enable us to confront the enemy head-on, hold our positions, and maintain possession of conquered ground. The armor of God gives us the advantage.

Strategy for the Battle

Verses 14-17 outline a series of statements detailing the strategy for the battle. Here is how we are to stand against the devil.

First, *we must stand convicted with truth:* "Having your loins girt about with truth." Girding up the loins is a common image used in the Bible to represent readiness for action. The long flowing robe of the typical attire of that time could easily impede the kind of mobility necessary for battle, and by hitching it up and securing the garment around the waist with a military belt, the soldier made himself ready to go. In this conquest for holiness, the belt that secures the freedom by keeping everything in place is the truth. The Word of God is the sword that the soldier will carry, and so this truth probably refers to the personal conviction of the truth that is believed, applied, and embraced. In other words, this is truth in the heart. If we are going to win victory in this battle, it is absolutely imperative that we personalize truth. We will not fight as we ought if motivated only by theological theories or practical principles. Internalizing the truth will enable us to maneuver safely through the battlefield. What Paul suggests figuratively, Jesus said literally: "And ye shall know the truth, and the truth shall make you free" (John 8:32). Since Christ is Himself the truth (John 14:6), He links knowing the truth to Himself: "If the Son therefore shall make you free, ye shall be free indeed" (John 8:36). It is ultimately the personal appropriation of Christ that frees us and keeps everything in place.

Second, *we must stand confident in justification:* "Having on the breastplate of righteousness." The breastplate is the armor covering the body from the neck to the thighs. This piece of armor protected the vital organs, one part covering the front and the other covering the back. Without the breastplate the soldier would be effectively naked, exposed to every thrust of the enemy. I emphasize that the back as well as the front was covered. I have heard some claim that it is called the breastplate because the back was not covered as a deterrent against retreat. Thankfully, that is not true. We certainly do not want to retreat, but remember that our enemy is not flesh and blood and that he does not necessarily confine his attacks to the frontline. God has provided us a protection against onslaughts from any direction. This protection is righteousness. I submit that this refers specifically to the righteousness of Christ that has been imputed to us. Personal righteousness would give little or no defense against the accusations of Satan or even our own conscience. But Christ's perfect righteousness secures us and protects us against every assault, whether from the outside or from the inside. "Who shall lay anything to the charge of God's elect? It is God that justifieth. Who is he that condemneth? It is Christ that died, yea rather, that is risen again, who is even at the right hand of God, who also maketh intercession for us" (Romans 8:33-34). Remember in Zechariah 3 how the Lord quieted the accusations of Satan against Joshua on the basis of His gracious justification. What God did regarding Joshua, He does for all His saints. Knowing and resting on our justification generates a confidence that cannot be shaken regardless of how strong the attacks against us. Nothing can penetrate the sure defense of justification.

Third, *we must stand committed to the gospel:* "Your feet shod with the preparation of the gospel of peace." This may be referring to special footwear studded for sure traction. Sureness of foot is essential in battle. We can relate to this in our day when footwear is so specialized. In my youth, "tennis shoes" were multifunctional; but today we have shoes specifically designed for walking, jogging, running, and every possible sport. Some would not dare think of running with jogging shoes. Well, we need to be as sensitive and even picky concerning what shoes we wear in our walk in sanctification. We must wear the gospel "spikes"–the shoes specifically designed for sanctification. It is the gospel that secures our peace, gives us the assurance of God's favor, and produces within us a joyful desire to walk with God. As believers individually and the church corporately move with the gospel, the gates of hell itself will be stormed. The gospel is both our defense and our offense.

Fourth, *we must stand concealed by faith:* "Taking the shield of faith." This word translated "shield" is literally a "door" and refers to the long shield that protected the whole body from head to foot. Unlike the breastplate that rested in place, the shield had to be held in the hand and wielded in whatever direction necessary to ward off the fiery darts. Using the shield effectively required constant vigilance and dexterity. The eyes had to be alert to every potential danger, and the hands had to be ready to move the shield to interrupt the dangerous missiles. In our spiritual battle, faith is the shield. Faith is the constant exercise of a regenerated soul that apprehends and receives all the provision that God has given to us in Christ by His Spirit. Faith is indeed the victory that overcomes the world, because faith is founded and grounded in Jesus Christ, the Overcomer. Faith in Christ is our only real protection. Faith lays hold of Christ and places Him and His cross between the enemy and us. There is no dart in the devil's arsenal that can penetrate and pass through Christ to us. Keep the shield up.

Fifth, *we must stand conscious of salvation:* "Take the helmet of salvation." The helmet was usually made of leather reinforced with metal, and it served to protect the head from blows. The verb "take" carries the idea of receiving what is offered by appropriating it to one's own possession. In this spiritual battle, we are deliberately to appropriate the salvation God has offered. The obvious connection between the helmet and the head suggests that it is the consciousness of the salvation that protects the mind. Wearing the helmet gives the assurance of salvation and keeps the mind set on grace. In simple terms, we are to be thinking about the gospel. Here we go again: Thinking determines behavior. So think right.

Sixth, *we must stand conquering with the Word of God:* "The sword of the Spirit, which is the word of God." The sword is the offensive weapon used to cut down and destroy the enemy. The only assault weapon that God supplies for us is His word applied by His Spirit. It is not the sword in the sheath that cuts; it is the sword unsheathed and brandished that puts the enemy to flight. Too many flash the sheath–a closed Bible–and expect victory. Only the open Bible that is known and applied has the power. The Lord Jesus showed this in His own temptation. Although He was the Son of God, He answered every temptation with a specific word of Scripture. With every thrust of the sword, the devil was silenced and finally compelled to flee. How important it is for us to know the Bible, to have its message in our hearts, so that we can immediately and skillfully use it at the very moment of temptation. "Thy word have I hid in mine heart, that I might not sin against thee" (Psalm 119:11). This is how to resist the devil.

Put on Christ

The New Testament uses another image to illustrate the connection between Christ and our sanctification: wearing Christ. "But put ye on the Lord Jesus Christ, and make not provision for the flesh, to fulfil the lusts thereof" (Romans 13:14; see also Galatians 3:27; Ephesians 4:24; Colossians 3:10). The form of the verb "put on" is significant. First of all, it is in the imperative mood, which directs the command to our will–we must obey. Second, it is in the middle voice, which stresses individual and personal involvement in the action–we must dress ourselves. This illustrates again the difference between justification and sanctification. Whereas in justification God graciously clothes us with the righteousness of Christ (Zechariah

3:4), in sanctification we have to dress ourselves with that same righteousness. The picture of wearing Christ flows obviously from the fact of our union with Christ. It makes sense that if we are in Christ, then Christ is what should be visible when we look in the mirror and when others see us. Dress always limits and defines activity. I love to hunt, but I would not think of wearing camouflage to church any more than I would wear a coat and tie to the woods. Similarly, there are certain places I will not walk in my Sunday shoes. If we are conscious of what we have on, we will be cautious about what we do. The spiritual application is direct. If we are conscious that we are wearing Christ–the garment of salvation and the robe of righteousness–then we will behave ourselves in a way that befits the dress. There are going to be things we will not dream of doing and places we will not dream of going if we have put on Christ. For the Christian, what to wear every day should be an easy decision.

THE PATTERN FOR SANCTIFICATION

God has provided everything that the Christian needs for spiritual life and godliness (2 Peter 1:3). He has commanded holiness and has implanted within the believer both the desire and the means to do those things that are pleasing unto the Lord. The question that remains is this: How do we know if we are doing what pleases the Lord? What is holiness? The wonderful thing is that God does not leave us to guess what to do. He has given us His Word as our rule for both faith and practice and His Spirit as our personal guide in both faith and practice. The Word and Spirit bring to light clearly the pattern for sanctification.

Conformity to Christ

Sanctification is imitating Christ. The ultimate objective of our whole salvation is that we might be conformed to the image of the Lord Jesus (Romans 8:29). The day is coming "when he shall appear" that "we will be like him" (1 John 3:2). According to John, that glorious transformation transpires because "we shall see him as he is." If seeing Christ is the catalyst to our consummate glorification, it is the secret to our progressive sanctification. The more we see Christ, the more we will be like Him. This is precisely what Paul says in what is perhaps the single greatest text concerning the pattern for sanctification: "But we all, with open face beholding as in a glass the glory of the Lord, are changed into the same image from glory to glory, even as by the Spirit of the Lord" (2 Corinthians 3:18). There is something transforming about seeing the Savior. When Moses saw the glory of the Lord, his face shone so gloriously that the people could not stand the brightness (2 Corinthians 3:7; Exodus 34:29-30). They knew that he had seen the Lord. So will it be for us as we behold Christ: Men will know that we have been with Jesus (see Acts 4:13).

What follows should go without saying, but let me say it nonetheless. If Christ is the pattern for sanctification, and being conformed to Christ is the consequence of seeing Him, it is essential that we look where He is. The only place we can find the real Christ is in the Word of God. That's the glass that reveals the Lord's glory. The real Christ is not a figment of the imagination or the portrait of an artist; He is the Living Word revealed in the written Word. Therefore, it is vital for us to be in the Word, daily searching for the Savior. He is our pattern for living. He is more than our example, but He is our example.

Obedience to the Law

It is easy enough to say, "Be like Christ." But what was Christ like? What made Him "holy, harmless, undefiled, separate from sinners" (Hebrews 7:26)? The answer is simply that He perfectly obeyed the law of God. By obeying it, He earned for us the perfect righteousness for our justification and revealed to us the way for our sanctification. Holiness is not some indefinable abstraction or man-defined code of conduct. It is a separation unto God and away from sin, the course for both being set down in God's law. Being conformed to Christ requires obedience to the law. "Fear God, and keep his commandments: for this is the whole duty of man" (Ecclesiastes 12:13). Simple enough.

That is, it should be simple enough, but sadly there is much confusion about the law of God among Christians today. Law has been made the enemy of grace. The consequences of this are manifold, but my concern here is how it has affected sanctification. Christians who desire to be holy and who are constantly being told to be holy are at the same time being told that the law is no longer applicable to this age. On the one hand, this has resulted in a libertarianism that piously permits believers to do virtually whatever they want with a clear conscience because they are under grace and not law. Sin is defined away. On the other hand, it has resulted in a strict legalism that adheres to endless lists of standards defined more by culture than by Scripture. Christians are put under the frustration and bondage of cultivating character traits and ticking off lists of conservative rules that seldom agree with the lists of other churches, institutions, or Christians. There is nothing really absolute. Both of these are spiritually deleterious, but I'm not sure which is worse.

A Scriptural perspective of the law is essential to our understanding and enjoyment of the gospel. The gospel has freed the believer in relationship to the law in three essential ways. First, *believers are free from the law as a means of earning life, merit, and favor with God.* Christ vicariously earned the necessary life, merit, and divine favor for all of His people. That liberates us from the oppressive pressure of trying to do enough to earn salvation and the constant frustration of knowing that we cannot possibly do enough to merit eternal life. Second, *believers are free from the penalty and condemnation of the broken law.* Christ vicariously paid the debt and suffered the penalty of the sin of His people. That liberates us from the oppression of guilt and fear of ever being condemned by God. We can live in the confidence that Jesus paid it all. Third, *believers are free from sin's power, having both the desire and the ability to obey the law as a way of life that pleases God.* Christ showed us the path to follow on that way. We should endeavor to keep the law not because we expect to gain divine favor, but because we have received divine grace. We should obey the law not out of rigid routine or heartless obligation, but out of love. For the Christian, the law is **not a way to life**, but it most certainly is **the way of life**.

The law defines the borders of holiness–the sphere of behavior pleasing to God. The first recording of the Ten Commandments–the summary of the moral law–underscores the proper perspective of the law for God's redeemed people (Exodus 20). Although the moral law was operative from the beginning, it was not written down until Mt. Sinai after God had redeemed the nation from the land of bondage. Had God given Moses the stone tablets at the burning bush and made obedience to the commandments the condition for deliverance, Israel would still be in bondage in Egypt. But He graciously delivered them by His immense power and the blood of the Passover. To a people already redeemed, God graciously gave the law to show how a redeemed people were to behave. For ancient Israel, the law was **not a way to life**, but **the way of life**. A saved people always have a heart desire to please the Lord, and the Lord does not leave a saved people wondering what pleases Him.

Let me illustrate it this way. I have two wonderful sons who are now grown men. When they were growing up, I believe they loved me and had a genuine desire to please me. I did not want my boys going through the frustration of wanting to please me but never knowing exactly what I wanted. So in my love for them, I established in my house what is called "Barrett law." They knew that so long as they behaved within the sphere of "Barrett law," I would be well pleased. "Barrett law" defined how Barretts were supposed to behave. Get the point. I did not find these kids somewhere and offer to them sonship if they would conform to "Barrett law." They were my sons by birth, and the house rules were for family. This is how we as the sons of God must view the law of God. The law is not the condition for our sonship; it is the rule for the family. It defines how Christians are supposed to behave.

The restraints provided by the law of God are part of the gospel of grace. How we view the law of God is an index to how we view God Himself. "For this is the love of God, that we keep his commandments: and his commandments are not grievous" (1 John 5:3). To come to Christ is to take His yoke, that which restrains and restricts. Grace in the heart makes the yoke easy and burden light (Matthew 11:28-30). It is indeed a pleasant yoke, but it is a yoke nonetheless.

Knowing how to interpret, apply, and obey the law of God is integral to our sanctification. It is outside the scope of this discussion to include any detailed study of the Ten Commandments–God's absolute standard for Christian ethics; I have included in the appendices, however, an article I wrote giving a general synopsis of the commandments that you might find helpful. As important as the law is, I want to be clear about this. Keeping the law does not sanctify us; we are sanctified by faith in Christ and all the provisions we have in the gospel. The law is not the means of sanctification; it is simply the sphere in which sanctification operates.

Sanctification is the certain and necessary effect of the gospel. We must use the means of grace God has given us, particularly the Word of God and prayer, to utilize all the provision that we have for victory over sin and Satan. Remember, it is the grace of God that has brought salvation to us that also teaches us to deny ungodliness and worldly passions and to live thoughtfully and righteously in this present age (Titus 2:11-12). Let us do so with the confidence that victory is possible. "Abstain from all appearance of evil. And the very God of peace sanctify you wholly; and I pray God your whole spirit and soul and body be preserved blameless unto the coming of our Lord Jesus Christ" (1 Thessalonians 5:22-23). As I finally bring this chapter to a close, I simply echo to Paul's prayer, "Amen."

CHAPTER 10

Glorification: The End of the Gospel

Not long after his conversion and call into the gospel ministry, the apostle Paul–most likely as a lesson in his own personal theological training by Christ (Galatians 1:16-18)–received a glorious vision in which he was given a personal tour of paradise, the third heaven, the special dwelling place of the omnipresent God (2 Corinthians 12:1-4). He confessed that he saw and heard things so remarkable that he was not permitted to remark about them. Although we don't know the details of what he saw, it is clear from his life and his ministry that he never got over what he saw. His sight of eternity influenced his sight of time. More aware of eternity than time, Paul could refer to his afflictions as light and momentary (2 Corinthians 4:17-18). That is astounding given the nature of his afflictions–multiple incarcerations and various life-threatening situations including beatings, stonings, and shipwrecks, as well as hunger, thirst and frequent physical and emotional weariness, pain and suffering (2 Corinthians 11:23-28). He knew that this life was not all there is; he had something glorious to look forward to. Assurance about eternity breeds confidence for time. Knowing that there is more to life than life is crucial.

What Paul knew for a fact via the heavenly vision, we also can know by faith in God's infallibly inspired Scripture, that "more sure word of prophecy" (2 Peter 1:19). We have something glorious to look forward to. As wonderful as the benefits of the gospel of grace are now, we haven't seen anything yet. As glorious as our salvation is, the best is yet before us. The same gospel that saves us now keeps us saved forever and assures us that the Paradise of God is our final destination. A sight of eternity will aid us greatly in our journey through our little bit of time. Certain glory is our end. Appropriately, the component of the gospel that concerns our final end is *glorification*.

The doctrine of glorification brings us full circle in our examination of the gospel chain. In our analysis of the gospel, we have attempted to stretch out the chain, looking at the individual links. As we come to glorification, it becomes clear that we really can't stretch out the chain after all. All the links are inseparably connected. Both ends are hooked together and padlocked by divine purpose, power, and resolve. This connection is rendered explicitly in the well-known biblically defined order of salvation. "Moreover whom he did predestinate, them he also called: and whom he called, them he also justified: and whom he justified, them he also glorified" (Romans 8:30). Paul uses the same past tense to designate each step in the whole chain. Our complete salvation is a "done deal." Our salvation that had its inception in eternity when the Father chose us in Christ ends in the same eternity when we join Christ, and the experience of our salvation becomes complete. Being complete in Christ means just that. In Christ we are completely saved: Not one part of redeemed man will ever or can ever perish.

When sin entered the world through Adam's disobedience, the consequent curse was complete. It extended to man's body, soul, and environment. The effects of sin were everywhere. At the same time God pronounced the curse, He announced His plan to reverse the curse through the Seed of the woman, the Messiah (Genesis 3:15). Christ's redemption is as extensive as the curse itself. Isaac Watts expressed this well in what we often sing at Christmas. "No more let sins and sorrows grow, nor thorns infest the ground; He comes to make His blessings flow far as the curse is found." Joy to the world! If the curse of sin extends to man's body, soul, and environment, then so does salvation from sin. While obviously including the soul, the doctrine of glorification concerns principally our new bodies and the new standard of living that we will forever enjoy in the immediate presence of our Savior and our God. Consider the summary statements of the creeds.

> The righteous . . . shall be fully and for ever freed from all sin and misery; filled with inconceivable joys, made perfectly holy and happy both in body and soul, in the company of innumerable saints and holy angels, but especially in the immediate vision and fruition of God the Father, of our Lord Jesus Christ, and of the Holy Spirit, to all eternity. And this is the perfect and full communion, which the members of the invisible church shall enjoy in glory. . . . (*Westminster Larger Catechism*, question 90)

> The souls of the righteous being then made perfect in holiness, are received into paradise, where they are with Christ and behold the face of God in light and glory, waiting for the full redemption of their bodies . . . At the last day, such of the saints as are found alive shall not sleep, but be changed . . . the bodies of the just, by his Spirit, [will be raised] unto honour, and be made comformable to his own glorious body. (*Baptist Confession of Faith*, Chapter 31, sections 1-3)

THE NEW BODY

Every one of us can confess along with the Psalmist that we are "fearfully and wonderfully made" (Psalm 139:14). The human body is indeed a divine masterpiece. When God made us, He did a good job; we, then, ought to be content with His creation. Yet, because of sin, death is working in us and will finally overtake us. In what is called the "Allegory of Old Age," Solomon graphically and poetically describes the aging process in which everything in the body wears out until ultimately the dust of our flesh returns to the earth (Ecclesiastes 12:3-7). Even without Solomon's inspired description of growing old, we would see its truth in the mirror and feel its reality in all the aches and pains of our bones. We have on one of the walls in our home a gallery of old family pictures. One is of my grandparents not long after their marriage. Another frame pictures them in exactly the same pose some fifty years later. The pose, however, is the only thing that is the same. Age affected them, and now they are both gone. The scary thing is that my wedding portrait is there as well. About thirty years have passed since that photograph was taken, and I have a hunch that to my grandchildren, I look just as old as my grandparents did to me. Soon I will be gone too. That's the way life has worked since death entered the world through sin (Romans 5:12).

But just as certainly as death entered the world, so did Jesus Christ, who came to "deliver them who through fear of death were all their lifetime subject to bondage" (Hebrews 2:15). Because of Christ and the complete salvation in Him, "the sufferings of this present time are not worthy to be compared with the glory which shall be revealed in us" (Romans 8:18). Therefore, we who are in Christ are to await with eager excitement the "redemption of our body" (Romans 8:23). The New Testament makes clear that this bodily redemption is just as much a part of the gospel of Christ as the spiritual aspects.

In setting forth Christ as the answer to all the problems of life Paul declared to the struggling Corinthians, "But of him are ye in Christ Jesus, who of God is made unto us wisdom, and righteousness, and sanctification, and redemption" (1 Corinthians 1:30). The syntax of the Greek actually isolates the word "wisdom" and defines it terms of the last three components: Christ is made unto us wisdom, even our righteousness, sanctification, and redemption. Wisdom refers ultimately to the ability to be pleasing and acceptable before God: Christ is what we need for that acceptance. Righteousness, sanctification, and redemption designate those aspects of salvation that deal with both our position and our experience–none of which exist apart from Jesus Christ. Righteousness refers to justification, our legal position before God in Christ. Sanctification refers to our experience of progressive holiness before God in Christ. Redemption brings the two together: it refers to the final glorification at which "time" our position of holiness and experience of holiness will coincide. We will come to our full completeness in Christ. What this new body will be like I don't exactly know. However, the Bible does reveal some of its extraordinary traits.

A Christlike Body

First, our new bodies will be just like Christ's glorified body. The New Testament assures us that our citizenship is in heaven "from whence also we look for the Saviour, the Lord Jesus Christ: Who shall change our vile body, that it may be fashioned like unto his glorious body" (Philippians 3:20-21). Our bodies that now limit us to a low estate of abasement, humiliation and struggle will by a divine act be refashioned into another form and placed in a most high estate. There is a significant lexical link between this promise and God's revealed purpose in our complete salvation. According to Romans 8:29, being conformed to the image of God's Son is the divinely predetermined destination of every true believer. What the Authorized Version translates as "fashioned like" in Philippians 3 and "conformed to" in Romans 8 is actually the same Greek word. God's purpose vouchsafes His promise.

Whereas now our conformity to Christ is the gradual process of our sanctification, then it will be the certain and fixed consequence of our glorification. The perfection that every believer desires will be every believer's ultimate end. Our daily, laborious pursuit of holiness toward Christlikeness will some day end in one indivisible moment when we miraculously and gloriously will be changed to be like Him (1 Corinthians 15:52). We will be like Christ when we see Him face to face as He is (1 John 3:2): Seeing Him is all it takes.

Too often speculation focuses on what we will be capable of doing in these new Christlike bodies. Will we able to walk through walls? Such speculation completely misses the point. I believe the crucial issue is not what we will be able to do, but what we will be incapable of doing. Whatever else is true about the new body, it will be a body in which we can no longer sin. That is the essence of being conformed to Christ.

A Real Body

Second, our new bodies will consist of real flesh. Job makes this clear in one of the most outstanding resurrection statements in all of Scripture (Job 19:25-27). After he affirmed his certain knowledge of his living Redeemer who would sooner or later come to the earth to vindicate him, he acknowledged that his long-awaited vindication might not come until after his death. He knew that the "upright shall have dominion…in the morning" (Psalm 49:14). "And *though* after my skin *worms* destroy this *body*, yet in my flesh shall I see God" (19:26). Notwithstanding the translation difficulties in the first part of the verse (evident from the italicized words in the English translation) and a significant interpretation question in the second part, I believe that the overall meaning is indisputable. I personally prefer the translation offered in the margin of most copies of the Authorized Version: "After I shall awake, though this body be destroyed, yet out of [from] my flesh shall I see God."

Both translations make it clear that by the process of natural corruption, death destroys the body. The interpretation question concerns the meaning of the preposition "from." Some interpreters suggest that this means that apart from his flesh, Job would see God. If this is the idea, it would refer to Job's confidence that his being absent from his body meant his being in the presence of God. Although I believe the theology and reality of that are true, grammatically and lexically I would prefer interpreting the preposition as referring to the vantage point from which Job would see God. This is the interpretation of the Authorized Version that translates the preposition as "in." This is why I consider it a great statement of resurrection hope. Even though Job's body was covered with agonizing sores and he knew that his flesh would soon rot off completely in the grave, he was nonetheless certain that **in his flesh** he would see God. It would be resurrected flesh, but flesh nonetheless. Let me define Job's theology in terms of Paul's. Job, who suffered so immensely in body, was "waiting for the adoption, to wit, the redemption of [the] body" (Romans 8:23).

Paul also expressed his desire for a new fleshly body. Although he was certain of the happiness of the intermediate state, he longed for the final consummation (2 Corinthians 5:1-8). The intermediate state refers to that time between death and resurrection during which the body lies dormant in the grave while the spirit is alive. The Bible knows nothing about soul-sleep or any unconscious existence after death. For sinners, to be absent from the body is for the soul to suffer in the torments and agonies of hell (Luke 16:19-31). Dead sinners are doomed to a future in which their resurrected bodies will unite with their souls to suffer and perish forever. For Christians, on the other hand, to be absent from the body is to be present with the Lord (5:8). Although Paul preferred a purely spiritual presence with Christ to an earthly separation from the Lord, he confessed that he did not want to be forever naked. He used a graphic image to illustrate his desire for eternal clothes. He groaned, "earnestly desiring to be clothed upon with our house which is from heaven: If so be that being clothed we shall not be found naked" (5:2-3). He defined that house from heaven as a "building of God, an house not made with hands, eternal in the heavens" (5:1). He contrasted that heavenly, eternal house with the "earthly house of this tabernacle" that was going to be dissolved (5:1). His point is clear. The skin of our flesh, which now houses us temporally, will be replaced with new skin that will last forever. Just as certainly as sinners will be cast bodily into the lake of fire to endure the torments of body and soul (Matthew 10:28), so will Christians reside bodily in heaven to enjoy the bliss of both body and soul.

A Distinct Body

Third, our new bodies, though real, will be different. First Corinthians 15, the great resurrection chapter, is the most thorough exposition in the Bible discussing the details of the glorified body. Paul emphasizes that certain kinds of flesh are good only for certain places. The kind of flesh that we have for earth is fit for earth, but it is not fit for glory (15:50). To inherit heaven requires a completely different kind of body, one that is spiritual and without corruption (15:44, 52-53). Left to self, man is incapable of changing the nature of his body. But that brings us again to the gospel; there is more good news. Christ has purchased for His people a new body with none of the sin-induced limitations of the old. In union with Christ, even our bodies will "bear the image of the heavenly" and will be supernaturally changed into the incorruptible, immortal bodies required for entrance into glory. This complete salvation is guaranteed by the certain gospel. Everything required for eternal life we either already have or will certainly have when the time comes that we need it.

If we are truly convinced of the shortness of time and the unending glory of eternity, we ought to be able to endure whatever temporary hardships or afflictions may fall to us. Most people can endure almost anything if they know the end is in sight. Unfortunately, far too many of us live as though time is more real than eternity, and we walk more by the sight of now than by faith in the end. How foolish it is for us to get so distracted and upset by temporal circumstances in the light of the "far more exceeding and eternal weight of glory" that awaits us. Christians ought always to live with the end in sight. Glory and our glorification are ahead.

A New Standard of Living

Not only will glorification provide for us bodies fit for glory, but it will relocate us to glory and set for us a whole new standard of living. Revelation 21 and 22 preview for us some of the features of Paradise, our final destination. It was the sight of this Paradise that so motivated Paul to live with eternity's values in view; it should do the same for us. Applying Paul's prohibition that prevented him from describing what he saw about Paradise to John's inspired description of Paradise causes me to believe that as fantastic as John's revelation is, it only touches the surface. Heaven will be the ultimate fulfillment and realization of every gospel promise.

Significantly, Revelation 21 begins with unmistakable covenant imagery and phraseology. Note particularly the references to the tabernacle of God, God's dwelling with His people, and the divine affirmation that God will be our God and we will be His people (21:3, 7). God initiated the covenant promises in the earthly Paradise that man lost because of sin. Throughout time He has given the evidences and tokens of His grace. But in eternity, every impediment to the unhindered fellowship and union between God and His people is removed, and full and complete salvation becomes the experience of every child of God. Heavenly Paradise will be our eternal home, and life will be forever different.

A New Home

As His crucifixion approached, the Lord Jesus comforted His disciples with this well-known and wonderful promise. "In my Father's house are many mansions: if it were not so, I would have told you. I go to prepare a place for you. And if I go and prepare a place for you, I will come again, and receive you unto myself; that where I am, there ye may be also" (John 14:2-3). John describes this mansion-filled place as "the holy city…prepared as a bride adorned for her husband" (Revelation 21:2). Similarly, in 21:9 he speaks in terms of "the bride, the Lamb's wife." Heaven's being described in terms of the bride is suggestive, touching on life as we know it.

Every husband has the duty and, hopefully, the desire to supply the needs of his wife. A home with adequate furnishings is one of those crucial necessities. As a husband, I acknowledge my duty, but I confess that my desire is greater than my resources. Christ, on the other hand, as the Husband of His Bride, employs all of His infinite, unlimited resources in providing for the church a home that surpasses imagination. In his vision of the new heaven and new earth, John saw for himself our mansions above and drew a verbal blueprint for us. Blueprints, however, only pict in flat dimension and never convey the full beauty of the finished structure. I can read Hebrew and Greek with some degree of ease, but I have to admit to near illiteracy when reading blueprints. I usually see nothing but unintelligible lines. Notwithstanding my architectural incompetence, I can discern three significant details about our new home.

(1) It will be a safe place. John directs much attention to the foundation, walls, and gates of the city (21:11-25). This place will be unshakable and impregnable. No force can topple it, and

no enemy can enter it. In fact, that the gate of the city will never be shut (21:25) indicates that there are no enemies to worry about anyway.

(2) It will be an expensive place. Verses 11 and 18 detail the glory and attractiveness of the city. Precious stones and pure gold are all over the place. Nothing of worth or beauty is spared; it will be a splendid and magnificent home.

(3) It will be a big place. Verse 16 gives the dimensions of the city as being foursquare, with its length, breadth, and height equal. John's point in supplying these measurements is not that we able to calculate the city's precise proportions, but that we be impressed with the obvious hugeness. There is room enough for all of Christ's redeemed people, and every space will be occupied.

As glorious as our new home will be, it does not distract from the glory of Christ. Rather, the glory of heaven points to Him. He is the Foundation, the Gate of entrance, and the Pearl of great price. All of the provisions for His bride are simply tokens reflecting His love and care. Any bride finds her ultimate happiness in her husband, not in the things he provides. So it will be that Christ's heavenly bride will find ultimate joy not in the luxuries of heaven, but in the presence of Christ. Not even this part of salvation can be understood or appreciated apart from the Lord Jesus Christ. He will be everything: the Alpha and Omega (21:6), the light and glory of heaven (21:23). My mind goes to my favorite verse of my favorite hymn.

The bride eyes not her garment,
But her dear Bridegroom's face;
I will not gaze at glory,
But on my King of Grace–
Not at the crown He giveth
But on His pierced hands.
The Lamb is all the glory of Immanuel's land.

A New Environment

Not only will our new home be great beyond description; it will be in the perfect "neighborhood." We now live in a world cursed by sin, influenced by Satan, and hostile to holiness. Our new world will be free from the curse, liberated from Satan's control, and conducive to holiness. This suggests the common definition of glorification in relationship to other key components of the gospel. Whereas justification frees us from the penalty of sin, and sanctification frees us from its power, glorification frees us from the very presence of sin. I want to suggest two facts concerning our new sin-free environment. I am only going to list the specifics.

Removal of the Effects of Sin

(1) The curse will be gone. Revelation 22:3 could not be more to the point: "And there shall be no more curse." No more thorns or thistles will infest the ground; no more obstacles will inhibit perfect service to God.

(2) Death will be gone. "And there shall be no more death" (21:4). Notwithstanding the wonderful truth that death has lost its sting for believers in Christ (1 Corinthians 15:55), it is the last great enemy that we face in this life. It is cause for many of the sorrows that we suffer as a fact of this life. Thankfully, the atoning death and triumphant resurrection of Jesus Christ put death itself to death: "Death is swallowed up in victory" (1 Corinthians 15:54).

(3) Sorrow and weeping will be gone (21:4). Weeping times and mourning times are during this life divinely allotted, designed to bring man to the fear of God (Ecclesiastes 3:4, 11, 14). Because even believers have the tendency to forget God during those odd times when everything seems to be going well, God graciously juxtaposes days of prosperity with days of adversity to bring us to an increased sense of dependence on Him (Ecclesiastes 7:14). But in our new environment in the actual presence of God, it will be forever impossible to forget Him. With our attention forever fixed on the Lord there will be no need for the memory-jarring sorrows. In that eternal day of prosperity, we can only rejoice.

(4) Pain will be gone (21:4). This is one of the advantages of our new bodies as well as our new environment. There will be

no more disease that can inflict us from within or oppression that can afflict us from without. In our complete redemption, we will know all the physical as well as the spiritual benefits of the atonement. Isaiah declared and Peter affirmed that we are healed by the "stripes" of Christ (Isaiah 53:5; 1 Peter 2:24). Without question, this refers to our spiritual healing, which the Psalmist defines as the forgiveness of sins (Psalm 103:3). But it includes physical healing as well. Significantly, Matthew appealed to the same Suffering Servant prophecy when commenting on Christ's healing of Peter's mother-in-law: "Himself took our infirmities and bare our sickness" (Matthew 8:17). There is indeed healing in the atonement of Christ. Although it may be the will of God for even the most godly of saints to suffer in body here, it is the will of God that no saint suffer there. Everything purchased by the blood of His Son becomes the possession of every saint. Christ redeemed our bodies, and the salvation of that redeemed body will be complete and perfect. The new, glorified body is not only incapable of sinning, it is also incapable of suffering.

Before I make a final observation concerning the removal of the effects of sin, I must digress briefly. I want to expand on something I have already alluded to in earlier chapters. Revelation 21:4 has been the basis of three of the four preceding statements. I want you to notice carefully how the verse begins and ends: "And God shall wipe away all tears from their eyes . . . for the former things are passed away." Death, sorrow, crying, and pain are the former things, and God's wiping away all tears is the umbrella statement that overshadows the whole. God wipes away all tears because with the removal of these tear-producers, there will be no more cause for tears. John puts the statement in a similar joyful context in Revelation 7:17. Significantly, Isaiah, who said it first, puts it in the same context of God's bringing His people to a festive celebration where death is swallowed up in victory (Isaiah 25:6-8). Every time the Scripture makes this comforting statement, it is in the context of our being in a new environment that is free from all the effects of sin.

I must say I am sick and tired of the common misuse and abuse of this wonderful text that applies it to God's wiping away tears after He has dealt with imperfect Christians at the Judgment Seat of Christ. Too many preachers have spawned the notion that when Christians stand before Christ at that day, it is God's last chance to "get" them before the bliss of eternity can begin. After they face guilt one last time, only then God will wipe away tears. I certainly agree that the thought of standing before Christ ought to produce a godly fear and desire for holiness, but any preaching or theology that uses guilt as the hammer to beat Christians into submission and turns the blessed hope of Christ's return into the panic of anxiety is a betrayal of the gospel. Not only does this interpretation becloud the gospel, but it also reflects a most careless and cavalier handling of Scripture. Never does Scripture place this statement in the context of judgment. No interpreter has the right to extract a statement from its context and apply it to whatever else he feels may intensify a desired application.

I'm finished with my digression; now I'm ready for the last observation.

(5) Hindrances and helps to worship and service will be gone. Twice this passage says, "There shall be no night there" (21:25; 22:5). It is the night that requires work to cease (John 9:4). Our new environment will be an everlasting day requiring no pause in our constant worship and service. Without weariness or natural fatigue, we will forever serve the Lord in unending praise. Neither will any temple be there (21:6). The temple–the symbolic abode of God–was a holy place designed as an aid to worship. With all of its attendant ceremonial rituals, the temple revealed how to approach God; nevertheless, it always barred complete entrance to His most holy presence. But in eternity, there will be no need for aids to worship or tokens of divine

presence because every spot will be holy and God's presence is real. Access to God through Christ leads to full entrance to glory. We will see Him directly with unclouded view. Not even the cloud of theophanic glory will obscure our sight. The glory of God and the Lamb will lighten the whole place (21:23).

Restoration of Paradise

The corollary to removing the effects of sin is the restoring of the blessings forfeited because of sin. Sin drove man out of earthly Paradise; grace restores man to eternal Paradise. Using the imagery of Eden, John highlights the full enjoyment of life and the refreshment that will mark our glorified life in the Paradise of God. Corresponding to the refreshing and fertilizing streams in Eden is "a pure river of water of life, clear as crystal, proceeding out of the throne of God and of the Lamb" (22:1). Whereas in Eden attention was directed to the four flowing streams (Genesis 2:10-14), in heaven attention is focused on the Head of the fountain from which all the blessings flow. From that fountain of the water of life, the Lord will give freely and abundantly (21:6).

Revelation 22:2 also refers to the heavenly tree of life. The cherubim with their flaming swords obscured our last sight of this tree. But in John's vision, the tree is freely accessible. Its luxuriant leaves and perpetual fruit symbolize the never-ending, abundant, and prosperous life for all who live there.

Unquestionably, the fact that "they shall see his face" (22:4) is the high-water mark of restoration blessing. When Adam sinned, his first move was to hide "from the presence of the Lord God" (Genesis 3:8). By his own depraved will, he forfeited his right to God's presence and fellowship. But in glory, with all of the resolve of our glorified wills, we will fix our gaze fully on the face of our Savior. It will be good to see the prophets, apostles, reformers and all our loved ones in heaven, but nothing will compare to our seeing Christ. "O that will be glory for me. . . . When by His grace I shall look on His face, that will be . . . glory for me." You know the hymn. Let the words sink in.

When all my labors and trials are o'er,
And I am safe on that beautiful shore,
Just to be near the dear Lord I adore,
Will through the ages be glory for me.

When, by the gift of His infinite grace,
I am accorded in heaven a place,
Just to be there and to look on His face,
Will through the ages be glory for me.

Friends will be there I have loved long ago;
Joy like a river around me will flow;
Yet, just a smile from my Saviour, I know,
Will through the ages be glory for me.

In Christ, we have a glorious end. Citizenship in the heavenly kingdom is certain for every person united to Christ, and it is reserved for believers alone. Revelation 21:27 issues sobering yet assuring words. "And there shall in no wise enter into it any thing that defileth, neither whatsover worketh abomination, or maketh a lie: but they which are written in the Lamb's book of life." To have our names in His book is essentially to have our names in His heart and His name on our foreheads (22:4). Christ knows those who belong to Him; He knows every particular member of His body, His bride. Not one of His redeemed people will be missing from heaven. Not one who has been chosen, called, and justified will fail to be glorified as well. Glorification is the certain end of the gospel. In Christ, the gospel works; it really and truly works.

CHAPTER 11

ASSURANCE: THE ENJOYMENT OF THE GOSPEL

My burden has been to reach this chapter. Not because it is the last chapter of the book, but because it addresses one of my principal concerns that has given impetus to this study from the beginning. I would dare to say that the most common sore spot in the hearts of believers that I have seen throughout the years of my ministry is the festering doubt that fuels the struggle over assurance of salvation. These struggles can be frustrating and spiritually debilitating. I know this not only by observation, but also by experience. My prayer and plan has been to guide Christians to a better understanding of the gospel with a view to an increased personal enjoyment of the gospel. Right thinking about the gospel produces not only right living in the gospel, but also a happy experience of it. Spiritual understanding fosters spiritual enjoyment. Assurance of salvation is not just wishful thinking or whistling in the dark; it is a sense of confidence that flows from the verities of the gospel. Assurance of salvation is the in-this-life enjoyment of gospel grace. If saving faith is our receiving and resting upon Christ alone as He is offered in the gospel, assurance of saving faith is our relaxing in Christ.

Any consideration of the issue of assurance must confront two problems. The first concerns those who claim assurance without legitimate or Scriptural warrant. Because of some professed decision in their past, they bank on invalid notions about the eternal security of saints and lock a claim on grace regardless of how they live. "Once saved–always saved" are magical words that supposedly give license to careless living without consciousness of God or any compulsion to holiness. Such assurance is neither Scriptural nor produced by the Spirit.

The second problem concerns those who have Scriptural warrant for assurance but fail to claim it. Through constant introspection, they wrestle and wonder if they have ever, will ever, or can ever have any real saving interest in Christ. Both the *Westminster* and the *Baptist Confessions* recognize the struggle and state in exactly the same words that "this infallible assurance doth not so belong to the essence of faith, but that a true believer may wait long, and conflict with many difficulties, before he be partaker of it" (Chapter 18, section 3 of both confessions). That is itself comforting, for I suppose that if assurance of faith was of the essence of saving faith, few believers could ever lay claim to a full assurance of salvation. Tragically however, some Christians have been taught that assurance of eternal security is the true evidence of saving faith. This has led to repetitive efforts to believe sufficiently enough to be secure. Attention focuses on the efforts of faith rather than the efficacy of the object of faith. Ironically, this teaching has turned faith into an obstacle to assurance rather than the effortless means of receiving Christ and enjoying the full salvation God offers in Him.

Although the exposition of the doctrine of security and assurance should knock out the false props of false professors (the first problem), my primary burden here is for genuine believers who are struggling (the second problem). However, I want to be clear that it is beyond my authority or ability to give assurance of faith to anyone. All I or any other preacher or teacher can do is to point men to Christ and what the Scripture says. The application of truth to the heart is ultimately and necessarily the work of the Holy Spirit. I say this because some well-meaning preachers have unwittingly caused more harm than good by giving assurance to those who are in fact not genuine believers at all. There are just causes for doubt, and not being in Christ is one of them.

Allow me a personal example that explains why I want to be so adamant on this point. My wife's testimony bears witness to the danger of preachers who take to themselves the work of the Spirit. As a young girl, she made a profession of faith and was baptized. Upon reaching her teen years, she became convinced in her own heart that she was not genuinely saved. When she approached her preacher for help, he convinced her that she must be saved because he had personally led her to the Lord. When the fears persisted, he baptized her again, claiming that would help confirm her faith. For years as the doubts plagued her, she would find fleeting consolation in the unfounded assumption that her preacher would not mislead her. And then for more years–though hiding it well–she was in total despair, knowing that she was not saved. But now the fear of what others might think kept her from coming to Christ–after all, she was married to a preacher and seminary professor. Thankfully, the gracious Holy Spirit, the Author of her struggling doubts, persisted until she set aside her pride, left her fears and came humbly and truly to the Savior. I will never forget the night I led my wife to Christ. The counsel she received would have been maleficent enough if she had been in a liberal or apostate church, but she was in a fundamentalist church with an avowed fundamentalist preacher with credentials from a fundamentalist school. I submit that regardless of the fundamentalist label, that preacher did not have a clue about the gospel. I can only wonder how many similar stories there are, and how many without such a happy ending.

So with these purposes in mind, I want to examine what the Bible says about the issue of assurance of faith and trust the Holy Spirit to apply the truth by affirming it in the soul of every genuine believer in Jesus Christ. It is possible for every believer *to enjoy the gospel.*

The Objective Basis for Assurance

I think that one of the main reasons so many Christians grapple futilely with the matter of assurance is that they are trying to find it in the wrong place. They keep looking inside rather than outside. The New Testament, indeed, commands us to examine ourselves to prove whether we are in the faith (2

Corinthians 13:5). We are obligated to obey that command as much as every other imperative to duty. But self-examination must not terminate in self, because introspection only proves personal worthlessness and failure. I don't know how a true believer, regardless of his personal maturity and practice of holiness, can ever look inside and be satisfied with what he sees. Even the apostle Paul, when considering the inner struggles of his own life, had to confess, "O wretched man that I am" (Romans 7:24). Proper self-examination always leads to and ends at the proper object of faith. Paul knew where his security was and, thankfully, directed every believer to the same confidence: "There is therefore now no condemnation to them which are in Christ Jesus" (Romans 8:1). Remember the vital principle I emphasized in the chapter on conversion: **The object of faith determines the value of faith**. Self-examination is not to measure how well we believe, but to affirm whom and what we believe. Christ and the gospel of grace give saving and sustaining value to faith. The more we know whom and what we believe, the more we can be sure of the salvation that Christ has secured for us. As faith increases, so will our level of assurance, but the objective basis for that assurance remains fixed and constant.

My point is simply that the basis for security rests outside ourselves; the assurance of security intensifies in proportion to our consciousness of the object of our faith. The best illustration of this that I have ever heard was in a sermon on the Passover from Exodus 12, in which the preacher compared two reactions to the tenth plague. Think what it must have been like that first Passover evening for all the firstborn of Israel. What was normally a position of privilege was not one that night. They had heard Moses putting them under the sentence of death on the one hand and then, on the other hand, pointing them to the shedding and the application of the blood of the Passover lamb for salvation. They witnessed the sacrifice of the lamb and the spreading of its blood on the doors to their homes, and then entered for the evening believing the word of divine promise, "When I see the blood, I will pass over you" (Exodus 12:13). My guess is that some tossed and turned in their beds, wondering if they would make it through the night alive and anxiously speculating: "Did Dad do it right?" I believe, though, that there were others who slept soundly, peacefully resting upon God's word of promise. The fact is that regardless of how well they rested, both groups made it through the night. One was sure, and the other was not; but they were equally saved. None perished where the blood of the lamb was applied. The basis for security was not that they saw the blood, but that God saw the blood and was satisfied. They were safe and sound because of the power and promise of that which was outside themselves. This is what I mean by the objective basis for assurance.

If we are to experience the full assurance of faith, it is imperative that we fix our thoughts on the unchangeable facts that provide the solid ground upon which we can confidently stand. All of the objective truths for assurance focus on God. From start to finish, "Salvation is of the Lord" (Jonah 2:9). Each Person of the Holy Trinity unfailingly fulfills His role in our salvation. Before I survey the Scriptural data, ponder these confessional statements that direct our attention to each of the Persons of the Godhead. The *Westminster* and *Baptist Confessions* are exactly the same, except for the helpful addition in the Baptist Confession to union with Christ and the oath of God (marked by brackets in the quotation).

> This perseverance of the saints depends not upon their own free will, but upon the immutability of the decree of election, flowing from the free and unchangeable love of God the Father; upon the efficacy of the merit and intercession of Jesus Christ, [and union with him, the oath of God,] the abiding of the Spirit, and of the seed of God within them, and the nature of the covenant of grace: from all which ariseth also the certainty and infallibility thereof. (Chapter 17, section 2 in both Confessions)

I suppose that in one place or another in the preceding chapters, we have considered something about each of the truths I am going to present here. Consequently, I will not go into great detail, but I do want you to see that assurance of faith, relaxing in the gospel, depends on unchangeable truth. So don't be put off by what may seem to be repetition; just put it all together for your own personal enjoyment.

The Authority of the Father

"Nevertheless the foundation of God standeth sure, having this seal, The Lord knoweth them that are his" (2 Timothy 2:19). God knows His people, and the Bible is unmistakable that the security of those people rests in the power of God. Peter opens his first epistle by blessing God the Father, whose mercy brought us to spiritual life (1 Peter 1:3) and whose power keeps us "through faith unto salvation" (1 Peter 1:5). The Lord Jesus assures all of His sheep that "no man is able to pluck them out of my Father's hand" (John 10:29). Although the Father's part in saving a people in Christ is multi-faceted, three truths stand out in my thinking as being particularly significant for our assurance.

The Immutability of His Election

Why is it that my first thought here is to justify my use of the word "election" and reconcile what the Bible says with all of man's finite and foolish misunderstandings? I'm not going to do it. Shame on us for making this doctrine a matter of controversy among God's people when the Bible always makes it a matter for confidence and consequent duty. In the chapter on adoption, we considered some important aspects of God's election according to grace (Romans 11:5) as well as some cautions concerning the abuse of the doctrine.

Therefore, all that I want to do at this point is encourage you to rest in God's eternal and unchangeable purpose in election as solid ground upon which to stand secure. Understanding it will remain beyond our comprehension, but believing it should be our joy. Remember that God never commands sinners to determine their election before they come in faith to Christ. But He does invite believers to consider their election as evidence of His grace. His choice of us did not depend on foreseen potential worth, merit or even faith on our part. His choice was gracious; it finds its reason in God and not in us. That's why we can rely on it. Saving us was God's idea and plan, and He is in control of the entire operation of the gospel.

However, it is not the isolated fact of God's election that is our salvation. God's election of sinners is always in reference to and in union with Jesus Christ (Ephesians 1:4), and it leads infallibly to faith in Christ. Any consideration of election that does not get to the gospel of Christ is unwise and unbiblical. See how Paul links God's decreed end–our election to salvation–to the only means whereby the elect will be saved–through belief in the truth. "Because God hath from the beginning chosen you to salvation through sanctification of the Spirit and belief of the truth: Whereunto he called you by our gospel, to the obtaining of the glory of our Lord Jesus Christ" (2 Thessalonians 2:13-14). God's purposed end always includes the necessary means to achieve that end. The Bible is explicitly clear that the believer's coming to Christ is evidence of the Father's will (John 1:13; 6:37, 44). The accomplishing of the means, therefore, testifies to the certainty of the end. God's election was not a hindrance to our coming to Christ for salvation; it was the reason we came. "According to the eternal purpose which he purposed in Christ Jesus our Lord: In whom we have boldness and access with confidence by the faith of him" (Ephesians 3:11-12). Our faith in Christ is the response in time to God's purpose in eternity. That is grounds for assurance.

It gets even better when we realize that God's eternal purposes are immutable; they cannot change. "Yea, I have loved thee with an everlasting love: therefore with lovingkindness have I drawn thee" (Jeremiah 31:3). God's love for us in His eternity caused Him in our time to draw us to Himself. In his famous discourse on God's election, Paul refers specifically to the Lord's special and selective love for Jacob as an example of sovereign grace. He quotes as evidence Malachi's record of God's remarkable declaration, "Jacob have I loved" (Romans 9:13; Malachi 1:2). Malachi, having started his prophecy with a statement of God's electing grace, records the Lord's own amazing application of this truth: "For I am the Lord, I change not; therefore ye sons of Jacob are not consumed" (Malachi 3:6). Those whom God has chosen are excluded from condemnation because the changeless Lord will not renege on His eternal choice and purpose. Therefore, the answer to Paul's question is wonderfully certain. His question is: "Who shall lay anything to the charge of God's elect?" (Romans 8:33). His answer: "For I am persuaded, that neither death, nor life, nor angels, nor life, nor angels, nor principalities, nor powers, nor things present, nor things to come, Nor height, nor depth, nor any other creature, shall be able to separate us from the love of God, which is in Christ Jesus our Lord" (Romans 8:38-39). Our salvation cannot fail of God's eternal purpose. He who eternally predestinated us will infallibly glorify us as well (Romans 8:29-30). This is the truth. We might as well enjoy it!

The Irreversibility of His Gifts

Here is another irrefutable truth about God that ought to give us assurance: "For the gifts and calling of God are without repentance" (Romans 11:29). God never regrets giving, and He never takes back what He gives. This has a dual focus that should encourage us.

God's Gift to Christians

God gave us Christ and all that is necessary for life in Him. The Scripture makes some remarkable statements. "For God so loved the world, that he **gave** his only begotten Son, that whosoever believeth in him should not perish, but have everlasting life" (John 3:16). "The **gift** of God is eternal life through Jesus Christ our Lord" (Romans 6:23). These two texts identify Christ and eternal life through faith in Christ as God's gracious gifts. It is for us by the help of the Holy Spirit to "know the things that are **freely given** to us of God" (1 Corinthians 2:12).

Peter brings Christ and life together and marks even the necessary faith as God's gift. Let's consider a few thoughts from his inspired exposition of the objective basis for our security. As you read the text, notice his emphasis on both God's giving and our receiving.

> Simon Peter . . . to them that have **obtained** like precious faith with us through the righteousness of God and our Saviour Jesus Christ: Grace and peace be multiplied unto you through the knowledge of God, and of Jesus our Lord, According as his divine power hath **given** unto us all things that pertain unto life and godliness, through the knowledge of him that hath called us to glory and virtue: Whereby are **given** unto us exceeding great and precious promises: that by these ye might be partakers of the divine nature, having escaped the corruption that is in the world through lust. (2 Peter 1:1-4)

Note first that God gives saving faith. The beginning of confidence is to realize that faith is not self-generated, but divinely given. This is evident from the description of believers as those who have "obtained like precious faith." Receiving presupposes a source from which something is received, and the rest of the passage clearly identifies God as the source. The exercise of faith would always be suspect if it were the product of personal resolve. We need to understand that faith is indeed a willful exercise, but it is not the product of the will. Faith is the God-given vehicle for appropriating the benefits of grace.

Another basis for confidence is to realize that all saving faith is the same. What the Authorized Version translates as "like precious" literally means "equal in value." I love this. The inspired apostle equates his faith with that of ordinary, common believers; he equates his with mine. God is no respecter of persons, and the requirements for entering into salvation are the same for all. There is no doubt about God's acceptance of Peter, and there can be no doubt about God's acceptance of every true believer with the same kind of faith equal in its saving value.

I confess, however, that it used to bother me to compare my faith with Peter's. How could my weak faith be compared to Peter's faith that enabled him to walk on water? I worried that I didn't have that equal-in-value faith. Obviously, though, it is not the degree or strength of faith that is equal between believers. I want you to see again that measuring faith will never lead to assurance. It was a happy day when it finally sank into my head and heart that it is the object of faith that makes all true faith equal in value. I may not believe as Peter believed, but I believe what he believed–Jesus Christ. God-given faith always terminates in Christ. Such God-given faith can never fail because Christ can never fail. God-given faith infallibly secures every believer.

Second, note from Peter's exposition that God gives sustaining grace. Grace does not save us and then leave us. It leads us more and more into the knowledge of Christ, the object of both saving and sustaining faith. Follow Peter's argument and you will see that God has given everything that we need for spiritual and supernatural life in union with Christ. This is grounds for confident security. If we are to enjoy assurance, we must be thoroughly convinced of what God has done and what He has given to make our salvation a reality. What He gives, He gives for good and forever. This is why Paul can say, "The **gift** of God is eternal life through Jesus Christ our Lord" (Romans 6:23). And why we can say, "Thanks be unto God for his unspeakable gift" (2 Corinthians 9:15).

God's Gift to Christ

Our security rests not only in the gracious fact that God gave Christ to us but on the amazing, incomprehensible fact that God gave us to Christ. In the eternal covenant between the Father and the Son in which the Father ordained the Son to be the Mediator and Savior, the Father promised a people to Christ for His being the sacrifice for their sins (see for example, Isaiah 53:10; Psalm 2:8; Hebrews 2:13). So with that joyous prospect before Him, Christ came to save His people from their sins by enduring the cross (Matthew1:21; Hebrews 12:2).

The Lord Jesus often referred to those given Him by the Father in contexts designed for our comfort and assurance. Explaining this is over my head, so let Bible speak for itself. "All that the Father **giveth me** shall come to me; and him that cometh to me I will in no wise cast out" (John 6:37). "My sheep hear my voice, and I know them, and they follow me: And I give unto them eternal life; and they shall never perish, neither shall any man pluck them out of my hand. My Father, which **gave them me**, is greater than all; and no man is able to pluck them out of my Father's hand" (John 10:27-29). "Father, the hour is come; glorify thy Son, that thy Son also may glorify thee: As thou has given him power over all flesh, that he should give eternal life to as many as thou hast **given him**" (John 17:1-2). "Holy Father, keep through thine own name those whom thou hast **given me**" (John 17:11). "While I was with them in the world, I kept them in thy name: those that thou **gavest me** I have kept, and none of them is lost"(John 17:12). "Father, I will that they also, whom thou hast **given me**, be with me where I am" (John 17:24). Just notice how many of these references occur in Christ's great High Priestly prayer for His people. The Lord's great argument in prayer was that God must in fact secure those He had given to Him. It is absolutely inconceivable and eternally impossible for the Father to turn a deaf ear to any request of His Son. Christ's prayer for us guarantees our eternal security.

Our inability to comprehend completely this covenant mystery should not rob us of the sure ground of assurance it provides. It should be simple enough for us to understand that God will not take away from His Son what He has given to Him.

The Inviolability of His Oath

The final truth about God that should contribute to our sense of security is the invariable fact that God always keeps His word; His promises are sure. It is not without significance that God reveals His word and promises in terms of covenant oath, the most solemn and inviolable expression of certainty. Jeremiah, for instance, records God's guarantee of an unbroken relationship between Himself and His people in terms of covenant promise. "And I will make an everlasting covenant with them, that I will not turn away from them, to do them good; but I will put my fear in their hearts, that they shall not depart from me" (Jeremiah 32:40).

The apostle Paul does the same in Hebrews 6:17-20. Interestingly, one of the most sobering warning passages in the New Testament ends with one of the most glorious declarations designed to lead true believers not to doubt, but to assurance. Here's the promise.

> Wherein God, willing more abundantly to shew unto the heirs of promise the immutability of his counsel, confirmed it by an oath: That by two immutable things, in which it was impossible for God to lie, we might have a strong consolation, who have fled for refuge to lay hold upon the hope set before us: Which hope we have as an anchor of the soul, both sure and stedfast, and which entereth into that within the veil; Whither the forerunner is for us entered, even Jesus. . . . (Hebrews 6:17-20)

The two immutable things by which it is impossible for God to lie are the counsel and the oath, which together equate with the Word of God. I think you understand that it is impossible for God ever to lie, but the reference to counsel and oath is emphatic language that puts in boldface the absolute verity of His word to aid the assurance of all who have placed their hope in Jesus Christ. Describing the hope as a sure and steadfast anchor with its flukes firmly fixed behind the veil (the symbolic reference to God's unique dwelling place) heightens the word of assurance. The word "sure" refers to that which is able to withstand outside pressure. The Christian's hope in Christ cannot successfully be assailed or disturbed outwardly. The word "stedfast" refers to that which is inherently firm and strong. The Christian's hope in Christ can withstand the inner assaults as well. The anchor imagery again reminds us of the importance of the object of faith. An anchor left in the boat or dangling overboard is useless. But when the anchor is cast into the murky waters and sinks beyond sight, all doubt concerning its weight and effectiveness dissipates when it takes hold on the bottom and secures the vessel. Here our anchor is taken by Christ and placed where we cannot perceive it with physical sight and where without Him we have no right to enter. But we can know that our anchor holds. There the anchor is so firmly fixed that it cannot be hauled back in. With one end of the anchor cable fixed to the believing heart and the other end fixed with Christ in heaven, the believer must ultimately be where Christ is. His being the forerunner into Heaven guarantees our certain entrance as well. We have God's word on it.

I want to refer to one final text that guarantees our salvation on the authority of God's word of promise. "The Lord is not slack concerning his promise, as some men count slackness; but is longsuffering to us-ward, not willing that any [of us] should perish, but that all [of us] should come to repentance" (2 Peter 3:9). I have put within brackets what is required from the logic of the context. I do this because the verse has been taken out of its context to argue theological issues that it is not addressing. Both Arminians and Calvinists have been guilty of isolating this verse and giving it their own peculiar slants to prove their interpretations. You can't do that. The issue of verse 9 is not the extent or design of the atonement, nor is it some supposed distinction between God's desire and His decree. The issue is the absolute assurance believers have that they will never perish in God's judgment. Verse 7 declares God's certain word and revealed will to bring the fire of judgment on ungodly men. There is a most wonderful and obvious contrast between those sentenced to judgment and those who will not perish in that judgment–a contrast between them and us. Just as certainly as sinners will perish, believers in Christ will never perish but will have everlasting life.

On the basis of God's attention to His promise and His unfrustratable will, believers are secure and have every right to claim the inviolability of the promise. God's word is forever settled, and not one part of it will fail its fulfillment (Psalm 119:89; Matthew 5:18).

The Accomplishments of the Son

Because the accomplishments of Christ constitute the heart of the objective basis for personal assurance, my remarks in this section could be either extremely brief or extremely detailed. I will keep them brief. At this point, I simply refer you to everything we have considered together in this study. I have tried to keep before you that every element of our salvation finds its locus in Jesus Christ: *We are complete in Him*. Every aspect of His person and His work contributes to our complete salvation: He is the essence of the gospel. I sincerely believe that the more we understand about the gospel–about all that Christ successfully accomplished by His life, death, resurrection, and ascension, about all that He is successfully accomplishing in His exalted Session, and about all that He will accomplish in His soon return–the more will be our confident assurance of salvation in Him. In Hebrews 10:19-23, Paul definitely links our thoughts of Christ and His successful accomplishments to boldness, assurance, and perseverance.

> Having therefore, brethren, **boldness** to enter into the holiest by the blood of Jesus, by a new and living way, which he hath consecrated for us, through the veil, that is to say, his flesh; And having an high priest over the house of God; Let us draw near with a true heart in **full assurance of faith**, having our hearts sprinkled from an evil conscience, and our bodies washed with pure water. Let us **hold fast the profession of our faith** without wavering; (for he is faithful that promised;). . . .

"Enough for me that Jesus saves, this ends my fear and doubt; A sinful soul I come to Him, He'll never cast me out. I need no other argument, I need no other plea, it is enough that Jesus died, and that He died for me." We look to Christ for forgiveness, for righteousness, for holiness, for merit, for acceptance, for eternal life, for assurance. He has it all. In union with Christ, we have it all. Look to Christ and enjoy.

The Application by the Holy Spirit

"Eye hath not seen, nor ear heard, neither have entered into the heart of man, the things which God hath prepared for them that love him" (1 Corinthians 2:9, referring to Isaiah 64:4). The apostle Paul echoes the prophet Isaiah in defining the gospel as that which is beyond human invention and natural reasoning. Because man could never conceive of such a message of grace that includes so many saving benefits and blessings, "God hath revealed them unto us by his Spirit" (1 Corinthians 2:10). The Holy Spirit is our divine Teacher whom we have received from God, "that we might know the things that are freely given to us of God" (1 Corinthians 2:12). The very fact that we have come to believe that Jesus Christ is the only way, truth, and life is a spiritual discernment possible only as a result of the operation of the Holy Spirit (1 Corinthians 2:13-14).

In the chapter on adoption, I discussed the role of the Holy Spirit as our ever-present internal witness of the personal interest that we share with Christ. Let me simply remind you here of two principal aspects of that work that directly relate to our objective basis for assurance. Paul brings the two aspects together in connection with God's uniting believers together with Christ. It is amazing how the inspired apostle can pack so much profound truth into such a compact statement. "Now he which stablisheth us with you in Christ, and hath anointed us, is God; Who hath also sealed us, and given the earnest of the Spirit in our hearts" (2 Corinthians 1:21-22). Notice the references to the sealing and the earnest. Paul refers to the sealing again in Ephesians 1:13 and 4:30–"after that ye believed, ye were sealed with that holy Spirit of promise" and "grieve not the holy Spirit of God, whereby ye are sealed unto the day of redemption." Remember that the image of sealing served three important functions: identifying something as genuine, rendering something secure, and marking something a personal property. The Holy Spirit does all three for every believer.

Paul refers to the earnest again in 2 Corinthians 5:5 and Ephesians 1:14. Remember that the earnest is primarily a commercial term that designates a down payment in guarantee of full payment to follow. In 2 Corinthians 5 Paul has just referred to the prospect of a glorified body and then refers in verse 5 to God's giving the "earnest of the Spirit" as the token guarantee of certain glorification. In Ephesians 1, Paul defines the Holy Spirit as "the earnest of our inheritance until the redemption of the purchased possession." Since Christ did not fail to acquire all that He purchased for His people, the Holy Spirit will not fail in applying all that the Son purchased and vouchsafing its full enjoyment. It is not surprising that the Lord Jesus spoke of the Holy Spirit as the Comforter who would testify of Him (John 15:26). The assuring work of the Holy Spirit always directs us to the full sufficiency of Christ. That's one way to distinguish between the doubts generated by self and Satan and those convictions generated by the Spirit. The Holy Spirit always directs attention and faith to Christ.

THE SUBJECTIVE EXPERIENCE OF ASSURANCE

The fact of the believer's security rests with God; that security is unchangeable, infallible, eternal, and equal for every Christian. The assurance of that security, however, is the privilege and the responsibility of the believer. It varies between true Christians and fluctuates even within the individual believer. The *Westminster* and *Baptist Confessions* are in total and verbal agreement concerning this matter. These are lengthy quotations, but well worth our meditation.

> This infallible assurance doth not so belong to the essence of faith, but that a true believer may wait long, and conflict with many difficulties, before he be partaker of it: yet, being enabled by the Spirit to know the things which are freely given him of God, he may without extraordinary revelation, in the right use of ordinary means, attain thereunto. And therefore, it is the duty of every one to give all diligence to make his calling and election sure, that thereby his heart may be enlarged in peace and joy in the Holy Ghost, in love and thankfulness to God, and in strength and cheerfulness in the duties of obedience, the proper fruits of this assurance; so far is it from inclining men to looseness. (Chapter 18, section 3 in both Confessions)

> True believers may have the assurance of their salvation divers ways shaken, diminished, and intermitted; as, by negligence in preserving of it, by falling into some special sin which woundeth the conscience and grieveth the Spirit; by some sudden or vehement temptation, by God's withdrawing the light of His countenance, and suffering even such as fear Him to walk in darkness and to have no light: yet are they never utterly destitute of that seed of God, and life of faith, that love of Christ and the brethren, that sincerity of heart, and conscience of duty, out of which, by the operation of the Spirit, this assurance may, in due time, be revived; and by the which, in the mean time, they are supported from utter despair. (Chapter 18, section 4 in both Confessions)

The Confessions' demand for believers to fulfill their individual duties in order to experience assurance simply repeats the demand of Scripture. Having outlined some of the great privileges of grace, Peter issues the imperative to those who share his like precious faith: "Give diligence to make your calling and election sure: for if ye do these things, ye shall never fall" (2 Peter 1:10). I need to make an important grammatical observation for you. So stay with me–it will be worth it. It is clear that Peter is referring to the believer's personal knowledge of security and not to the believer's obligation to make himself secure. The voice of the verb "to make" is significant. Voice is that aspect of the verb that defines the subject's relationship to the action. Greek has three possible voices. The active voice indicates that the subject performs the action (e.g., "he hit the ball"). The passive voice indicates that the subject receives the action (e.g., "he was hit by the ball"). The middle voice indicates that the subject performs the action with a special interest or application to himself (e.g., "he hit the ball for himself"). In this text, Peter uses the middle voice: "Give diligence to make your calling and election sure for yourself." There is a world of difference between having to secure ourselves in grace and making sure for ourselves that we have received grace. Securing ourselves in election would be impossible; knowing that our election and calling are sure is wonderfully possible. We don't have to make it sure for God. Remember the foundation of God stands sure. The Lord knows those who are His, and He gives the instructions whereby we can know it too.

The question is how we can know for certain. Before I suggest two biblical answers to that question, let me remind you not to evaluate the subjective evidences of grace independently from the objective realities of grace. I don't want you to think that I keep harping on this point unnecessarily. It is just that I am acutely conscious that ignoring the objective truths of gospel grace has caused a great many of the spiritual struggles within believers. I'm afraid that too many assurance-seeking Christians jump into the duty of 2 Peter 1:10 without beginning their diligent efforts where Peter begins–at the divine supply of grace centered in the knowledge of Jesus Christ (1:1-4). I hope that if we have learned anything from our study of the gospel, it is that no part of it is ever separated from Christ. Assurance of salvation does not result from the power of positive thinking; it flows from the power of the gospel of Jesus Christ. Since I have addressed the following two subjective evidences of grace in our previous discussions, I will only highlight them here to encourage you to see their implications and relevance to the enjoyment of assurance.

Persistent Faith

Although the Lord is the Author and Finisher of our faith (Hebrews 12:2), we are the exercisers of it. An inseparable link exists between God's work in our salvation and our response to that work. Eternal election, for instance, is the work of God. But the evidence of election is the saving faith of those chosen. Understand the connection: If we are divinely chosen in Christ, we will believe in Christ. If we believe in Christ, we can know we are elected in Christ.

Likewise, eternal security is the work of God. But the evidence of eternal security is the continuing faith of those kept by the power of God. Here is the logic. If we are eternally secure, we will believe. If we believe, we are eternally secure. Eternal security is the end; perseverance of faith is the means to that end. It should be simple enough. In the chapter on conversion, I noted the biblical emphasis that saving faith is always present–it continues to believe. It may be weak at times and is never perfect, but it never stops trusting Christ. It is Christ who gives value even to the weakest of faith. Therefore, don't look for assurance in the amount of your faith, but in the object of it. I've said that before, and I say it again.

Pursuit of Holiness

Grace never leaves a man where it finds him. I've said that before, too. But the grace that has made us new creatures in Christ, causing old things to pass away and all things to become new, is going to show itself in the way we live (2 Corinthians 5:17). The path to assurance of faith will follow the path of holiness and Christlikeness. This, for instance, is Peter's line of reasoning in 2 Peter 1:5-11, where he suggests two crucial principles.

First, true believers must complement grace. Follow the logic of Scripture; it is always precise and necessary. In verses 1-4 Peter makes some remarkable statements about God's grace that supplies in the knowledge of Christ all we need for life and godliness. Verse 5 begins, "And beside this, giving all diligence, add to your faith." The word "giving" occurs only here in the New Testament and has a rather transparent meaning in the Greek, "to bring in alongside." Because of the grace received, the believer must bring in alongside that grace the exercise of intense and earnest zeal to add some things to God-given faith. Grace does not exempt the saint from responsibility; rather, it gives the ability and demands the effort to pursue holiness. As though in choral harmony, the believer is to complement his faith with virtue, knowledge, temperance, patience, godliness, brotherly kindness, and charity. These virtues are not sequentially perfected before the next is added; they are all in some degree coincidental to the life of faith. It is beyond my purpose to expound each of these characteristics, except to say that sharing in the divine nature demands their demonstration (2 Peter 1:4). Verses 8-9 make it clear that these virtues are necessary for the conscious assurance of faith. "For if these things be in you, and abound, they make you that ye shall neither be barren nor unfruitful in the knowledge of our Lord Jesus Christ. But he that lacketh these things is blind, and cannot see afar off, and hath forgotten that he was purged from his old sins." Don't miss the connection to the knowledge of the Lord Jesus Christ.

Second, true believers can confirm grace. If the marks of grace are present, assurance of grace is possible. The criterion for this subjective assurance is clear: "If ye do these things" (1:10). Good works are not the ground of election and calling but the proof of it. God's calling and man's living always go hand in hand: The mark of grace is a transformed life. The Scripture never holds out assurance to those who are persistently and continuously living in sin. It is always sin, as the Confessions noted, that precludes the enjoyment of assurance. But the desire for and the presence of fruit are good signs of the working of grace. And notwithstanding the certain imperfection in all of our good works, God will be content with them because they are done in union with Christ. We have to keep this in mind.

The content of this subjective assurance is clear as well: "Ye shall never fall: For so an entrance shall be ministered unto you abundantly into the everlasting kingdom of our Lord and Saviour Jesus Christ" (1:10-11). It is possible to have the assurance that we cannot fall into ultimate destruction and ruin and that we have heaven opened and waiting for us. Interestingly, the word translated "add" in verse 5 is the word translated "ministered" in verse 11. Just as the believer complements [supplies] his life with Christlike virtue, so God complements [supplies] heaven with believers. Holiness belongs in the life of the believer, and the believer belongs in heaven.

The Scriptures affirm positively that assurance of faith is attainable based on objective truths and that it is confirmed by a pious life. It is possible to be saved and know it. John wrote his first epistle with the express purpose of bringing believers to certain knowledge of eternal life. "These things I wrote to you who are constantly believing on the name of the Son of God in order that you might know that you are constantly having eternal life, and in order that you might continue to constantly believe on the name of the Son of God" (1 John 5:13, my translation). The reception of grace is the logical basis of a holy life, and a holy life is the logical assertion of the reception of grace. Salvation is indeed a pledge of eternal life, but it is more. It is the governing principle of life. The more we consciously allow it to govern, the more we can be sure of its promises. The more we utilize the means of grace–specifically the prayerful use of the Word of God–the greater will be our sense of security. Right thinking about the gospel produces right living in the gospel, which in turn produces confident enjoyment of the gospel. It is my prayer for you and for me that the Holy Spirit will teach us more and more of what we have in Christ to enable us to relax in Him.

Conclusion

Why we do what we do is often more important than what we do. Ask a child, regardless of his age, why he did something, and almost invariably his response will be, "I don't know." This answer is quite annoying to parents and usually generates the more probing question concerning what in the world the child does know. Unfortunately, many Christians give the same childish response when faced with the issues of Christian living. Ask many believers why they do certain things–even the right things–and in their heart of hearts they have to acknowledge that they do not know. They do certain things and avoid doing other things more out of blind habit than out of conscious conviction. Living the Christian life without the proper motives tends to produce a rigid, although perhaps comfortable, routine that knows little, if any, real spiritual joy. Without the "why's," Christianity is little more than a lifestyle that is somewhat out of step with most of society. The "why's" of Christian living are found in Christian theology. Doctrine defines life; understanding and applying doctrine motivate life. Right thinking produces right living.

I am a fundamentalist. I was born and raised in a fundamentalist environment, was educated in a fundamentalist institution, and have served within fundamentalism for all of the almost thirty years of my ministry. I totally agree with the fundamentalist creed that whatever the Bible says is so. As a Christian fundamentalist, I stand convinced that the Bible is the only rule for faith (what to believe) and for practice (what to do). I love the Bible. Although my conscience dictates my fundamentalism, there are some things about typical fundamentalism that distress me. Even within traditional fundamentalism, Christianity has been reduced to nothing more than the observance of certain principles and rules that externally, but not internally, mark the difference between faith and infidelity. I have had students over the years who know the rules of proper conduct and appearance, but whose only motive for conforming to those standards has been the fear of rebelling against God-established authority, a common theme for sermons. These same students were often incapable of defining any of the essential doctrines of the faith. I will never forget a young woman sitting in the front row of one of my classes who wept uncontrollably and joyously when she learned for the first time what it meant to be justified and accepted by God in union with Jesus Christ. I was simultaneously happy and sad. Happy that she grasped the truth. Sad that she had never heard it before, even though she was raised in fundamentalism.

There seems to be such widespread ignorance of what the Bible says. I have heard fundamentalist preachers virtually brag about their ignorance of theology while boasting about the practicality of their ministries. Who more than a fundamentalist, with his "Whatever the Bible says is so" creed, ought to devote his attention to knowing the great doctrines of the Bible and especially of the gospel as the foundation of life? A fundamentalist should be one who has knowledge of the truth coupled with unyielding, uncompromising convictions concerning those doctrines that are vital to the Christian faith.

This is why I have written this book. My motive and my desire are that Christians might "grow in grace, and in the knowledge of our Lord and Saviour Jesus Christ" (2 Peter 3:18). Nothing is more basic to spiritual growth than understanding and enjoying the fundamental truths of the gospel of saving grace that center directly and uniquely in Jesus Christ. This book is nothing more than a back-to-the-basics approach to Christian living. In every endeavor of life the basics are essential. Reading the most sophisticated literature depends on knowing the alphabet. The most advanced mathematical procedures depend on the basic principles of addition and subtraction. So it is that successful Christian living depends on fundamental truths of Christ and the gospel.

There is, however, a flaw in my analogy. I can read and write well enough without a conscious thought about the alphabet. Even as I am now writing on my Macintosh PowerBook, I am typing without conscious thought of where the letters are located on the keypad. In fact, if I thought about it, it would probably slow me down tremendously. But it is impossible to live the Christian life successfully and joyfully without conscious thinking about Christ. The more we think, the better we will do. Growing in grace and in the knowledge of Christ is not advancing beyond the basic gospel truths of the death and resurrection of Christ. On the contrary, Christian growth depends on sticking as close to the cross and empty tomb as we possibly can. It has been my premise throughout this gospel survey that right thinking about the gospel produces right living in the gospel. Putting the "why" into Christian living will put the joy into it as well.

It has been my contention that all of salvation relates to and flows from the Savior, Jesus Christ. Salvation in Christ is complete, and we are complete in Him. The Bible defines from different perspectives what it means to be saved so that we can put it all together to see how great a salvation we truly have. Although the gospel of salvation is a unified whole, the Scripture at various times draws attention to its individual components that combine to form the whole. I have used the analogy of salvation's being like a chain consisting of several inseparable links with both ends hooked as well. In this study, I have tried to examine some of the key links in the gospel chain with the aim of aiding both growth and confidence in grace. Of necessity and on purpose, there have been themes of the gospel message that appear in virtually every chapter. Of necessity, because none of the elements of salvation exist independently. On purpose, because I want you see how important it is to think about the Person and work of Christ in the application of all truth.

It is my prayer that God will use this survey of the basics of the gospel to increase our realization that there can be no vital experience of Christianity without the conscious application of Jesus Christ. I explained in the Introduction that I chose the title of this book from Paul's declaration to the Colossian church that all who have received the Lord Jesus Christ as their Savior are "complete in Him" (Colossians 2:10). Paul's theme throughout his letter to the Colossians was the pre-eminence of Jesus Christ.

What a theme that is for a book. What a theme that is for life. If I have in any way been a guide to your seeing Christ and your completeness in Him and to your understanding and enjoyment of the gospel, I give my humble thanks to the Lord.

APPENDICES

APPENDIX 1

JUSTIFICATION AND SANCTIFICATION

Although sanctification be inseparably joined with justification, yet they differ, in that God in justification imputeth the righteousness of Christ; in sanctification his Spirit infuseth grace, and enableth to the exercise thereof; in the former sin is pardoned; in the other, it is subdued: the one doth equally free all believers from the revenging wrath of God, and that perfectly in this life, that they never fall into condemnation; the other is neither equal in all, nor in this life perfect in any, but growing up to perfection. (*Westminster Larger Catechism*, question 77)

DISTINCTIVE ASPECTS

Justification	Sanctification
A judicial act outside the believer	A moral work inside the believer
Imputed righteousness	Imparted righteousness
Concerns legal position	Concerns daily experience
Restores rights as children of God	Renews in God's image
Removes guilt of sin	Removes pollution of sin
Cancels penalty of sin	Defeats power of sin
A single completed act	A continuing process
No change in character	A gradually changed life
Equal standing for all believers	Different stages of progression

SHARED ASPECTS

Although justification and sanctification are theologically distinct, they are practically inseparable. Sanctification is the necessary effect of justification. Sanctification is living in the reality of justification.

Both require the grace of God.

Both require faith in the blood and righteousness of Jesus Christ.

Both require the operation of the Holy Spirit to apply God's grace and Christ's merit.

APPENDIX 2

WHO FOUGHT THE BATTLE OF JERICHO?*

By Michael P. V. Barrett

Finally, Israel was in Canaan. The previous generation had failed to enter the land of promise because of unbelief. Nothing had changed in the forty years since the first spy report detailing the bounties and the dangers of the land. It was still a land flowing with milk and honey, and it still had those intimidating cities fortified to the heavens. The test of faith that their ancestors failed now confronted this generation. Since the day Israel left Egypt, they were enrolled in the school of faith with one test after another. For forty years God had been teaching His redeemed people vital lessons about Himself, His power, His promises, His provisions, and their necessary faith and obedience. The Lord, who led the way through the wilderness, had now brought His people miraculously across Jordan. As soon as they crossed the Jordan and stood on the threshold of the promised inheritance, they saw the towering walls of Jericho. From every human analysis, Jericho was an immovable obstacle to possessing the land. From God's perspective, Jericho was another classroom to teach these would-be warriors important lessons before they settled in the land. They had to learn that every victory depended on God. Jericho would fall not because of military strength, but because of divine purpose and intervention. God's fighting the battle of Jericho taught ancient Israel and teaches Christians today that spiritual victories are both God's intent and provision for His people. This written history is an inspired textbook for spiritual learning. The narrative of Jericho's fall suggests three significant lessons.

---

*Reprinted with permission from *Biblical Viewpoint*, XXVI (November, 1992), 24-32

A LESSON IN SACRED JUSTICE

Known as the city of palms (Deuteronomy 34:3), Jericho appeared to be an oasis of pleasure, prosperity, and security. Contrary to appearance, it was a city doomed to destruction. Jericho's fall testifies to God's holy justice and the consequences of sin. It is a picture of the final judgment when God will shake more than brick and mortar (cf. Hebrews 12:26). It is a warning to every sinner that none can stand in the day of judgment. Jericho's fall teaches three important lessons about God's justice that every sinner should know.

God's Justice is not Capricious

Just before Moses died, he preached an eloquent sermon warning the nation against the sin of self-righteousness when they began to experience the blessings of Canaan (Deuteronomy 9). He made it clear that although there were several reasons why God was going to give them the land, their goodness was not a factor. In addition to fulfilling the covenant promise (9:5) and listening to Moses's intercession (9:26), God revealed that they were to possess the land and dispossess its inhabitants because of the wickedness of the Canaanites (9:4, 5). Just as years later Assyria and Babylon would be the Lord's weapon in executing judgment against Israel, so now Israel was the ordained rod of God's anger against the Canaanites. The destruction of Jericho was the beginning of the decreed extermination of these wicked people. The Lord's instructions made it clear that none were to escape (Joshua 6:17, 21).

If the destruction of Jericho and its inhabitants teaches any spiritual lesson, it is that the wages of sin is death. Both the Bible and archaeological evidence give evidence of the total depravity and perverseness of these people. The very name of the city, related to a word meaning "moon," suggests that Jericho may have been a center of that astrological religion so common in the ancient world. Not only idolatry, but oppression, fornication, and injustices of every sort characterized their way of life. That they were pagans did not remove their responsibility before the Lord.

All souls belong to the Lord, and He declares that the sinning soul will die (Ezekiel 18:4). Every soul that perishes receives exactly what has been earned. To receive from God what one deserves is a fearful thought for sinners of every age.

Those that defend the Canaanites as innocent victims of Israeli savagery fail to recognize the theology of the extermination. To charge the Old Testament as being sub-Christian because of this divine order to kill all the Canaanites is to deny the holy justice of God. It is neither pre- nor sub-Christian that God must and will judge every sinner; it is God's Word for every age that warns against falling into the hands of an angry God. In addition to the manifold evidence of the Old Testament about the heinous sins of these doomed people, the book of Hebrews gives some insight that silences every accusation against God and any defense of the inhabitants of Jericho: they perished because they did not believe (Hebrews 11:31). What Rahab heard and believed about the God of Israel all the city heard (see Joshua 2:9-11). What they heard, however, they did not mix with faith. From every perspective they were without excuse before the Lord. One of the great lessons from Jericho is that God's judgments are always righteous; no sinner, whether from ancient Jericho or modern America, can claim innocence before the most holy Lord.

God's Justice is Patient

The prophet Nahum declared that "The LORD is slow to anger, and great in power, and will not at all acquit the wicked . . ." (1:3). The destruction of Jericho illustrates this truth well. The ruins of what many believe to be Jericho (Tell es Sultan) are some of the oldest in the world. In fact, many scholars identify this as the world's oldest city. Occupation levels indicate the existence of a thriving city hundreds of years before Abraham began his faith-tour of the land of promise. When the Lord spoke to Abraham about the land and future of his seed, He postponed Abraham's possession of Canaan because the "iniquity of the Amorites" was not yet full (Genesis 15:16). Hundreds of years have passed, and finally the sin of these people was full. The time of judgment had come. In the years of God's long-suffering, this city had prospered and had multiple reasons to repent. They had most likely witnessed the rising smoke from Sodom's destruction on the horizon. They had certainly heard of God's judgment on the Egyptians and Transjordan peoples. But while others were falling, they seemed to be exempt. The fall of Jericho warns sinners that the postponement of God's judgment does not mean pardon. God may delay His execution, but when it comes it comes suddenly and without remedy (Proverbs 6:15). Jericho's fall warns sinners to seek the Lord while He allows Himself to be found (Isaiah 55:6).

God's Justice is Irresistible

Joshua 6:1 describes Jericho as "straitly shut up" (i.e. closed and staying closed). They assumed that they were safe and secure. They were confident that no weapon could either penetrate the gate or break down the double-walled barrier. Archaeological evidence from Tell es Sultan and other Palestinian cities indicates that the Israeli spies did not exaggerate their descriptions of these fortified cities. But however intimidating and mighty their defenses were against human invasion, strong fortifications were absolutely nothing before the Lord. The walls of Jericho fell at God's command. The spiritual lesson is clear. No sinner can stand against the judgment of God. It is folly to believe that the walls of self-righteousness can stand when the judgment trumpet sounds. Any foundation of hope other than God Himself is insecure and unstable. Jericho's fall illustrates Jeremiah's declaration, "Cursed be the man that trusteth in man, and maketh flesh his arm . . ." (17:5).

A Lesson in Saving Grace

In wrath, God remembers mercy (see Habakkuk 3:2). Perhaps even more outstanding than the miraculous destruction of Jericho's walls is the miraculous deliverance of Rahab's life and soul. Jericho fell, but Joshua spared Rahab and all that belonged to her (Joshua 6:22-25). Rahab's salvation testifies to the power of saving grace that can transform the greatest sinner into a believing saint. Rahab, the harlot, was a lesson to Israel and to the church that although none deserve the least of God's favor, none are beyond the reach of His grace. The narrative of Rahab's salvation makes three significant statements about God's saving grace.

Grace Finds the Sinner

Of the eight times the Scripture mentions Rahab by name, five times it designates her as the harlot (Joshua 2:1; 6:17, 25; Hebrews 11:31; James 2:25). This frequent reminder of her occupation highlights the depth of her sin and magnifies the beauty of grace that is greater than sin. Among a cursed people, Rahab was a chief among sinners. From every appearance she was, like every sinner, without hope. She was alienated from the commonwealth of Israel; she was a stranger to the covenant of promise. God, however, had placed the scarlet cord around Rahab long before the spies instructed her to hang the cord from her window.

When God has a purpose to save, He always supplies the means to accomplish His purpose. God has promised that all those that call in faith upon the name of the Lord will be saved. Calling with faith, however, depends on hearing the Word of God, and hearing depends on a preacher. God sends preachers to proclaim the necessary message (see Romans 10:13, 14). This is exactly the means to faith illustrated in Rabab's conversion. God with saving purpose directed the spies to Rahab's house. Interpreters have offered various reasons why the spies entered the harlot's house. Some suggest it was by chance; others suggest that the spies thought the town prostitute would be privy to vital information; others suggest that the harlot's house would have been the natural and logical place for visitors to remain anonymous. If that was their reasoning, it was certainly wrong because they were detected as soon as they arrived (Joshua 2:2). Without doubt the spies had orders to find out as much as possible about the city for the coming battle. Notwithstanding those orders, with reference to Rahab they were preachers, not spies. They had a word for Rahab from the Lord. Significantly, both the Old and

New Testaments suggest this truth when they declare that Rahab hid *messengers* (6:25; James 2:25). Grace found a great sinner and gave the message necessary for salvation.

Grace Awakens the Sinner

Not only does grace find sinners, it changes sinners. Rahab, the harlot, became Rahab, the believer. Hebrews 11:31 declares that it was "by faith" that "the harlot Rahab perished not with them that believed not." The narratives in Joshua 2 and 6 reveal that Rahab proved her faith both by confession and in conduct. First, she acknowledged her conviction concerning God's power (2:10), God's glory (2:11), and the prospect of God's mercy (2:12, 13). Then, she demonstrated her faith by what she did: she hid the spies (6:25). This is the point that James underlines: Rahab acted like a believer. Her hiding the spies was testimony to her denying self, forsaking the old life, and seeking her share with God's people. For Rahab, old things had passed away and all things had become new.

Grace Honors the Saint

Rahab's salvation illustrates well the truth that God rewards those who diligently seek Him. Joshua 6 focuses on two great aspects of Rahab's salvation. First, God delivered her from the penalty of sin. Jericho fell and all the inhabitants of the city died in their sins, but Rahab escaped (6:22). Although this was deliverance from physical death, it typifies clearly the exemption from spiritual death that belongs to all who rest their faith in the Lord. Second, God delivered Rahab's family (6:23). This is Achan in reverse. Achan's sin led to the loss of his family; Rahab's faith led to the saving of hers. This household salvation did not just involve the immediate family, but the generations that followed. In fact, Matthew's Gospel reveals that Rahab became part of the family line that ultimately led to Christ (1: 5, 6). What a lesson in grace this is. Rahab, a brand plucked from the fire, was rescued from the muck of depravity and placed on the firm foundation. Rahab's salvation assures sinners that they need never despair of grace.

A LESSON IN SANCTIFYING POWER

If Rahab's salvation was a lesson in how to be free from sin's penalty, the destruction of Jericho is a lesson in how to be free from sin's power. Israel's conquest of Canaan is a significant type of the believer's battle with sin. The battle of Jericho was the first of many conflicts. The battle plan was instructive not only for Israel as they prepared to take possession of their land inheritance, but for all believers as they take possession of the spiritual inheritance that rightfully belongs to them. Four principles surface in Joshua 6 that teach important lessons about sanctification.

The Promise of Victory

The Book of Joshua begins with the sweeping pledge to Joshua that "every place that the sole of your foot shall tread upon, that I have given unto you, as I said unto Moses" (1:3). Israel's possession of Canaan was linked inseparably to God's promise. The Lord had first given the promise hundreds of years earlier to the patriarchs, had repeated it to Moses and the people brought out of Egyptian bondage, and now He renewed it to Joshua and the generation that would begin to enjoy the fulfillment. After God led the nation safely through Jordan to the threshold of the promise, they stood before Jericho. What had been a theoretical enemy now was visibly real. The Lord encouraged the people immediately by making the general promise specific: "See, I have given into thine hand Jericho, and the king thereof, and the mighty men of valour" (6:2). The past tense of the verb "I have given" highlighted the certainty of the promise and generated confidence in the definite application. Before the army took the first step around Jericho, they had the assurance of victory.

The parallels to sanctification are significant. Just as God promised Israel victory over the Canaanites, He has promised believers victory over sin. For instance, in discussing the implications of union with Christ, the apostle Paul made some sweeping statements: those in Christ have been freed from sin, and sin no longer has dominion over those in Christ (Romans 6:7, 14). These are wonderfully great promises. The first step in sanctification, dying to sin and living to righteousness, is to know that God has both purposed and promised victory for every believer. Christians should also learn from Jericho that the promise of victory is not abstract theory. God's promise that Jericho would fall was not a new promise, it was simply the specific application of the general word. There is no specific sin that stands outside God's general promise that sin no longer has dominion.

The Presence of the Enemy

Although the Lord guaranteed His people possession of the promise, the Canaanites did not voluntarily give up their claim to the land. Jericho was defiantly occupying the place of promise. This strong, fortified city shut its gates (6:1), secured itself, and dared Israel to attack it. It seemed to be a hopeless situation for Israel. They certainly did not have the means, the weaponry, the experience, or the ability to conquer this enemy. Humanly speaking Jericho had more going for it than Israel. Had Joshua ignored the divinely revealed battle plan against Jericho and decided to storm the city on shear desire and zeal, Jericho would have continued to stand.

The situation is similar in the Christian's daily battle. Although Christ has fatally bruised the serpent's head, defeated sin and every enemy, and guaranteed victory, sin remains in the world and dares believers. Sin will not give up its territory without a struggle. The Devil goes around as a roaring lion, and sin with seducing strength stands in the way of holiness. No amount of zeal or raw will power can win victory over sin. Christians must realize that by themselves and in themselves they have no chance against the dominion of sin. The presence of sin must be placed within the certainty of God's promise. Believers will enjoy victory only as they follow the divinely revealed battle plan.

The Power of God

God's promises are always sure because of God's power. Defiant Jericho became a token that God had the ability to make every promise good. The detailed plan for Jericho's fall and execution of that plan certainly included human involvement, but the nature of that involvement served to accent God's involvement (6:3-16). What happened to Jericho was a miracle. Although Jericho stood as an immovable obstacle to Israel, it was absolutely nothing to God. His might was greater than Jericho's. It is significant that God's plan for defeating Jericho focused on the ark of the covenant (6:4, 6, 7, 8, 9, 11, 12, 13). The ark with its mercy seat was the important symbol of the Lord's presence with His people and the visible reminder of the necessity of atonement. It was only as the Israeli army remained in union with the ark that they saw Jericho fall.

So it is in sanctification that the power for victory resides in the Lord. Sin is far stronger than any Christian, but it is not stronger than Christ. The New Testament declares that the cross work of Jesus Christ marked the end to sin's power (see Colossians 2:14, 15; Hebrews 2:14, 15). The power over sin resides in the blood of the Savior. Victory is possible only as believers look to that blood and their union with Christ in each battle with sin. This truth makes little sense to natural reasoning, but neither did marching around Jericho.

The Practice of Faith

Hebrews 11:30 says, "by faith the walls of Jericho fell down, after they were compassed about seven days." God said Jericho would fall; Israel believed God; they acted in the reality of what they believed. Faith is never passive. It lays hold on the truth of God's word and acts in obedience to that word. This cooperation between God and Israel in Jericho's destruction parallels nicely the process of sanctification. Although the power for victory over sin is in Christ and His blood, the believer is not passive in claiming that victory. Sanctification is not a holy zap by which the Christian becomes holy in experience. There must be a cooperation between the believer and God's Spirit who applies the benefits of Christ. By faith the Christian must look to Christ and his part with Christ and then live in the reality of that victorious union. Paul's argument for holiness in Romans 6 follows this order precisely: know about union with Christ (vv. 4-6); reckon or appropriate personally the benefits of that union (v. 11); stop sinning (vv. 12, 13). To try to stop sinning without reference to personal union with Christ is as much folly as Israel's storming Jericho without reference to the Lord's provision and promise.

In view of all the lessons from this passage, there is little doubt as to who really fought the battle of Jericho. The Lord Himself was the Commander-in-chief. This episode of Jericho's fall teaches that it is not vain to trust the Lord. When He promises victory and prescribes the course to that victory, those who believe the promise and follow the course will enjoy the victory. The walls of Jericho fell in such a way that God's power was undeniable. The text says essentially that the wall fell under itself (6:20). It did not fall outward or inward, but downward. There was no rubble for the army to maneuver through or over on its straight ahead march into the city. It disappeared in the ground as if in an elevator shaft. It was indeed a miracle. It should be noted as well that the entire wall did not fall: only that portion directly in front of the parading army. The rest of the wall remained, preserving Rahab's house and preventing any escape for those doomed to judgment. Every detail of God's purpose was accomplished.

APPENDIX 3

UNION WITH CHRIST: THE GROUND OF SANCTIFICATION*

By Michael P. V. Barrett

Natural reasoning always perverts the truth. Paul's exposition of justification by faith on the merits of Jesus Christ raised the absurd question "shall we continue in sin, that grace may abound?" (Rom. 6:1). With forceful language, the apostle expressed his denial of that perverted reasoning. Being justified freely by grace demands purity and holiness in life. Receiving Christ's gracious deliverance from sin's penalty and guilt in order to remain in sin's power and domination is as illogical as it is perverse. Throughout his epistles, Paul exhorts converts to be holy because the gospel applied to the heart not only rescues the soul from condemnation, but also it inclines the soul in the direction of righteousness. Paul's argument for Christian holiness based on the application of the gospel is nowhere more compelling than in Romans 6.

Just as the atoning work of Christ is the ground of the sinner's justification, so is it the ground for the saint's sanctification. Justification has fixed the Christian's legal position and standing before God. In Christ, the believer stands before God as holy as Jesus Christ Himself. This is imputed righteousness. Sanctification is the believer's becoming in experience what the grace of the gospel has purposed him to be. Sanctifying grace enables the Christian to live piously–to live in the reality of what he is in Christ. This is imparted righteousness. Whereas justification is a single legal act or declaration of God, sanctification is a continuing work of God that progressively matures during the lifetime of every justified saint. Theologically, it is imperative to maintain the distinction between justification and sanctification. Practically, it

*Reprinted with permission from *Biblical Viewpoint*, XXII (April, 1988), 29-36

is imperative to demonstrate the inseparable connection between the two truths. Sanctification flows necessarily from justification. Paul links these two aspects of salvation by demonstrating how the sacrifice of Christ is the ground for each.

While most Christians agree that holiness should mark the life, there are differing views concerning how to achieve that holiness. Unfortunately, many of the suggestions for obtaining victory over sin are based on psychological tricks to increase personal resolve and determination to win over temptation. Efforts in sanctification that are founded on personal resolve and will power are doomed to failure and frustration. It is imperative to return to the biblical theology of sanctification. Romans 6 reveals this important theology. Paul essentially argues that right thinking about the gospel produces right living. His order of reasoning is clear. First, there must be a knowing of certain truths by experience (6:3, 6). Second, there must be a reckoning of those truths by faith (6:11). Third, there must be a doing of the truths by obedience (6:13). This order cannot be successfully altered. The key truth that gives motion to sanctification is the believer's union with Jesus Christ.

The Fact of the Union with Christ (6:3, 4)

There is no chance for holiness apart from spiritual union with Jesus Christ. This truth marks an essential difference between biblical Christianity and every other religion. Whereas in natural religion men try to live holy lives in order to get to God, in true Christianity men live holy lives after God has gotten to them.

Paul first expresses the believer's union with Christ in terms of baptism. He asks the Roman Christians whether they were ignorant of the nature and design of baptism. His reference must be to spiritual baptism, for no amount of water can effect the spiritual union that this passage describes. To see this as water baptism is to see baptismal regeneration, and no orthodox view of baptism tolerates the notion of saving grace in association with the act of the church ordinance. Rather, the apostle refers to that gracious act of the Holy Spirit where we are "all baptized into one body," the body of Christ (see I Cor. 12:13). The basic significance of this spiritual act is that it creates a vital, intimate union with the Savior Himself. Although the mechanics of this union remain an inexplicable mystery to the finite mind, it is nonetheless a real union. The implications of this union boggle the mind and would be unbelievable if they were not the authoritative assertions of God Himself. God's Word declares that the believer's acceptance by God is "in the beloved" (Eph. 1:6). The believer is positioned in Christ by an inseparable union. This position with Christ is so certain that the believer is blessed "with all spiritual blessings in heavenly places in Christ" (Eph. 1:3). United with Christ, the believer is where Christ is.

In this text Paul emphasizes that the believer is united to the death of Christ. When Christ died, the believer died in Him. Every believer, therefore, partakes of all the benefits that Christ accomplished by His atoning death. Christ purchased the believer's justification, adoption, assurance of divine forgiveness, peace, joy, and eternal life; and the list of benefits for both this life and the life to come goes on. This passage reveals that the Christian's holiness or sanctification was one of the benefits accomplished by Christ's death. Indeed, Christ gave Himself for the church "that he might present it to himself a glorious church . . . holy and without blemish" (Eph. 5:27).

Having stated the reality of union with Christ (verse 3), Paul reflects on the consequences of that union (verse 4). This spiritual baptism effected a burial with Christ. In the physical realm, burial is the means to dispose of the old corpse, to remove it from the presence of the living. It effects a separation. In the spiritual realm, burial with Christ involves a separation from the world, the kingdom of Satan. Although living in the world, the Christian is not of the world. Life in Christ demands and enables separation from the world (see I John 2:15-17). One aspect of sanctification is dying more and more to sin, living separate from evil.

Once the Christian was dead in sin; now he must be dead to sin by virtue of his association with Christ.

The consequence of death and burial with Christ is life. Christ, having died, rose again. His resurrection was the certain and necessary consequence of His atoning death. Similarly, a new and holy life is the certain and necessary consequence of the believer's dying with Him. Newness of life is a reality in Christ. That is a fact. Sanctification is nothing more than living in the reality of what we have in Christ.

THE DESIGN OF UNION WITH CHRIST (6:5-7)

In verses 5-7 Paul confirms and expands his preceding thoughts by revealing the design of union with Christ. Sharing in Christ's death means sharing in Christ's victory and life. Verse 5 defines the condition of the Christian: "If we have been planted together in the likeness of his death." The apostle's language in stating the believer's condition is significant. By using the simple condition formula, Paul assumes the reality of the protasis or "if clause." By substituting the word "since" for "if," the force of this construction is more evident. It is an established fact that the believer has been planted with Christ in His death. Planting is a new image that Paul uses to describe the nature of union with Christ. The word has the idea of a common origin, things that are born or produced at the same time, things that grow together. The perfect tense of the verb used in the protasis suggests that this planting was instantaneous and final with results that continue. Being well rooted in Christ produces an inevitable experience. The apodosis or "then clause" defines what that continuing, inevitable experience is. Since the believer is planted with Christ in His death, he will be "of the resurrection." The future tense that occurs in the apodosis is a future of obligation; it refers not simply to what will happen, but what must happen. There is a certainty of sequence between the protasis and the apodosis. Because the one is true, the other is absolutely certain. Christ's death and resurrection secured for every believer a necessary and certain life. That life involves not only escape from sin's penalty but also cleansing from sin's guilt, power, and pollution.

The design of this union with Christ's resurrection relates to sanctification and is specifically stated in verse 6, where Paul remarks on the knowledge of the Christian. The word for "knowing" involves more than merely head knowledge or creedal affirmation; it refers to a personal experience of gospel truths. There must be a vital experience of the old man's crucifixion with Christ. The old man designates the old depraved nature that is thoroughly corrupted with sin. Union with Christ involved a joint crucifixion of the Savior and the believer's sin. Indeed, to pay the penalty of this sin was the reason Christ died. Having established the experiential association between "our old man" and Christ's crucifixion, Paul uses two different purpose formulas to show the design of the union. First, the union was in order to destroy the body of sin. This sinful body most likely is synonymous with the old man. The old man was crucified in order to destroy itself with all its corruption. Second, the union and destruction of the old man was in order that the believer might not be servant to sin. To live free from sin is to fulfill the purpose of salvation. This second stated purpose is the practical evidence of the theology of the first stated purpose. Because of Christ's death, the Christian is no longer in bondage to sin. Outside of Christ the sinner is in slavery to sin, a state of misery and bondage from which he cannot free himself. Sin is a terrible master that has sufficient power to coerce and control in spite of the sinner's best intentions or efforts. But in Christ are the basis and reason for and only hope of victory over sin's dominion. Because Christ destroyed sin's dominion by His death and because the believer was united to that death, it is illogical that the believer should continue under sin's control.

In verse 7 Paul summarizes the result of this union for the Christian: for the one who died has been justified from sin. Judicially, union with Christ's death frees the believer from sin's penalty. Subjectively, union with Christ's death frees the believer from sin's power. Prophetically, union with Christ's death will free the believer from sin's presence. This mystical union effects a radical change. To be in Christ is to be free, to "be free indeed" (John 8:36). Freedom in Christ is freedom to be and do what outside of Christ was impossible. To live under sin's control is to fail to use the freedom that Christ has purchased by His atoning death. Freedom from sin is not just a possibility; it is a reality in Christ. To understand this is to understand the basis of sanctification.

THE APPLICATION OF UNION WITH CHRIST (6:8-14)

All theology has application. God never reveals truth just to satisfy man's curiosity or answer his reason. Theology must make its way from the head to the heart and then to practice or it has been abused. Conversely, there can be no proper Christian practice unless there is a theological basis. Realizing the vital connection between doctrine and duty, Paul applies the theology of union with Christ to the experience of the everyday conflicts with sin. In theory, the Christian has victory over sin. In practice, how is that victory to be experienced?

The link between theology and practice is faith. Twice in verses 8-14 the apostle uses the vocabulary of faith to give impetus to his practical instructions. First, he uses the word "believe" (v. 8). Once again Paul uses a simple condition to assume the reality of the protasis in this conditional sentence. Since it is a fact that we died with Christ, we are constantly believing (present tense) that we will live with Him. This faith rests firmly on Christ. The value of faith is always determined by the object of faith. Just as Christ is the object of justifying faith, so must He be the object of sanctifying faith. Sanctification does not progress because of self-determination or will power; it progresses as Christ and the benefits of His sacrifice are appropriated by faith. In verses 9 and 10 Paul demonstrates the sensibility of such faith in Christ by directing attention to facts about the Savior's death and resurrection. He describes the permanent life of the risen Christ to show that the Christian's new life must be permanently free from sin's domination. Believing that there is victorious life in Christ is not just wishful thinking; it is reality.

Second, he uses the word "reckon" (v. 11). This word means to consider or regard something as being true. This word emphasizes the vital appropriation of what is believed. It is one thing to believe something to be generally true; it is another thing to regard it as personally true. What the Christian is to reckon is the same thing he is to believe: deadness to sin through union with Christ. This is the doctrine that Paul had set forth in the opening verses of the chapter. It is true; therefore, the believer must acknowledge the personal relevance of the truth. The Christian must consider himself to be in experience what he is positionally and legally in Christ. The believer must never lose sight or thought of what he is and what he has in the Lord Jesus Christ. It is noteworthy that this word "reckon" occurs also in connection with the doctrine of justification (see Rom. 4:3-4). However, in justification God is the subject of the verb. He looks at the merits of Christ's atonement and considers the sinner who believes in Christ to be legally free from sin. In sanctification, the saint looks at the same merits of Christ's atonement and considers himself to be experientially free from sin. Faith is the victory because faith lays hold of Christ.

Knowing the truth and believing the truth lead to doing the truth. In verses 12-14 Paul issues the imperatives not to let sin rule and not to yield to sin's domination. Unfortunately, many interpreters begin their explanation of sanctification with the imperatives of verses 12 and 13. To tell anyone not to sin without explaining where the ability not to sin comes from can only breed failure and discouragement in the efforts toward holiness. It must be emphasized that successful obedience to these commands is possible only because of what Christ has done and because of the inseparable union that Christ has with His people.

Although victory over sin is possible because the atonement defeated sin and Satan, the Christian nonetheless has to do his part in realizing victory. The believer is not passive in sanctification; indeed, he cooperates with God as he continually dies to sin and lives to righteousness. The Christian's responsibility in sanctification is essentially twofold. On the one hand, he is to refuse submission to sin. In verse 12 Paul gives the admonition that sin should not so reign that we would obey its lusts. The word "lust" refers to those cravings and desires generated by sin. To allow these sinful inclinations to dominate and direct the life is contrary to God's desire for our conformity to Christ. Believers must resist sin's rule. In verse 13 Paul continues this aspect by commanding Christians not to yield themselves to become agents for unrighteousness. This word "yield" simply means to put at someone's disposal. To put self at sin's disposal is nothing more than surrendering to sin's domination. To surrender to sin's persistent domination is to become a traitor. "No surrender to sin" must be the Christian's battle cry. The tense of this prohibition is significant; it is the present imperative, which in prohibition requires the ceasing of an act assumed to be in progress. "Stop surrendering to sin!" The very grammar of the text conforms to daily experience. Every Christian knows well that the conflict against sin rages constantly. One victory over sin's temptations leads only to the next temptation. In daily experience, the one united to Christ's triumphant death can never let the guard down.

On the other hand, the Christian is to submit to God. This is the positive element in sanctification: living unto righteousness. Paul uses the same word "yield" to refer to this positive aspect. Every Christian is to place himself at God's disposal, to surrender to God and the cause of righteousness. Whereas Paul used the present tense to express the prohibition against yielding to sin, he uses the aorist imperative to command allegiance to God. The use of the aorist does not preclude the idea of a continual yielding, but it emphasizes the urgency and necessity of the action. This is the proper course of action for those who are alive from the dead. Regeneration has given the Christian a new nature, a new inclination, a new power. It is by virtue of this resurrection power that willing submission to God and willing rejection of sin are possible.

Paul concludes this section with the explicit declaration that sin will "not have dominion" (v. 14). The Greek word for "have dominion" is the verb form of the root meaning "lord" or "master." Christ's people are free from sin's lordship because they are under grace and not law. Paul is not inserting here a dispensational observation about the church age; he is making an observation that is vitally necessary for victory over sin. The word law does not refer here to the Mosaic era or the Old Testament at all; it designates, rather, the principle of doing. This statement of being under grace and not law parallels Paul's question to the foolish Galatians: "Having begun in the Spirit, are ye now made perfect by the flesh?" (Gal. 3:3). It is impossible to achieve victory over sin merely by striving to do things. All of salvation is by grace. Sanctification is God's gracious working just as justification is God's gracious act. Too often Christians today behave like the Galatians of Paul's day. They realize that they come into salvation by grace through faith in Christ. But for whatever reason, they attempt to live the Christian life by self-power without reference to the grace of the gospel. Paul reminds such as these of the grace of God, which in this entire context finds expression in the atoning sacrifice of Christ. Paul's instructions concerning sanctification can be reduced to this: "Do not go beyond the cross." When temptations come, we should consciously direct our thinking to the cross of Christ and what He accomplished for us. It is impossible to yield to sin while at the same moment placing ourselves at the disposal of God. Right thinking about the gospel will result in right behavior. To forget about the gospel in the daily battle against sin is to enter the conflict unarmed. We stand little chance against sin by ourselves. Lewis Jones, the hymn writer, reflected well Paul's theology of sanctification: "Would you o'er evil a victory win? There's wonderful pow'r in the blood."

Sanctification is not a divine "zap" that automatically makes the believer irreversibly holy. It is a lifelong battle that requires the saint to lay hold by faith of the victory that Christ has accomplished on the cross and actively enjoy that victory by living as though it is really true. The Christian's daily battle with sin is much like ancient Israel's conquest of the Promised Land. Over and again God told the people to possess the land because He had driven out the Canaanites from before them. Although God had won the victory, the Israelites had to cross the Jordan and fight the Canaanites in deadly battle. The Canaanites did not roll over and play dead or pack their bags and leave voluntarily just because Israel entered the land; they fought for their land. The Canaanites were naturally stronger than the Israelites, and the Israelites stood little chance against them in their own strength. But, believing God had given them victory, they entered and fought in the light of that certain victory. Similarly, Christ has already achieved our victory over sin. But sin does not disappear from us just because we are saved. It does not give up its territory without a fight. If we attempt to fight by ourselves, defeat is certain because sin is much stronger than we. But if we enter the conflict claiming Christ's victory and our part in it, sin and Satan must flee from us.

God's Law: The Absolute Standard for Ethics*

By Michael P. V. Barrett

By definition ethics are the rules or standards that govern conduct. It is ironic that society as a whole laments the tragic absence of ethical behavior while at the same time rejecting any fixed standards that would give definition to ethics. We live in a day when every one does what is right in his own eyes, yet there is no concept of what is really right or wrong. The result is turmoil and moral anarchy. If there is such as thing as ethical behavior, there must be such a thing as absolute standards. The absolute standard is God and His revealed law. However, the ungodly's attitude about God's law seems never to change. The Lord said to wicked and wayward Israel through the prophet Hosea, "I have written to him the great things of my law, but they were counted as a strange thing" (Hosea 8:12). Sinners still regard God's law as strange and outmoded. Sadly even Christians, who ought to know better, have ignored God's law for various reasons and as a result even they drift along in a sea of self-conceived liberty. Although all men are under obligation to live according to God's law and set standards, Christians above all others should live and move and choose their daily course within the parameters set by God's absolutes.

The Purpose of the Law

Christianity is not just a religion; it is a vital personal relationship with Jesus Christ that determines and demands a certain way of life. Nothing in the life of a Christian can be separated from that relationship. Right thinking about the Gospel, its grace,

*Reprinted with permission from *Biblical Viewpoint*, XXX (April, 1996), 19-27

and its implications will produce the right, ethical conduct. The Christian's purpose in life is essentially threefold and the fulfillment of this purpose will always result in ethical behavior. First, he is to glorify God. "Whether therefore ye eat, or drink, or whatsoever ye do, do all to the glory of God" (1 Corinthians 10:31). Second, he is to enjoy God forever, as the Psalmist declared "God is the strength of my heart, and my portion for ever" (Psalm 73:26). Third, he is to be conformed to Christ. "For whom he did foreknow, he also did predestinate to be conformed to the image of his Son, that he might be the firstborn among many brethren" (Romans 8:29). Without Christlikeness, there is no way a Christian will either glorify God or experientially enjoy Him. Indeed, the glory of God is seen perfectly in the face of Jesus Christ (II Corinthians 4:6) and it is by looking in God's Word to see the Lord's glory that believers are changed into that glory (II Corinthians 3:18). Being like Christ, glorifying and enjoying God are not vague directions that God sets before His people. On the contrary He has made the means to the end very clear. He has given His Word, the only rule for faith and practice. God's law serves to help the believer fulfill his goal. He has also given His Holy Spirit to guide in the implementation and application of that Word.

God's moral law, which is summarized in the ten commandments, is the capsule statement of God's absolute requirements. Indeed, the Lord Himself is at the very heart and center of the moral law because it reflects and declares His very nature. Consequently, Paul declared that this law is "holy, and just, and good" (Romans 7:12). The law serves many functions. Its demand for perfect obedience not only condemns sinners before the righteous God but is the schoolmaster that leads men to Christ whose perfect active and passive obedience is the only ground for a sinner's acceptance before God. This evangelical function, however, does not exhaust the law's purpose. Once delivered from the penalty of the broken law and the requirements of the law for spiritual life, the believer whose obligation is to holiness must live within the sphere of the law. The grace of the Gospel does not give the Christian the right to do whatever he desires. To come to Christ is to be under a yoke. It is an easy yoke, but it is nonetheless a yoke (Matthew 11:28, 29). The Gospel has loving boundaries (II Corinthians 5:14), and for the genuine believer living within those boundaries is pleasurable (I John 5:3). The liberty of the Gospel involves freedom from the law as the means of gaining divine favor, freedom from the law's penalty and guilt, and the freedom to be holy. Holiness is not some abstract, indefinable virtue. Holiness is living according to the precepts of God's law. Nothing should be more desirable for a Christian than to do those things that are pleasing unto the Lord. God's law defines the sphere of pleasing behavior. Christians must endeavor to keep the law, not in order to gain divine favor or salvation (that would be legalism), but because they have received divine grace (that would be sanctification). Those in Christ are free from the law as a means of life, but they are not free from the law as a way of life.

The Meaning of the Law

The ten commandments are at the heart of the Mosaic covenant inaugurated at Mt. Sinai. They were central to the Israelite theocracy of the Old Testament, and the Lord Jesus made it clear in His teaching that the ancient code is equally valid for the Christian faith (Matthew 5:17-37; 19:16-20). In addition to recognizing the timeless validity, Christ also demonstrated the proper method of interpreting the commandments: the individual statements include within them all degrees and forms of the represented prohibition or command. The surface requirements of the law are clear. What God forbids should never be done, and what God commands should be done. But spirit of the law goes beyond the surface. Included in a prohibition is the demand for the converse duty. Included in a duty is the prohibition of the converse sins. Included in a duty or prohibition are not only all the "same kind" issues, but also the causes, means, and provocations associated with it. This hermeneutic that recognizes the spirit as well as the letter of the law is essential and makes the application of the commandments to the Christian profoundly simple.

If the ten commandments (literally ten "words") are the summary of the moral standards and requirements of God, then Christ beautifully summarized the commandments when He demanded total love for God and "self" love for neighbors (Matthew 22:36-40). Not only does this set in capsule man's duty, but it suggests the principal divisions in the law: man's duty to God and man's duty to man. Through these laws God clearly reveals to man, and particularly to His people, the conduct that is pleasing to Him. These laws define the sphere of ethical behavior.

Man's Duty to God

The decalogue begins with a preamble, which, though not one of the ten words, constitutes a vital part of the whole. God identifies Himself as Jehovah, who redeemed the people from the bondage of Egypt (Exodus 20:2). Thus, the Lord highlights the covenant relationship that He had with His people and "justified" His right to issue the following demands. It was the Exodus that demonstrated to Israel that Jehovah was their God and they owed their existence to Him. Because of what God had done, His people were obligated to live a special way before Him. It is significant that God gave these stipulations, not as the condition for their deliverance from bondage, but as the means for their living as a redeemed people. Even then, the law was not to be a means of life, but a way of life for God's people. Remembering their redemption would create within them an attitude toward the Lord that would make obedience both necessary and pleasurable. It is no less true for the Christian that a sincere acknowledgment of God's saving and faithful acts must inspire obedience and total, humble devotion. A saving, vital, personal relationship to God through the Lord Jesus Christ is the foundation for proper living. Right thinking about this sets the heart toward right living before God and man.

First Commandment (Exodus 20:3). The purpose of the first commandment is to obtain exclusive allegiance to Jehovah. It obviously requires knowing and recognizing the Lord to be the one true and living God and to worship and glorify Him as He deserves. As the only true and living God and as the God of covenant grace and mercy, the Lord will not tolerate divided worship; He must be the sole object of devotion. This commandment addresses every manifestation of our worship, obedience, and submission to Him. Its inclusiveness should guard against any and all offensive behavior and motivate pleasing conduct outwardly and meditation inwardly. The last two words, "before me," are important in understanding the full force of the commandment. The expression refers to personal presence, but can also have overtones of hostility or defiance (cf. Genesis 16:12; Psalm 21:12). Literally "to my face," the phrase is not unlike the similar statement in colloquial English "in your face." Anything that distracts from or competes with the absolute devotion to God is a defiant insult to the great God who made us and the gracious God who saved us. This commandment demands that everything else and everyone else be subservient to the Lord. It is only as He occupies His rightful place in the heart of His people that they can hope to live right in other areas. If this is not right, nothing will be right.

Second Commandment (Exodus 20:4-6). Whereas the first commandment identifies the object of worship, commandments two through four specify the way to worship. This commandment, specifically, involves prohibitions that forbid worshipping images of Jehovah. God forbids the making of images of any sort and especially those in the form of created beings. The word translated "graven image" refers to something manufactured from wood or stone; however, it frequently describes images in general regardless of the manner of their manufacture. The expression "likeness" refers to any form capable of being seen. Together the words eliminate all possible physical representations of God. God is Spirit and true worship must be in spirit and in truth. It is impossible to represent the infinite God by the finite notions of man. There is always the danger that the form may receive the worship in lieu of what it symbolizes. The vehicle of worship becomes the object of worship. The application and extent of this commandment is far-reaching. It forbids devising and using any religious worship that is contrary to God's revealed order. It demands observing and keeping pure all that God has ordered for true worship. This commandment makes it clear that it is possible to worship the right God in the wrong way. Too often the church worships the grandeur of its formalism, the distinctives of its denominationalism, or the methods and techniques of its zealous service more than God Himself. The result is idolatry. The basis for this prohibition is the jealously of God. In His fervent zeal for His name, His law, and His people, God will not tolerate wrong worship. That God inspects and punishes the successive generations of violators and esteems and blesses those that obey suggests the seriousness of this commandment.

Third Commandment (Exodus 20:7). The third commandment prohibits the misuse and abuse of the divine name. The significance of the name in the Old Testament is well known, and the name of God is particularly important. Not only does the divine name reveal characteristics of God's nature, it also stands by association for the very person of the Lord. Consequently, this commandment creates something of a paradox. Although Jehovah revealed His name and Himself so that His people might know Him intimately, this special knowledge could be the source of danger if misused. God makes it clear that He will not tolerate the empty, purposeless use of His name for any reason.

This commandment has far-reaching implications. It certainly includes the ignorant, vain, irreverent, wicked mentioning or using His name or perfections by blasphemy or sinful cursing. It demands that in speech, thought, and action His person be regarded with holy reverence and honor. The creature must not trifle with the holy Creator. The command also prevents using God for personal gain. Man must not manipulate God for private purposes. In the ancient world "name magic" was common as men would invoke the name of their god to somehow sanction the action or seduce their deity to do what they wanted it to do. Although modern "incantations" may take a different form, the selfish use of religion is as common today as ever. Too often the world mentions God in order to sanction and promote some activity or program. Even Christians, sadly, sometimes attempt to use God to their advantage. Often the divine gift of prayer becomes a vehicle for gratifying personal interests as God is coaxed into a particular course of action. Such violates this commandment that demands respect, fear, and subservience to the holy name. This commandment includes any use of the divine name for empty or worthless reasons.

Fourth Commandment (Exodus 20:8-11). The fourth commandment requires the keeping of the Sabbath. The verb "to remember" denotes not only a mental recall, but, more importantly, a willful acknowledgment. Consequently, the statement in Exodus is virtually the same as in Deuteronomy that commands the "keeping" or "observing" of the Sabbath day. Although the Sabbath principle existed from creation, this is the first injunction to keep it holy. Perhaps the biggest misconception involving this fourth word concerns the meaning of the term Sabbath. In spite of the association of the word in this context with the seventh day, the term does not inherently refer to the seventh day. The word comes from a root that means "to cease." Simply, the Sabbath is a day which stops or a day which marks or sets a limit. It is a day of cessation, regardless of the day of the week so designated.

This day was to be kept holy. The basic idea of this verb signifies separation or withdrawal. The Sabbath is a day that is set apart from all others. Verses 9-11 describe the manner and purpose of separation. If the Exodus and Deuteronomy passages are considered together there are two significant and related reasons why the Sabbath is required. The commandment positively states that work is to be done for six days. According to Exodus, the Sabbath day is to be free from all labor because of the example God established at creation; He rested. According to Deuteronomy, the Sabbath is to be observed because God delivered His people from bondage. The Sabbath is a day of rest and remembrance. Relief from the mundane affairs of life allows the time for proper reflection and worship of the Lord for who He is and what

He has done. It takes time and a proper frame of mind to worship, and the Sabbath provides both.

Although the day of weekly Sabbath has changed, there is still a Sabbath for the Christian. Just as the Old Testament weekly Sabbath looked back to the Exodus, the day of redemption, so the Christian Sabbath looks to that eventful day, the resurrection of Christ, which guarantees redemption. The Christian also must set himself apart from the labors and happenings of everyday existence in order to worship the Lord effectively. By setting aside those things that are lawful and necessary on other days and making it the delight of the heart to spend time in public and private worship and in performing with true heart works of necessity and mercy, the Christian will enjoy His God and find the necessary impetus to serve His God with fervent zeal. Suffice it to say that God deserves constant worship and praise. However, in His providence He has given us other things to do that demand our time and attention. In His law, He has set aside a time when we can and must give our full attention to Him. Without such a day, that kind of worship is not possible. Unfortunately, there are many Christians today who have interpreted or reasoned the fourth commandment away. That is tragic and dangerous. It is not my purpose in this article to defend or expound the Sabbath controversy; perhaps, I will in a future issue.

Ethical behavior begins with the right relationship to God. Man cannot be right or do right with his fellow man unless he is first right with the Lord. The first four commandments set the guidelines of right behavior before the holy God. These are the first absolutes of ethical behavior.

Man's Duty to Man

Whereas the summary of the first four commandments is to love God with all our heart and soul and might, the summary of the last six is to love our neighbor as ourselves and to do to others what we would have them do to us (Matthew 22:39; 7:12).

Fifth Commandment (Exodus 20:12). The fifth commandment is the fitting link between the two divisions of the decalogue.

This word requiring the honoring of parents sets forth the family as the primary social unit and establishes the principle that submission to all divinely ordained authority is necessary. Obedience to God's authority representatives on earth is tantamount to obedience to God Himself. The word "honor" expresses the attitude and behavior required toward parents. The word's use in the Old Testament indicates that the concept involves both an internal attitude and an external expression (cf. Psalm 50:15; Numbers 22:17). The honor for parents is an internal reverence and gratitude that expresses itself in obedience and other external acts. Because honoring is internal as well as external, it is not always humanly possible to determine whether it is genuine. Only God knows the heart that motivates any action. An important aspect of this commandment is the promise of long life to those who obey. A comparison of this promise with the punishment mentioned in Exodus 20:5 establishes an important principle: religion is a family affair. Those successive generations being visited (literally, "investigated") by God in regard to iniquity no doubt followed the idolatrous example of their fathers. Deuteronomy 4:40 extends the promise of life and prosperity to those who obey to their children also. Consequently, those who receive this promise attached to the fifth commandment are those who follow the instruction and example of their parents.

The scope of this commandment extends beyond the family unit to the duty man owes to other relationships as well: to inferiors, superiors, and equals. The rest of Scripture demonstrates this wide scope of application. Paul says that we are to submit ourselves to one another in the fear of God (Ephesians 5:21). Peter says that we are to "Honour all men. Love the brotherhood. Fear God. Honour the king" (I Peter 2:17). Again Paul says, "be kindly affectioned one to another with brotherly love; in honour preferring one another" (Romans 12:10). It is necessary to search the Scriptures to define all the specific duties we owe to our several relationships.

Sixth Commandment (Exodus 20:13). The sixth commandment prohibits the illegal taking of life. The proper understanding of this word depends on the meaning of the verb "to kill." There are four words in the Old Testament which mean "to kill." The two most common words are often interchangeable and occur in similar contexts. They occur 1) in connection with the killing of enemies (both personal and political), 2) in reference to killing in war, 3) in the execution of criminals deserving of capital punishment. In contrast, the decalogue verb occurs only in personal situations. It never refers to killing in war and, with one possible exception, never denotes capital punishment (Numbers 35:30 where the "eye for an eye" principle occurs). Therefore, to use this command as an injunction against capital punishment or military service is illegitimate. It is significant that human life, either expressed or understood, is always the object. The main difference between this verb and the others is that it refers to illegal killing, whether intentional or unintentional. Although both types of murder are prohibited, it is significant that the Old Testament makes provision in the cities of refuge for those guilty of unintentional murder (Exodus 21:14). In contrast, not even clinging to the horns of the altar could protect those guilty of intentional murder (I Kings 2:28, 34). This corresponds to Christ's statement in Matthew 5:21, which stresses the evil attitude of malice rather than the actual act. Sinful anger, hatred, desires for revenge would all be precluded by the command. The positive side of this prohibition would include the thoughts and expressions of compassion and kindness, readiness for reconciliation and willingness to forgive. Needless to say, the full compliance to this command encompasses virtually every aspect of good behavior toward fellow men.

Seventh Commandment (Exodus 20:14). The seventh commandment prohibits all sexual impurity. Strictly speaking, committing adultery refers to the violation of the marriage bond. The serious nature of this sin is evident from its penalty: death (Exodus 22:15). Although the specific word is restrictive, it is here representative of all sexual sins. Perhaps the Lord singled out adultery as the chief expression of sexual impurity because it involves unfaithfulness to a relationship as well as fornication. Despite the fact that general acts of fornication outside marriage are not punishable by death in the Old Testament theocracy, the Scripture, nonetheless, views them as serious transgressions. Christ again shows the full intent of the law when He declares the thought apart from the act to be a violation (Matthew 5:28). Paul equates abstaining from fornication as a integral part of God's will for the Christian's sanctification (I Thessalonians 4:3). Obedience to this commandment demands purity in body, mind, affections, communication, and behavior. It requires that attention be given to modesty and care be exercised to avoid whatever would generate temptations to moral uncleanness. Living in this modern, perverse society that has elevated immorality and promiscuity to normal behavior means that Christians, who are bound to God's absolute standard of right and decency, must be on constant vigil to guard the senses and flesh.

Eighth Commandment (Exodus 20:15). The eighth commandment prohibits theft and thereby protects rights of others. As in all the commands, the extent of the prohibition goes beyond the obvious. Not only would this include the robbery of things, but also fraudulent business ventures, breaking of contracts, violations of trust between parties, or any sort of dishonest gain, whether financial, material, temporal, or in personal reputation.

Ninth Commandment (Exodus 20:16). The ninth commandment prohibits whatever is prejudicial to the truth. It promotes truthfulness between men, particularly as it relates to the giving of testimony. The principal statement is forensic, but the application embraces all of life. The word translated "false" has the general idea of deceit. When Moses expounded on the commandments in Deuteronomy 5, he changed the word to a term that signifies something empty or without foundation. In so doing, he expanded the commandment to include not only false testimony, but anything that is not conducive to the propagation of truth. Lying seems to be the first recourse of action from the home to the school to the workplace to the media to the halls of government. Trust has given way to justified suspicion. Isaiah's woeful description of his day has far too many parallels to modern society:

> For our transgressions are multiplied before thee, and our sins testify against us: for our transgressions are with us; and as for our iniquities, we know them; In transgressing and lying against the LORD, and departing away from our God, speaking oppression

> and revolt, conceiving and uttering from the heart words of falsehood. And judgment is turned away backward, and justice standeth afar off: for truth is fallen in the street, and equity cannot enter. Yea, truth faileth; and he that departeth from evil maketh himself a prey: and the LORD saw it, and it displeased him that there was no judgment (Isaiah 59:12-15).

God hates lying wherever it occurs. Christians must learn to love and practice truth whatever the cost.

Tenth Commandment (Exodus 20:17). The tenth commandment requires man to be content with his condition and prohibits the envying of another's possessions or lot in life. Interestingly, this commandment along with the first creates a thematic inclusio. Whereas commandments two through nine state the injunctions in terms of external behavior that encompass internal attitudes, the first and last focus immediately and directly on the attitude of heart. The word "covet" has the general idea of desire and does not imply something inherently evil. Such desire becomes sinful when it is generated and nourished by discontent with what God has ordained for our personal estate and when with envy and inordinate affections toward what God has given to others we despise for them what we would desire for ourselves. Obedience results from the total satisfaction that one's position in life is sovereignly and providentially in the hands of God and from the assurance that God's demonstrates His goodness and His presence regardless of the situation (Philippians 4:11; Hebrews 13:5).

God does not change, and His moral standards do not change. The principles of worship and moral conduct revealed in the decalogue will forever be what God requires and expects from His people. Obedience is the proper response to God's love and the proper evidence of ours. Christ said, "If ye love me, keep my commandments" (John 14:15). Proverbs, the book of divine wisdom, says "He that keepeth law, happy is he" (29:18). That is significant because Proverbs, perhaps more thoroughly than any other part of Scripture, defines and directs the wise in the ways of moral and ethical behavior in every sphere of daily life. Whether the world agrees or not, God's moral law is the only rule for truly ethical behavior.

Scripture Index

CHAPTER 2
CHRIST

CHAPTER 6
JUSTIFICATION

CHAPTER 7 RECONCILIATION

CHAPTER 8 ADOPTION

CHAPTER 10
GLORIFICATION

CHAPTER 11 ASSURANCE

APPENDIX 3
UNION WITH CHRIST: THE GROUND OF SANCTIFICATION

APPENDIX 4
GOD'S LAW: THE ABSOLUTE STANDARD FOR ETHICS